Channels of Desire

Channels of Desire

Mass Images and the Shaping of American Consciousness

STUART EWEN and
ELIZABETH EWEN

McGraw-Hill Book Company

New York / St. Louis / San Francisco / Auckland / Bogotá
Guatemala / Hamburg / Johannesburg / Lisbon / London / Madrid
Mexico / Montreal / New Delhi / Panama / Paris / San Juan
São Paulo / Singapore / Sydney / Tokyo / Toronto

To Fran, Roger, Scotty, and Sol

First McGraw-Hill Publication, 1982

3 4 5 6 7 8 9 10 11   BKP BKP   8 9 8 7 6 5 4

ISBN 0-07-019848-9 (PBK)
0-07-019850-0 (H.C.)

LIBRARY OF CONGRESS CATALOGING IN PUBLICATION DATA

Ewen, Stuart.
    Channels of desire.
    Includes bibliographical references and index.
    1. Advertising—Social aspects—United States—
History. 2. Consumers—United States—History.
3. United States—Popular culture. 4. National
characteristics, American—History. 5. Fashion—
History. I. Ewen, Elizabeth. II. Title.
HF5813.U6E95   303.4'84   81-23634
ISBN 0-07-019850-0   AACR2
ISBN 0-07-019848-9 (pbk.)

Book design by Roberta Rezk.

CONTENTS

Acknowledgments

WITHOUT DOUBT, the issues, developments, and concerns raised in this book would not have come to our attention were it not for the groundwork laid by J. P. Morgan and Karl Marx. Beyond these two, a number of people have been particularly helpful to us in the writing and conceptualization of this book.

Karen Kearns conducted the interview with Anna Kuthan, under the auspices of the oral history project of the City University of New York. Laura Schwartz also provided us with rich interview materials.

Maria Spicciatie has been a patient and helpful friend, putting in long hours preparing the manuscript, making valuable editorial suggestions along the way. For her efforts we offer our deepfelt thanks. Others who worked on typing the manuscript include Maria Resurreccion and Marie Estime. Nancy Lane and Wayne Friedman offered valuable research assistance.

Over the years spent writing this book, we have been enlightened by the ideas and warmed by the support of Ros Baxandall, Herb and Anita Schiller, Eric Perkins, Steve Fraser, Stanley Aronowitz, Harry and Elaine Scott, Fred Ewen, Gail Pellett, Fina Bathrick, Andy Ewen, Paul and Wini Breines, Linda Gordon, Phyllis Ewen, Evan Stark, Margaret Schrage, Catherine Low, Onita Hicks, Sam Rosenberg, Larry Shore, Carmen Monteblanca, Bob Stanley, Allen Hunter, John Ehrenreich, and Kathryn Yatrakis. The friendships of M. J., Stolie, Pasta, and The Turk have sustained us through our wars with this book.

Much of our involvement with the cultural issues raised in the following pages was encouraged by the insights of teachers. For this we thank William Taylor, Loren Baritz, Herb Gutman, Harvey Goldberg, and George Mosse. We also remember the teachings and brilliant rage of Hans Gerth and Michael Cherniavsky.

To our students at Hunter College and the State University of New York College at Old Westbury, we offer our gratitude for their enthusiasm and their criticism while many of the ideas in this book were being worked out.

Tim Yohn, our editor at McGraw-Hill, has been a fine person to work with.

Our children, Sam and Paul Ewen, have provided us with a critical and illuminating perspective on our work. Without them, this book would not have been possible.

To our parents, Roger and Fran Wunderlich, Scotty and Sol Ewen, we dedicate this book. Their lives and those of *their* parents (Anna and Harry Scott; Mike and Rosa Campanile; Mollie and Sam Ewen; Hortense and Reginald Wunderlich) span the great transformation to which this book addresses itself.

Stuart and Elizabeth Ewen
New York City, Fall 1981

Prologue
In the Shadow
of the Image

MARIA AGUILAR was born twenty-seven years ago near Mayagüez, on the island of Puerto Rico. Her family had lived off the land for generations. Today she sits in a rattling IRT subway car, speeding through the iron-and-rock guts of Manhattan. She sits on the train, her ears dazed by the loud outcry of wheels against tracks. Surrounded by a galaxy of unknown fellow strangers, she looks up at a long strip of colorful signboards placed high above the bobbing heads of the others. All the posters call for her attention.

Looking down at her, a blond-haired lady cabdriver leans out of her driver's side window. Here is the famed philosopher of this strange urban world, and a woman she can talk to. The tough-wise eyes of the cabby combine with a youthful beauty, speaking to Maria Aguilar directly:

Estoy sentada 12 horas al dia.
Lo último que necesito son hemorroides.

(*I sit for twelve hours a day. The last thing*
I need are hemorrhoids.)

Under this candid testimonial lies a package of Preparation H ointment, and the promise "Alivia dolores y picasonas. Y ayuda a reducir la hinchazón." (Relieves pain and itching. And helps reduce swelling.) As her mind's eye takes it all in, the train sweeps into Maria's stop. She gets out; climbs the stairs to the street; walks to work where she will spend her day sitting on a stool in a small garment factory, sewing hems on pretty dresses.

*   *   *

Every day, while Benny Doyle drives his Mustang to work along State Road Number 20, he passes a giant billboard along the shoulder. The billboard is selling whisky and features a woman in a black velvet dress stretching across its brilliant canvas.

As Benny Doyle downshifts by, the lounging beauty looks out to him. Day after day he sees her here. The first time he wasn't sure, but now he's convinced that her eyes are following him.

*   *   *

The morning sun shines on the red-tan forehead of Bill O'Conner as he drinks espresso on his sun deck, alongside the ocean cliffs of La Jolla, California. Turning through the daily paper, he reads a story about Zimbabwe.

"Rhodesia," he thinks to himself.

The story argues that a large number of Africans in Zimbabwe are fearful about black majority rule, and are concerned over a white exodus. Two black hotel workers are quoted by the article. Bill puts this, as a fact, into his mind.

Later that day, over a business lunch, he repeats the story to five white business associates, sitting at the restaurant table. They share a superior laugh over the ineptitude of black African political rule. Three more tellings, children of the first, take place over the next four days. These are spoken by two of Bill O'Conner's luncheon companions; passed on to still others in the supposed voice of political wisdom.[1]

*   *   *

Barbara and John Marsh get into their seven-year-old Dodge pickup and drive twenty-three miles to the nearest Sears in Cedar Rapids. After years of breakdowns and months of hesitation they've decided to buy a new washing machine. They come to Sears because it is there, and because they believe that their new Sears machine will be steady and reliable. The Marshes will pay for their purchase for the next year or so.

Barbara's great-grandfather, Elijah Simmons, had purchased a cream-separator from Sears, Roebuck in 1897 and he swore by it.

*   *   *

When the clock-radio sprang the morning affront upon him, Archie Bishop rolled resentfully out of his crumpled bed and trudged slowly to the john. A few moments later he was unconsciously squeezing toothpaste out of a mess of red and white Colgate packaging. A dozen scrubs of the mouth and he expectorated a white, minty glob into the basin.

Still groggy, he turned on the hot water, slapping occasional palmfuls onto his gray face.

A can of Noxzema shave cream sat on the edge of the sink, a film of crud and whiskers across its once neat label. Archie reached for the bomb and filled his left hand with a white creamy mound, then spread it over his beard. He shaved, then looked with resignation at the regular collection of cuts on his neck.

Stepping into a shower, he soaped up with a soap that promised to wake him up. Groggily, he then grabbed a bottle of Clairol Herbal Essence Shampoo. He turned the tablet-shaped bottle to its back label, carefully reading the "Directions."

"Wet hair."

He wet his hair.

"Lather."

He lathered.

"Rinse."

He rinsed.

"Repeat if necessary."

Not sure whether it was altogether necessary, he repeated the process according to directions.

Late in the evening, Maria Aguilar stepped back in the subway train, heading home to the Bronx after a long and tiring day. This time, a poster told her that "The Pain Stops Here!"

She barely noticed, but later she would swallow two New Extra Strength Bufferin tablets with a glass of water from a rusty tap.

* * *

Two cockroaches in cartoon form leer out onto the street from a wall advertisement. The man cockroach is drawn like a hipster, wearing shades and a cockroach zoot-suit. He strolls hand-in-hand with a lady cockroach, who is dressed like a floozy and blushing beet-red. Caught in the midst of their cockroach-rendezvous, they step sinfully into a Black Flag Roach Motel. Beneath them, in Spanish, the words:

Las Cucarachas entran . . . pero non pueden salir.
(In the English version: Cockroaches check in . . . but they don't check out.)

The roaches are trapped; sin is punished. Salvation is gauged by one's ability to live roach-free. The sinners of the earth shall be inundated by roaches. Moral tales and insects encourage passersby to rid their houses of sin. In their homes, sometimes, people wonder whether God has forsaken them.

* * *

Beverly Jackson sits at a metal and tan Formica table and looks through the *New York Post*. She is bombarded by a catalog of horror. Children are mutilated . . . subway riders attacked. . . . Fanatics are marauding and noble despots lie in bloody heaps. Occasionally someone steps off the crime-infested streets to claim a million dollars in lottery winnings.

Beverly Jackson's skin crawls; she feels a knot encircling her lungs. She is beset by immobility, hopelessness, depression.

Slowly she walks over to her sixth-floor window, gazing out into the sooty afternoon. From the empty street below, Beverly Jackson imagines a crowd yelling "Jump! . . . Jump!"

*   *   *

Between 1957 and 1966 Frank Miller saw a dozen John Wayne movies, countless other westerns and war dramas. In 1969 he led a charge up a hill without a name in Southeast Asia. No one followed; he took a bullet in the chest.

Today he sits in a chair and doesn't get up. He feels that images betrayed him, and now he camps out across from the White House while another movie star cuts benefits for veterans. In the morning newspaper he reads of a massive weapons buildup taking place.

*   *   *

Gina Concepcion now comes to school wearing the Jordache look. All this has been made possible by weeks and weeks of afterschool employment at a supermarket checkout counter. Now, each morning, she tugs the decorative denim over her young legs, sucking in her lean belly to close the snaps.

These pants are expensive compared to the "no-name" brands, but they're worth it, she reasons. They fit better, and she fits better.

*   *   *

The theater marquee, stretching out over a crumbling, garbage-strewn sidewalk, announced "The Decline of Western Civilization." At the ticket window a smaller sign read "All Seats $5.00."

*   *   *

It was ten in the morning and Joyce Hopkins stood before a mirror next to her bed. Her interview at General Public Utilities, Nuclear Division, was only four hours away and all she could think was "What to wear?"

A half hour later Joyce stood again before the mirror, wearing a slip and stockings. On the bed, next to her, lay a two-foot-high mountain of discarded options. Mocking the title of a recent bestseller, which she hadn't read, she said aloud to herself, "Dress for Success. . . . What *do* 'hey like?''

At one o'clock she walked out the door wearing a brownish tweed jacket; a cream-colored Qiana blouse, full-cut with a tied collar; a dark beige skirt, fairly straight and hemmed (by Maria Aguilar) two inches below the knee; shear fawn stockings, and simple but elegant reddish-brown pumps on her feet. Her hair was to the shoulder, her look tawny.

When she got the job she thanked her friend Millie, a middle manager, for the tip not to wear pants.

* * *

Joe Davis stood at the endless conveyor, placing caps on a round-the-clock parade of automobile radiators. His nose and eyes burned. His ears buzzed in the din. In a furtive moment he looked up and to the right. On the plant wall was a large yellow sign with THINK! printed on it in bold type. Joe turned back quickly to the radiator caps.

Fifty years earlier, in another factory, in another state, Joe's grandfather, Nat Davis, had looked up and seen another sign:

A *Clean* Machine Runs Better.
Your Body is a Machine.
KEEP IT CLEAN.

Though he tried and tried, Joe Davis' grandfather was never able to get the dirt out from under his nails. Neither could his great-grandfather, who couldn't read.

* * *

In 1952 Mary Bird left her family in Charleston to earn money as a maid in a Philadelphia suburb. She earned thirty-five dollars a week, plus room and board, in a dingy retreat of a ranch-style tract house.

Twenty-eight years later she sits on a bus, heading toward her small room in North Philly. Across from her, on an advertising poster, a sumptuous meal is displayed. Golden fried chicken, green beans glistening with butter and flecked by pimento, and a fluffy cloud of rice fill the greater part of a calico-patterned dinner plate. Next to the plate sit a steaming boat of gravy, and an icy drink in an amber tumbler. The plate is on a quilted blue placemat, flanked by a thick linen napkin and colonial silverware.

As Mary Bird's hungers are aroused, the wording on the placard instructs her: "*Come Home to Carolina.*"

* * *

SHOPPING LIST

paper towels
milk
eggs
rice crispies
chicken
snacks for kids (twinkies, chips, etc.)
potatoes
coke, ginger ale, plain soda
cheer
brillo
peanut butter
bread
ragu (2 jars)
spagetti
saran wrap
salad
get cleaning, bank, *must pay electric*!!!

* * *

On his way to Nina's house, Sidney passed an ad for Smirnoff vodka. A sultry beauty with wet hair and beads of moisture on her smooth, tanned face looked out at him. "*Try a Main Squeeze.*" For a teenage boy the invitation transcended the arena of drink; he felt a quick throb-pulse at the base of his belly and his step quickened.

In October of 1957, at the age of two and a half, Aaron Stone was watching television. Suddenly, from the black screen, there leaped a circus clown, selling children's vitamins, and yelling "Hi! boys and girls!" He ran, terrified, from the room, screaming.

For years after, Aaron watched television in perpetual fear that the vitamin clown would reappear. Slowly his family assured him that the television was just a mechanical box and couldn't really hurt him, that the vitamin clown was harmless.

Today, as an adult, Aaron Stone takes vitamins, is ambivalent about clowns, and watches television, although there are occasional moments of anxiety.

These are some of the facts of our lives; disparate moments, disconnected, dissociated. Meaningless moments. Random incidents. Memory traces. Each is an unplanned encounter, part of day-to-day existence. Viewed alone, each by itself, such spaces of our lives seem insignificant, trivial. They are the decisions and reveries of survival; the stuff of small talk; the chance preoccupations of our eyes and minds in a world of images—soon forgotten.

Viewed together, however, as an ensemble, an integrated panorama of social life, human activity, hope and despair, images and information, another tale unfolds from these vignettes. They reveal a pattern of life, the structures of perception.

As familiar moments in American life, all of these events bear the footprints of a history that weighs upon us, but is largely untold. We live and breathe an atmosphere where mass images are everywhere in evidence; mass produced, mass distributed. In the streets, in our homes, among a crowd, or alone, they speak to us, overwhelm our vision. Their presence, their messages are givens; unavoidable. Though their history is still relatively short, their prehistory is, for the most part, forgotten, unimaginable.

The history that unites the seemingly random routines of daily life is one that embraces the rise of an industrial consumer society. It involves explosive interactions between modernity and old ways of life. It includes the proliferation, over days and decades, of a wide, repeatable vernacular of commercial images and ideas. This history spells new patterns of social, productive, and political life.

This book, in its various essays, attempts to plumb the social history that stands behind the apparent immortality of a consumer society; its universe of commodities; its priorities; its social forms. The pages that follow offer some historical suggestions aimed at telling some of the story by which these disparate events, these "insignificant" details and occurrences, took hold as the facts of life.

Part One

The
Bribe
of
Frankenstein

1 / *Gears of Progress*

TO HUMAN CONSCIOUSNESS, the epoch of the machine is one of hope and horror, ambiguous and confusing. While at one moment technology is equated with progress and the promise of a world of plenty, free from toil, in the next it evokes the vision of a world gone mad, out of control, the vision of Frankenstein.

In Mary Wollstonecraft Shelley's tale, on the verge of creating his terrible offspring, Victor Frankenstein sees only its utopian potential. Pondering his ability to replace kinship with science in the creation of life, the doctor proclaims:

> So much has been done . . . more, far more, will I achieve: treading in steps already marked, I will pioneer a new way, explore unknown powers, and unfold to the world the deepest mysteries of creation.[1]

This is the voice of eighteenth-century Enlightenment. The universe makes sense and it can be known, mastered, by its laws. Such knowledge of nature's secrets, once grounds for expulsion from Paradise, pointed Christendom toward the ultimate perfectability of human existence, as the "Great Mechanic" of the heavens gave way to the greater mechanic (and entrepreneur) on the ground.

Yet it is not long before Dr. Frankenstein's pride turns to a terror born of his own creation. The highly articulate monster of Shelley's story, betrayed by his father's fears, turns on his ambivalent creator with foreboding. He issues the following expression of a familiar technological predicament: "You are my creator," he says, "but I am your master." Then, for those of us not fully apprised of the extent of his mastery, he warns: "*I will be with you on your wedding night.*"[2]

The tale is recurrent within the industrial era. In one updated version, the film *Demon Seed* tells the story of a computer-monster that appropriates for itself all of the prerogatives of its creator. Securing its creator's home, the computer moves to help itself to the scientist's wife, raping her and impregnating her with the embryo of a new and ominous species—one that places humankind itself in jeopardy.[3]

Although the main theme in the Frankenstein legend lends itself to an Oedipal interpretation, the terror the story evokes should not be understood as purely or primarily sexual: neither is it purely or primarily about existence. Despite the undefined social relations expressed by the legends of Frankenstein, there is a particular social relation implicit within the legend. Historically, the story of human initiative as it is displaced by the demands of the "machine" is reflected most generally in the experience and consciousness of class. It is in the formation of the industrial working class that the visionary lullaby of technology is broken by the din of an ensuing nightmare. If the "machine" brings terror and pain to the human soul, it is because, for most people, the "machine" is not theirs. As "free laborers," they are but a part of it, pieces within a controllable universe that is out of their control.

Yet if for some the "machine" has provided a metaphor for domination, for others it has represented a guiding principle by which they might dominate. For an emerging bourgeoisie, the "machine" was no mere piece of equipment. First and foremost it was a way of perceiving the world. Historian Carlo Cipolla has argued that by the mid-seventeenth century, "the mechanization of the world view" was well underway. The machine provided a "reference-idea" by which the world could be understood, possessed, and mastered. In universities, speculative and contemplative philosophy and "traditional scholarship" were undercut by an "experimental and mechanical" philosophy, the aim of which was, very simply, "(t)he whole 'management of this great machine of the world.' "[4]

Long before the rise of factory capitalism and the extensive use of power-driven machinery, the "machine" represented—within evolving bourgeois thought—a vision of a world in which all human and material resources, even the power of creation, constituted a "complex apparatus of interrelated and moving parts."[5] In the nineteenth century, with the mammoth growth of industrialism, the stark contrast between the machine as a "reference-idea" and the machine as a social instrument of production became painfully apparent. Manchester, England, and other industrial hell-holes revealed to a growing factory population the specter of "dark Satanic mills"—the impoverishment, disease, and squalor of working-class lives alongside the "wonders" of the machine age. Yet even amid the manifest contradictions created by industrial capitalism, machines themselves would often be publicly exhibited, not only as examples of scientific development, but as totems to the vision of a manageable universe. The "Corliss Engine," a gargantuan device exhibited at the Philadelphia Centennial Exposition (1876), was only one example. The engine, displayed in a tabernacle to industry, gave middle-class onlookers a modern religious experience. Viewers of the engine were often reduced to tears in its awesome presence, swept away by the apparition that they were witness to the power of the universe, tamed and harnessed by reasonable, enlightened science.[6] Separated from its industrial context, and enshrined within a house of secular worship, the engine stood as testimony to a world which could be controlled.

Behind this notion of a totally manageable world, there was an implicit cultural premise. For the world to be apprehended as a well-oiled machine, one must assume that the intricate fabric of daily life itself can be controlled by those who understand its workings. Within this entrepreneurial conceit lies the imperative to develop a means by which the law, knowledge, information, transactions, and priorities of an expanding world market economy can be regulated: a *technology of discourse*. The ability to accumulate, package, and disseminate knowledge represented the formation of new networks of understanding, prefiguring the slow abolition of autonomous and indigenous popular forms of "culture."

For more than five hundred years, the growth of capitalism has depended on the ability to manage and distribute standardized knowhow and information. "Mass communication" is not an isolated phenomenon of twentieth-century capitalism, sustaining and reorganizing a society *previously* defined by the rise of factory production and discipline and by the development of heavy machinery. For capitalism, mechanical production and image-making have long shared the same quilt. Though the rise of machinery, utilizing interchangeable parts and proliferating standardized goods, preceded the development of modern communications technology, it was the technology of communications that, within Europe by the mid-fifteenth century, offered the prototype for the machine age, for the era of factory industrialism. The first printing presses were ensembles of skills and tools from an artisan tradition. Scribal skills and papers, combined with artisan punches and a modified winepress, produced a mechanism that permanently altered social definitions of work and production. This mechanism—*the printing press*—was the first mass-production machine, and by the late fifteenth century it represented the most dramatic contrast available between the localized, erratic tempo of customary life and the worldly promise of capitalist enterprise. Not only were early print shops capitalist operations; some were *factories*. By 1480, less than forty years after Gutenberg's initial enterprise, the Koberger Press in Nuremberg employed a hundred men, operating twenty-four presses.[7]

To a large extent, the history of printing coincides with the history of an emergent world commerce; they were often intertwined. It is no coincidence that the first printer in the English language, William Caxton, was also the leading English wool merchant (*mercer*) at Bruges, Belgium. Printing enabled commerce to develop a more universal and consistent language, appropriate to mobile, contractual transactions. Printing could standardize texts and disseminate information and imagery in ways impossible within the constraints and imprecisions of the traditional scribal culture. Printing was a tool of revolution by which world commercial networks could be established and maintained; by which a mobile economy could be underwritten and secured.[8] Herbert Schiller has noted that in today's world, the integration of capitalism is ensured by the maintenance of a world information order.[9] Already by the sixteenth century, the printed word was, to a large extent, the connective tissue of what Immanuel Wallerstein has termed "the modern world system."[10]

Yet the machinery of print was not, from its inception, the sole or implicit monopoly of an unfolding world commerce. The power to reproduce and spread ideas and information served a variety of social forces and possibilities. Print was also a revolutionary, democratic tool, central in the unraveling of old, feudal seats of authority and power. The spread of knowledge and literacy that came in the wake of printing reached far and wide. Beyond its service in the development of commercial enterprise, print raised the possibility of a transportable popular discourse, explosive in the context of feudalism.

Throughout most of feudal Europe, the written word had been a monopoly of the Church. Books were rare and costly, handwritten, slowly and individually, by scribes. Within such a world, literacy was unusual, limited to those clerics who had access to scribal texts. In addition, texts were for the most part written in Latin. While the clergy could read and understand them, they were indecipherable to those limited to vernacular tongues. This monopoly over the word gave the clergy enormous power, for they reserved the right to interpret what others could not read or understand. This power was particularly significant in the reading of the Bible.

The Bible was the Word of God, the universal law, but its interpretation was left to those privileged few who could read it. Within the context of feudal Catholicism, biblical interpretation tended to underwrite the immense social, political, land-holding power of the Church. Exegesis underwrote structures of hierarchy and authority. Vast chasms between the material abundance of Church and nobility and the scarcity experienced by peasants were represented as the immutable order of things. Salvation came from obedience to that order. According to the predominant clerical reading of the Bible, social inequity was the way of God. The sufferings of the poor were humankind's payment for *original sin*. Those who sat comfortably at the heights of social power did so, it was asserted, as a divine right; they were agents of God.

While feudal power was often held and defended by the sword, it was justified by the word. The monopoly over *the word,* over literacy, and over the ability to interpret what was read, was the fundamental aspect of rule.

Even before printing developed in the mid-fifteenth century, there were some radical challenges to this structure. If exclusive access to the word of God was used to justify the position and privilege of an often profligate clergy, attempts to break that monopoly stood at the heart of social revolt. In England, John Wycliffe and the Lollards (literally, "Babblers") moved against the monopoly over the word in the early fourteenth century. Preparing a vernacular translation of the Bible, and consequently breaking the Latin cipher of the Church, Wycliffe went throughout the countryside, reading the Bible aloud, *in the vernacular*. Whereas the Church limited access and interpretation to a clerical elite, Wycliffe and the Lollards sought to spread access to the Bible among people customarily banned from the power of interpretation. The results were explosive. With the word of God in the hands of the people, Church hegemony and practices came under simultaneous attack. Implicitly democratic, the Lollard movement undermined Church possession of the word and its interpretation. The spread of literature, the opening-up of arenas of interpretation, cut deep into the traditional fabric of power. Denounced by Pope Gregory XI and later condemned by a synod in England, Wycliffe was branded a heretic, his writings and translation banned.

Printing made this democratic impulse behind Wycliffe's heresy all the more realizable. Within less than a hundred years of Gutenberg's first printed Bible, vernacular translations were widespread throughout Europe. In addition, a wide variety of literature began to appear in the vernacular, not only accessible to more and more people, but able to be interpreted in terms of those people's experience and perspective.

For increasingly mobile sectors of the European population—not just merchants, but also artisans, low-level civil servants, and rural and an emerging urban poor—the demand for printed, vernacular literature plowed into the static, entrenched soil of the feudal order. The spread of vernacular literature, and of literacy, enabled individuals to spread knowledge and ideas, to interpret the world in their own terms. Alongside commercial networks of printed materials, a radical vernacular tradition began to emerge. The reproducible and transportable capacities of print offered vast possibilities of popular knowledge and expression. Written knowledge, once the exclusive domain of elites, now might reach and permeate populations held down by ignorance. The power to speak through the printing press provided the link between literacy and struggle. Beyond serving as a tool of mercantilism, print was a tool of emancipation; much of the early history of printed materials is that of a vernacular literature of protest and revolt; of popular sentiment and activity. In addition to a commercial intelligence, printing expanded access to democratic ideas, notions of individual and natural rights.

Literacy and access to the printed word were cardinal elements in the overturning of social systems predicated on popular ignorance. For centuries following the development of the printing press, access to the word was an essential demand among people attempting to break the chains of autocracy.

One of the most eloquent and penetrating discussions of the liberating powers of literacy was voiced by the great black abolitionist Frederick Douglass. For Douglass, raised in slavery in Maryland, access to the word was a critical device of freedom. In his autobiography, *My Bondage and My Freedom,* he tells the story of his own acquisition of literacy, and some of the revealing lessons he learned along the way. As a boy, Douglass would frequently overhear his mistress reading the Bible aloud. Innocently, and without knowledge of the consequences, young Douglass asked her to teach him, so that he too might read from the Bible.

> . . . the dear woman began the task, and very soon, by her assistance, I was master of the alphabet, and could spell words of three or four letters. My mistress

seemed almost as proud of my progress, as if I had
been her own child; and, supposing that her husband
would be as well pleased, she made no secret of what
she was doing for me. . . .

Douglass continues, describing her husband's response:

Master Hugh was amazed at the simplicity of his
spouse, and probably for the first time, he unfolded to
her the true philosophy of slavery, and the peculiar
rules necessary to be observed by masters and mis-
tresses, in the management of their human chattels.
(He) . . . forbade the continuance of her instruction;
telling her, . . . that the thing itself was unlawful; that
it was also unsafe. . . . To use his own words . . . he
said, "if you give a nigger an inch, he will take an ell";
"he should know nothing but the will of his master,
and learn to obey it." "Learning will spoil the best
nigger in the world"; "if you teach that nigger—
speaking of myself—how to read the bible, there will
be no keeping him"; "it would forever unfit him for
the duties of a slave"; . . . "if you learn him now to
read, he'll want to know how to write; and this accom-
plished, he'll be running away with himself." Such
was the tenor of Master Hugh's oracular exposition of
the true philosophy of training human chattel; and it
must be confessed that he very clearly comprehended
the nature and the requirements of master and slave.

For Douglass, the consequences of Master Hugh's ora-
tion were explosive and liberating:

The effect of his words, *on me,* was neither slight or
transitory. His iron sentences—cold and harsh—sunk
deep into my heart, and stirred up not only my feelings
into a sort of rebellion, but awakened within me a
slumbering train of vital thought. It was a new and
special revelation, dispelling a painful mystery, against
which my youthful understanding had struggled, and
struggled in vain, to wit: the *white* man's power to
perpetuate the enslavement of the *black* man.[11]

Douglass' words cut to the heart of the matter. As literacy had been a province of power among feudal clergy, slavery in the United States also depended on the exclusive literacy of whites, in order to maintain dominion over blacks. Access to the word—the ability to read, write, interpret and spread ideas through print—was essential to the emancipation of blacks from the generations of bondage. Not only does Douglass speak to the emancipatory powers of literacy, he also illuminates the reluctance, on the part of ruling elites, to allow literacy and knowledge to spread beyond themselves.

Increased popular access to the word also inspired new interpretations. Often these interpretations were at odds not only with the feudal past, but with the outlook of new, commercial forces as well. If the predominant idea of a "world-machine" was consistent with the concentration of property and power in the hands of a few, radical appropriations of the printing press offered a different, more egalitarian world-view. Writing in 1649, Gerard Winstanley, a revolutionary English pamphleteer and a leader of the "True Levellers" (also known as "Diggers"), for example, offered a different view of creation, one challenging the traditional notion that poverty was the legacy of original sin:

> In the beginning of time, the great creator, Reason, made the earth to be a common treasury, to preserve beasts, birds, fishes and man, the lord that was to govern this creation. . . . Not one word was spoken in the beginning that one branch of mankind should rule over another. . . . But . . . selfish imaginations did set up one man to teach and rule over another. And thereby . . . man was brought into bondage, and became a greater slave to such of his own kind than the beasts of the field were to him.[12]

Winstanley's words give us a good sense of the explosive capacity of vernacular printing. If in the traditional, clerical interpretation, poverty was the mark of sin, Winstanley sees property as sin, the result of bloody thievery. His reading of "creation" makes no allowance for autocratic control over land; Winstanley's God created the world as a "common treasury," motivated by Reason, not by vengeance against sinful humanity. Against a society marked by vast disparities of poverty and wealth, Winstanley appropriated the Bible on behalf of a world in which "the poorest man hath as true a title and just right to the land as the richest man." Diverting from definitions of *freedom* that accentuated the mobile needs of a commercial bourgeoisie, Winstanley posited a worldview in which "true freedom lies in the free enjoyment of the earth" for all.

Pamphlets, like those penned by Winstanley, were printed in the fields of battle, amidst the Puritan revolution. Articulated in an accessible vernacular, they reached a population formerly proscribed from textual interpretation. By the latter years of the eighteenth century, this vernacular tradition of pamphleteering was an essential component in the flourishing of popular movements. In the words of Thomas Paine, for example, vernacular literature and increasing literacy merged with sensuous glory. *Common Sense,* published by Paine in January 1776, represented the triumph of the vernacular as a potent and compelling revolutionary form, one that spoke to and touched the experiences of its readers. Like Winstanley's, Paine's vernacular is a voice of Reason, an assault against tyranny. Its imagery, compelling and inspirational, was also accessible, written in terms that could be understood by nearly anyone:

> O! Ye that love mankind! Ye that dare oppose not only the tyranny but the tyrant, stand forth! Every spot of the Old World is over-run with oppression. Freedom hath been hunted round the globe. Asia and Africa have long expelled her. Europe regards her like a stranger, and England hath given her warning to depart. O receive the fugitive, and prepare in time an asylum for mankind.[13]

Paine's words offered an explosive, vernacular, political language, words waging war against the tyranny of British rule. The ability to spread the word, rooted in the rise of a vernacular literature and literacy, was essential to the popular mobilization for the American Revolution.

Douglass, Winstanley, and Paine were powerful representatives of a vernacular literary tradition, rooted in the development of print, given impetus by developments that made printing presses relatively cheap and extremely portable. Simultaneous to the spread of printing throughout much of Europe was the circulation of an "underground" literature, using the new technology of discourse as a weapon against dominant structures of power and authority. The early history of the print media was not one of a monolithic commercial development, but of a battleground upon which struggles for social power and popular initiative were hotly contested.

Yet alongside the flowering of this vernacular tradition, the most widespread implementation of print was in the accumulation, reproduction, and transmittal of information essential to an unfolding world market. Well into the nineteenth century, one of the most pervasive uses of printing was the dissemination of commercial intelligence. Long before the "newspaper" became known as a popular form of diversion, it was a vehicle of commerce, passing privileged mercantile dispatches from branch office to branch office; from port to port; from seller to buyer and back again. As the mechanic on the ground inherited the creative powers of the mechanic in the sky, so too did the mysterious word and law of God give way to a worldly word and law, informed largely by the priorities of commerce and industry.

By the 1830s, in the United States, this commercial tradition in print took a new turn. Appealing to an increasingly literate working class, and contending with a potentially dangerous vernacular tradition, farsighted entrepreneurs began to develop a mass medium that was commercial in outlook and orientation, but that absorbed a vernacular idiom. The development of the "penny press"—a mass-circulation, commercial press—was the embryo of the twentieth-century mass media. As commercial ventures, these newspapers appropriated a common form of speaking, appealing to a wide, literate audience. Employing newswriting formulas that couched stories in fantastic, moralistic, and authoritative terms, these newspapers moved from being the limited, commercially oriented information sheets of the past, into commercial forms of popular entertainment and disclosure. Commerce was developing a popular "audience." While these papers built their readership by connecting their parlance to the terms of popular, urban experience, they were also vehicles that celebrated the mechanical world-view of the entrepreneurs. In the pages of this press, commercial enterprise was enshrouded in the magical liturgy of "progress." Science and invention were heavily promoted, presented in ways to capture the imaginations of a readership whose day-to-day confrontations with technological development might be considerably less entertaining. Newspapers offered readers a way of interpreting their world; moral lessons about urban life; fantastic visions of worlds unknown; authoritative renderings of things to come.

Yet commercial information was still an exclusive currency within an expanding market economy. Commercially supported newspapers represented a hybrid between entrepreneurial interests and popular, vernacular forms of expression. Meanwhile, other forms of communication were promoted to provide exclusive channels for commerce. The early development of the telegraph, and later the wireless, reflected this priority.

While the first officially sent telegraph message— "WHAT HATH GOD WROUGHT"—suggested an invention that stood above pecuniary interests, it is noteworthy that the lines along which this message was sent were laid beside the roadbed of the Baltimore and Ohio Railroad between Baltimore and Washington, D.C. As new telegraph lines were established within the United States, they relentlessly followed the routes of commerce (or *war,* when required), providing a means for high-speed passing of information, analogous to the speed of carriage provided by the rails. Reflecting the centrality of communications to the rise of industrial America, the first major industrial monopoly (Western Union) was established over the field of telegraphy; the integration and control of commercial and requisite military information were at stake. By 1867, a specialized adaptation of the magnetic telegraph had been developed in the form of the stock ticker; once again, communications technology had elaborated upon the infrastructure of the "great machine of the world." It had done so using wires and code, circumventing the explosive lines of battle encompassed by the vernacular.

Following the pattern by which American telegraph and rail lines coincided, the British control of a global, oceanic empire was similarly integrated by the introduction of submarine telegraph cables. In 1851 a cable was laid across the English Channel from Dover to Calais. By 1864, another stretched to the Persian Gulf, providing near-instantaneous commercial and military contact between England and India; and 1866 witnessed the successful laying of a trans-Atlantic cable. By 1871 (less than thirty years after the first overland lines had been established), the telegraphic cohesion of Empire was achieved with an underwater line to Australia.

The early development of the "wireless" had a similar pattern. Years before radio was commercially promoted as a vernacular medium of mass entertainment and impression, it was advanced by its developers as a refinement of the commercial orientation of telegraphy, allowing, for the first time, ship-to-shore communication. Wireless, like telegraph, was seen as a way of unifying and protecting commercial interests, for the carrying of market and military intelligence. Beyond Marconi, the prime developers of radio patents in the United States included the Navy and the United Fruit Company; both saw radio as essential to coordinating their operations.[14]

By the end of the nineteenth century, the consolidation of information into a basic form of currency had become a keystone in the structuring of a capitalist world economy, and in the establishment and maintenance of corporate industrialism. If Frankenstein provides us with a telling metaphor for a technological world out of reach and out of control, it is the development of communications systems, to a large extent, that has placed this world beyond the networks of popular discourse. Throughout its historical genesis, the apprehension of industrialism as a monster, as a machinery possessed of a pernicious intelligence, against which popular motives appear virtually helpless, owes much to the presence and elaboration of communication technologies. If print had once been a field of conflict between a vernacular and a commercial tradition, by the mid-nineteenth century the commercial tradition prevailed, in the process appropriating the vernacular, with the rise of mass-circulation newspapers.

By the dawn of the twentieth century, capitalism had come to mean an integrated, increasingly monopolistic interpenetration of market, scientific knowhow, industrial and finance capital, and communications networks. Channels of popular sensibility and desire were themselves subject to the encroachments of a marketable vernacular. For triumphant industrial and finance capitalists, this was a moment when the management of the world-machine seemed almost within reach, when (to quote Victor Frankenstein, once more) "unknown powers . . . (and) the deepest mysteries of creation" seemed there for the taking. Yet as the mechanical world-view became tangible in its formal structures, it

was far from established within the social relations that
guided them. If anything, the social experience of industrialism put the lie to the utopian idiom in which the
world-machine had been articulated. The years leading
up to 1900 were not only times of extreme exploitation
and industrial hardship; they were also a time of concerted growing anticapitalist resistance and organization.
The fantasy of a smoothly running mechanical world was
eroded by the dislocation and unrest that it provoked.
Beneath the reference-idea of capitalist development as a
machine was a history of what Marx once termed "reck-
less terrorism." Capitalism, he reiterated, "comes into
the world dripping from head to foot, from every pore,
with blood and dirt."[15] For the industrial working class,
and for those caught in the ever-widening sweep of capitalist dominion, it was a development that spelled continual and multiplying social crisis. Culture, social life,
were torn apart. As the machine represented a guiding
principle for a maturing bourgeoisie, for those in its path
it was the embodiment of the "white terror," threatening
life itself.

For the industrial working class at the turn of the
twentieth century, the social crisis was manifest and
immediate. The sanguine and utopian rhapsodies of a
new machine age were drowned out by the mechanical
din of the shop. The bourgeois celebration of the machine was answered by a multitude of voices, drawing
once again from the tradition of a radical vernacular. The
contradictions and irony of the mechanical world-view
can be heard in the words of Yiddish poet Morris
Rosenfeld, writing of the sweatshops of New York
City's garment industry:

> The machines in the shop roar so wildly that often I
> forget in the roar that I am; I am lost in the terrible
> tumult, my ego disappears, I am a machine, I work and
> work and work without end. I am busy and busy at all
> time. For what and for when? I know not and ask not!
> How should a machine ever come to think?[16]

Rosenfeld chants the subjective anguish of proletari-anization. While the roar of the machines and the disci-pline of the time clock signal the root of despair, and stir the motive to retaliate, exploitation is understood not in the numerical terms of dollars and hours, not in the terms of the machine. The ironic phrasing ''I am a machine'' is a recognition that mechanical routine is an attack on the essential integrity of the subject. The revolutions of the machine, so glorious within the liturgy of bourgeois thought, are revealed as an abomination for those who must follow their drumming.

2 / The Capture of the Eye

BY THE END of the nineteenth century, in the United States, the dissonance between the visionary celebration of the "machine" and the actual experiences of those employed in the mechanical processes of industry had reached crisis proportions. Labor militancy was on the rise and its socialist or syndicalist outlook posed a radical challenge to that of the "world-machine." Consistent with the traditions of the past, much of this militancy found expression in a critical and incendiary vernacular: song, poetry, journalism, political manifesto. While the ideology of mechanical progress permeated entrepreneurial thought, popular perceptions of the machine, and of capitalism itself, grew bitter and seditious. A torrent of antagonism was, more and more, carried by the channels of working-class opinion.

The 1905 *Manifesto* of the nascent Industrial Workers of the World (I.W.W.) offered a depiction of the machine that clashed sharply with the dominating ideology, challenging the very social relations that upheld it:

> The *great facts* of present industry are the displacement of human skill by machines and the increase of capitalist power through concentration in the possession of the tools with which wealth is produced and distributed.

Within such an arrangement, it was argued, the mechanical world becomes an arena of human degradation and destruction:

> As human beings and human skill are displaced by mechanical progress, the capitalists need use the workers only during that brief period when muscles and nerves respond most intensely. The moment the laborer no longer yields the maximum of profits, he is thrown upon the scrap pile, to starve alongside the discarded machine.[17]

Linked as they were to a flowering of revolutionary working-class activity, such ideas jammed the works of the "world-machine" outlook. They challenged the notion that the world could be mastered through the social application of mechanical principles, arguing that it was necessary to serve social needs, not vice versa.

Within the context of such combat, the commercial appropriation of the vernacular took on an increasingly important role in the forging of a modern, industrial ideology. Responsive to an environment shaken by proletarian rage and organization, commercial organs of public communication began to offer ideological concessions to the sway of popular desire. The idiom of a controllable "world-machine" became increasingly encoded with a vision of social promise. While the priorities of the marketplace continued to be asserted, they were phrased in the terms of the general good. "Industrial democracy" and social reform, previously the slogans of those opposing capitalist rapacity, began to enter the commercial dialect.

To an extent, the stage had been set for this development in the 1830s, with the emergence of the "penny" newspapers. As a mass-circulation press, its accomplishment had been based on the ability to translate the vernacular into a viable commercial form. The appeal to common experiences and perceptions provided an essential conduit between commercial institutions and the consciousness of an urban working class. During the latter decades of the nineteenth century, this fusion of perspectives provided the groundwork for a new, socially responsive iconography of capitalism, ostensibly more liable and accountable to its population.

From the mid-1870s to the '90s, caught in a period of economic stagnation, American industry and federal policy pursued an increasingly aggressive search to expand markets and prosperity. As the domestic frontier was closing, the United States embarked upon assembling a world empire. Surely such a direction required, in a renewed sense, a deep commitment to the idea of a manageable "world-machine." Yet domestically—confronting a surge of class upheaval—the "machine" adjusted its verbiage in the direction of social amelioration, of defusing the roots of social discord. It was a "machine" that, in the name of effecting a more pacific home front, developed a public face that disowned the cold calculation of the mechanical world-view—at the same time pursuing it, internationally, with a vengeance. The "machine," and particularly the decisive machinery of mass communications, would hereafter serve as the public champion of universal possibility and well-being.

Communications assumed a new "progressive" phraseology, espousing the goals of social improvement and change, a palliative to demands being voiced by an increasingly militant working-people's movement. Continuing to develop a sophisticated apparatus as a passageway for privileged intelligence, communications technologies also increasingly entered into the spheres of public discourse. Underwriting a "socially minded" vision of capitalism, media technologies began to emerge, more and more, as the public vehicles of such a vision. The "yellow" journalism of William Randolph Hearst and Joseph Pulitzer, coming to prominence in and around the 1890s, foreshadowed the essential role of *the image* within the new, social strategy of capitalism. These papers made innovative and extensive use of illustration, bold typeface, and sensationalistic style to command the eyes and minds of their readership. The *photo-*

graph provided a model for the desired journalistic impact: objective, true-to-life, mesmerizing. The photographic model for objectivity gave Hearst and Pulitzer a vital command over the popular sensibility.[18] The mobilization of a visual world expanded the commercial terrain of the printed vernacular, and made it even more accessible. Yellow journalism gave corporate imagery an inspired voice, couched in the idiom of social conscience. The papers put together a broad audience, posing as champions of the industrial poor and downtrodden, helping to forge the image of the United States as a refuge for those scorned by the rest of the world. Pulitzer's New York *World* mobilized a fund-raising campaign to erect Bertholdi's Statue of Liberty on its pedestal in New York's harbor, a mischievous promise to incoming immigrant labor. *"Give me your tired, your poor, your huddled masses yearning to breathe free. . . ."*

Carefully orchestrating and defending an image of capitalist America as a land of social promise, Pulitzer and Hearst were also propaganda architects for the imperial conquests that would underwrite that promise. It has often been simplistically stated that Hearst and his New York *Journal* brought about the Spanish-American War to aid in a circulation war with Pulitzer's *World*. Yet the war propaganda fomented in both of their papers represented a wide-ranging political and commercial strategy, within which the circulation of newspapers was but a small component. Building up a war fervor by printing a rash of articles decrying "Spanish atrocities" against "freedom-loving" Cubans, Hearst erected a massive, socially conscious smokescreen behind which American capitalism took hold of a Caribbean and Pacific empire. The journalism of the yellow variety provided the requisite imagery for a new corporate perspective, linking the humanistic principle of a "full dinner pail" at home with aggressive and militaristic cultivation of markets abroad.

The yellow press, along with other emerging agencies of mass impression, was a pioneer in the widespread dissemination of photographic and other pictorial imagery. In the early years of this century, the camera, particularly motion pictures, best revealed the charismatic social possibilities of communications technology. The camera was a powerful mechanism for conveying fantasy and suggesting transcendence; its imagery employed a powerful, visual vernacular, understandable even to immigrants unable to speak English. Yet at the same time, in its ability to codify and capture an objectivist "truth" it was also a powerful mechanism of order and control.

Reflecting progressive corporate thought of the time, *Scientific American* discussed the invention of the movie camera in its encyclopedic publication *The Book of Progress,* a three-volume work that appeared in 1915.[19] Here the movie camera is situated first in a long catalog of industrial accomplishments, discussed in two entries on movie technology.

The first entry ponders the rise of the movies as a popular entertainment, one particularly appealing to the urban, immigrant work force: the initial movie audience. The article is lyrical about cinema's ability to portray an altered vision of reality, and its ability to enlist the senses in such a vision:

> Here, at last, is the magic of childhood—appearances, apparitions, objects possessed of power of movement and of intelligence. . . .
>
> For the motion picture does for us what no other thing can do save a drug, or, in slight degree, long, long training. . . . It eliminates the time between happenings and brings two events separated actually by hours of time and makes them seem to us as following each other with no interval between them. Unconscious of this sixth sense of time, *because it is so much a factor of our daily lives,* ignorant of the fact that it is this and not our eyes alone which have been tricked, we leave

the darkened theater with wonder in our hearts and admiration on our lips.[20] [Emphasis added]

Consistent with the way we see *advertised* goods today, the machine is ripped from its association with the monotone of the workplace; it is not the vehicle of direct commercial transaction.[21] Revealing a significant break from the customary, capitalist use of communications technology, this machine enacts a symbolic assault on the conventions of *time* that rule in a society where people make money, live, by selling their time. *The Book of Progress* consecrates cinema as the carrier of utopian possibility. While integral to the marketplace, this is a machine that apparently wages war on the "machine." It offered, in its imagery, the language of dream in theatrical darkness; the possibility of escape from the constraints of industrial ritual and routine. If the "machine" was, as in Morris Rosenfeld's poem, an attack on the integrity of the subject, the motion picture was a product framed in the imagery of a newly integrated subject, one that evoked transcendent desire within the whirring of its gears. Consumable leisure was ennobled as a subjective answer to the discipline of the "machine." Appropriating, to some extent, the language of the unconscious, of dream and of myth in its imagery, the movie camera could dissociate itself from the tedium of the mechanical process, and realign itself with those realms of existence repressed by the harsh rationalism of "world-machine" ideology. Like the medium in a seance, film crossed the boundary of material existence, evoking a spiritual world. Among the first to use cinema—and earlier, the "magic lantern"—as a public form of entertainment were magicians. It was a part of the spirit world they concocted, the "illusions" by which they captivated their audiences. Later on, these magicians contributed to the development of movie "special effects," further elaborating the link between cinema and apparent miracle.[22] To audiences embroiled in the banality of the mechanical routine, the movie camera was a machine that intimated transcendence and escape. For *The Book of Progress,* this capacity was basic to its achievement.

The second entry on the movie camera in *The Book of Progress* was in stark and sobering contrast to the first, discussing the development of a particular adaptation, the "Gilbreth Chronometer." This device was, essentially, a moving-picture machine linked to a clock. Invented by management expert Frank Gilbreth, this movie camera was used in performing time-motion studies on industrial workers. In the wake of a rhapsody on the ability of the moving picture to lift people from the time constraints of industrial life, the following description of Gilbreth's movie camera appears:

> Every film [frame] reveals the successive positions of a workman in performing each minute operation of the task entrusted to him. The position of the chronometer pointer in successive films indicates the length of time between successive operations. These films are studied under a microscope, and a careful analysis of each operation is made to develop the standard time for each. . . .

> Any workman may, for a time, deceive an inexperienced efficiency engineer . . . but *the camera cannot be deceived.* . . . The film records faithfully every movement made, and subsequent analysis and study reveals exactly how many of these movements were necessary and how many were purposely slow or useless.[23] [Emphasis added]

Implemented within the realm of production, film becomes a mechanism of bald social control. As the movies constituted a consumable form of leisure, predicated on escape, this movie camera reinforced the entrepreneurial ideal of an objective "world-machine" from which no variation or escape is possible. Broken from and doing battle with the relentless rhythms of the industrial machine, it is at the same time a faithful servant to capitalist order—on one hand as a transcendental vehicle of mass illusion, on the other, an instrument of "truth" ("*the camera* cannot be deceived"). Its hold on truth consumes our own.

In this and other examples of communications technology, the dialectic of mass culture is manifest. For popular consumption, leisure, the technology is the carrier of visionary escape. Elsewhere, the technology performs, organizes, stores surveillance. We become data, facts, in the "world-machine." Here the traditional use of communications technology continues unabated. Mechanical control is maintained as the reference-idea of capitalism.[24]

The unity of illusion and control, presented by *Scientific American* in 1915, has established the terms that have characterized industrial culture in the twentieth century. This is a theme, a concern, that runs through the essays that follow. This pattern has informed the development of the "consciousness industries." Machinery is both the monster of Frankenstein and the bribe by which that monster is endured. The mass media and the industries of fashion and design, through the production and distribution of imagery, have reconciled widespread vernacular demands for a better life with the general priorities of corporate capitalism. The growth of the advertising industry, beginning in the 1920s, is *the* fundamental expression of this development. Built on expanded production and the economic potential of consumer markets, advertising created the imagery, the aesthetic, of a social-democratic capitalism, one that understood and would claim to solve the most basic contradictions of modern life.

Within this altered landscape, technologies of communication stand prominently. If previously they had served as a bloodstream nourishing the "world-machine," in the decades leading up to the twentieth century they emerged, more and more, as vehicles by which capitalist culture offered a way out. Altering the meaning of industrial social control, communications technologies were employed to convey an intelligence that was seemingly at odds with the mechanical discipline of industrial productivity.

Part Two

Consumption as a Way of Life

1 / "The System Is the Solution"

THE SCENE OPENS: A pair of hands interlocking the pieces of a three-dimensional wooden "Chinese" puzzle. As the puzzle is solved, a softly modulated man's voice explains that most "industrial problems" or "business problems" are actually "communications problems."

Businessmen and industrialists, take note! An effective, well-designed, integrated system of *communicating* is the key to a smoothly running enterprise.

At last the disembodied hands complete their task. The puzzle is complete. Behold! It has formed the logo of the American Telephone and Telegraph Company, the largest corporation on earth.

Now the screen goes black, and a white-lettered message crosses it, proclaiming:

The system is the solution.

Like stars in the firmament.

This television ad ran for some time during evening national news broadcasts. As people within a highly technological, consumer society, the message addresses us as a philosophical statement about the world in which we live. A quintessential example of the communications industry's self-projected image, it offers total control as a positive ideal, an absolute good. Elsewhere, the same corporation claims that its channels provide us with the wherewithal to "reach out and touch someone." Families are kept together, friendships maintained as we purchase the services of AT&T.

The image, the commercial, reaches out to sell more than a service or product; it sells a way of understanding the world. The basic premise is that in a corporate, industrial world, it is the agencies of communication that provide the mechanisms for social order. The notion appeals to the businessman's desire for effective management. For the rest of us, as mobile, often isolated individuals in an industrial consumer society, it promises that which is increasingly elusive: kinship and community.

Mass imagery, such as that provided by AT&T, creates for us a memorable language, a system of belief, an ongoing channel to inculcate and effect common perceptions, explaining to us what it means to be a part of a "modern world." It is a world defined by the retail (individualized) consumption of goods and services; a world in which social relations are often disciplined by the exchange of money; a world where it increasingly *makes sense* that if there are solutions to be had, they can be bought. Such reminders as those seen in the above ad are commonplace. Consumption is our way of life.

Commercial imagery—ads, packaging, public relations, film, television, and so on—plays an ongoing part in the reinforcement of this way of life. Yet for us, images merely reaffirm that which is structured within the terms of existence. A question—rarely addressed within commercial depictions of the world—remains. How did this way of life come about? Also, since as mass imagery plays such an important role in our kind of society, what role has it played historically in the directing of people into consumption as a way of life, a way of understanding?

2 / *An American Metamorphosis*

AS A seven-year-old girl, Anna Kuthan worked in a small textile factory in Czechoslovakia. She was born into a world of home production and self-sufficiency, but with her leaving home, her daily labors already represented a compromise with a new unfolding world of mass production. Each day she went to the factory, and applied her small young body to the task of unloading bales of cotton, sent there from a faraway place called Texas, in the United States.[1]

These bales of cotton provided Anna with more than her childhood labors; they also gave her a first glimpse of America. On the wrapping of each bale, a colorful lithographed label provided her with a utopian vision of the world from which they had come. In the "big beautiful pictures" she saw a vision that contrasted sharply with the tedium of her own daily chores. They showed "the plantation and the colored people, you know, pictures of how everybody worked and was happy." The children in the factory in Czechoslovakia looked at these pictures each day, weighing them against the hardships of their own experience. For the time being, the pictures served to bring a piece of beauty into their lives. "We got them off nicely," she recalls, "and we decorated everything" with them. But the labels also provoked the wellsprings of desire, pointing her, and others of her generation, toward America as a place to go, to live: "Oh my God! I save every picture and I was always saying I wish I could get to this country. I was dreaming already about this country."

But from the perspective of years of life in America, she found—in this instance—a fissure between image and reality.

> I came to this country and worked with the colored people and hear about and read about the history of the slaves and everything. . . . Then I realize that— Oh my God—how they have to work on the big plantation in the cotton fields, all those black people and children for nothing . . . you know, like slaves.

Nevertheless, the images had stood by themselves: promising and alluring. A way of life was heralded by a colorful label, pasted on the side of a cotton bale, and planted in the imagination of a seven-year-old Czech girl in the first few years of this century.

It was during the First World War that, as a young woman, Anna Kuthan came to Vienna, where she took work as a domestic servant to a wealthy Viennese woman. One of Anna's jobs was to pick up Red Cross packages filled with goods from America, and bring them to the home of her employer. Even though, as a domestic servant, she was denied access to these provisions, she saw the packaging in which they arrived. Like the labels on the cotton bales, those she saw on the Hecker's flour, the Nestlé's cocoa, and the Carnation milk helped to form in her mind a vision of America as a land of plenty:

> I saved all the labels, even from the Hecker's flour. I says, "Oh my God, they must have everything so good if they pack everything so good. If I could only come to this country."

While she was permitted to save the labels from empty containers, their contents were forbidden. "The lady locked everything up," she tells us. She could only imagine that wondrous goods must reside within such brightly decorated packaging. One day, she remembers, her questions were answered. Her employer was away from the house and had forgotten to lock up the provisions. This was Anna's moment of discovery:

> You know what I did? I just put the can in my mouth and it was dripping like honey right in my mouth. And one, two, three she opened the door. I says, "It's inside already, you can't get it out of me!" I got a taste for it. I never forgot it.

After the war was over, Anna made her pilgrimage to the United States. Her experiences of denial and getting caught in the act of stealing were constantly on her mind. To a large extent, she recalls, what she saw in America was a dream come true:

> When I came to this country, the first thing I see is those big stores. I said, "There is the Hecker's flour . . . there is the condensed milk!"
>
> I was married. . . . One day I was shopping and I came home. [My husband] says, "What happened to you?"

She responds:

> "All the things I bought in the stores . . . what I got in Vienna and I could only dream about, not even taste it. And here I see it on the shelf. I bought everything and I'm gonna go there every day and I'm going to buy it!"

As a domestic servant in Vienna, Anna Kuthan saw the consumer products of America as magical objects. Here were the fruits of the land sealed mysteriously in beautified vessels, with painted scenes gracing their outsides. Never before had she seen such things. When, on the occasion described above, she was able to taste from one of these enticing containers on the sly, her experience only served to verify the magic. Like honey the milk flowed past her lips! Yet what was magic for her had for others become a means of day-to-day survival. Already, among the elite of European society, American exports were beginning to make their mark on everyday existence. The terms of luxury were being redefined, and they were coming in cans.

For Anna these cans took on great significance. Beyond their mystical properties, they were concrete embodiments of her own deprivation, of what she desired. From the home of her employer she could take the gaily colored cans, emptied of their content. She was allowed to keep the packaging—the image of a good life—but was denied its contents. The brand names of this new, consumer economy became symbols of her own denial, her class-bound status; they also became channels for her desires, emblems of a world denied, embodiments of wishes unfulfilled. Mere objects, mass-produced in factories, held a highly personal significance; they were benchmarks of servitude, carriers of fantasy. The stolen taste of these products was, in part, an impetuous attempt to break through that world of denial; to assert her own needs and tastes. Before Anna ever set foot in America, her subjectivity had become intertwined with the brand names and products of a young and burgeoning consumer society. Through these she came to understand and define "America."

Arriving in the United States, Anna found these objects of denial flamboyantly displayed in store windows and in advertising. They beckoned to her as symbols of a heretofore unfulfilled expectation. Hecker's flour sacks and Carnation milk cans stared out at her with a promise: What had been denied to her as a servant in Vienna, or as a child laborer in Czechoslovakia, was now available for her own consumption. It was only up to her and her ability to buy. The availability of these products, even on the shelves of stores in which she shopped, was symbolic of a new social position. She was becoming a "free consumer" in an increasingly universal, consumer marketplace. The new constellations of the consumer economy defied the class-bound world of Europe; what was possible only for the upper class in Europe was for her a part of the storehouse of goods that might be purchased for money wherever one turned.

Tears streaming down her face, Anna Kuthan rushed into the grocery store to buy with her small earnings the goods that had become so important, so pregnant, in her previous history. The ability to buy these goods in America was not just an objective act of consumption; it was an act of transcendence, and the realization of a new social status. The brand names and trademarks of America's flowering consumer society formed a historical unity in Anna's passage from a European domestic servant to a new consumer in an industrial society. The image, along with more conventional means of transport, was a vehicle for historical travel.

Anna Kuthan's experience was widely shared. For many people, abroad and even in rural America, the proliferation of mass images provided an introduction to a new way of life promised by industrial America. One such introduction was a flyer circulated and posted in Italy's *mezzogiorno* (southern tier) at the turn of the century, addressed to a decimated peasantry plagued by taxes and rents, historical victims of the ascendancy of the industrial north. One of countless circulars inviting viewers to come to America, this flyer was distributed by woolen manufacturers' agents from Lawrence, Massachusetts, and showed a "picture of a mill on one side of the street and a bank on the other—and workers trooping from one to the other with bags of money under their arms." Linking "ancient utopian motives" to an as-yet-unknown future in industrial America, this ad functioned as an initiation into the terms of *modernity*.[2]

Likewise, within the United States, many rural people who moved into the industrial cities of the north had held similar hopes. Herbert Gutman tells us of an advertisement distributed among black Alabamans during a Kansas coal strike of 1896–97:

> WANTED! COLORED coal-miners for Weir City, Kan.,
> district, the paradise for colored people. . . .
> Special train will leave Birmingham the 13th.
> Transportation advanced. Get ready and go to
> the land of promise.[3]

Industrial wages held a utopian promise for many freedmen historically denied any claim to the land. Wages could provide the wherewithal for former slaves to return south and establish, for the first time, a sovereignty on the land—a hope instilled by the broken promise of Reconstruction: "Forty acres and a mule."

Unlike the later ad from AT&T, which assumes a viewership well-schooled in the logic of the consumer metropolis, these flyers—wooing people from one world into another—offered an unknown, which—through an image—promised to alleviate the hardships of immediate experience. It is only fitting that the first contact with an emerging consumer society should have come in the form of an advertisement, an artifact so characteristic of such a world.

The flyer, and the broad ensemble of alluring imagery to which it belonged, offered a first glimmer of a distant society where industrial development and a triumphal ideology of *progress* were forging new and unfamiliar precepts of survival. America was not a land where existence proceeded according to the venerable laws of nature. Industrial growth was premised on the taming of the natural world; molding it to the expansive imaginations of technological dreamers. Man would create a *nature* of his own, beyond that to which people had historically been bound. Unbeknownst to these peasants, whose axioms of survival had been instructed by a reciprocal engagement with the land, they were beckoned to a place where the transcendence and domination of nature was a project of loud-spoken and evangelical proportions. The world that called was one without a peasantry; its landed wealth had been amassed by means of large-scale capitalist agriculture.* The world that called was one where basic goods came from no apparent source. The ecology of the land, and the finger-knowledge of home and workshop production, were memories in the process of being annihilated.

While the America depicted in the circulars offered itself as a land of money and of promise, we cannot assume that the circulars were understood in their own terms. Millions came to the "land of dollars," but they did not necessarily want to abandon the "old culture." Because they needed and sought money does not mean that they consciously embraced a world-view in which

---

* Though the United States had (and still has) an agricultural working class, it was (is) a class that was largely assembled as integral to a cash-crop economy. From its beginnings, America had built much of its economic vitality on the foundation of a capitalist agriculture. Slavery in the Americas, standing at the heart of the development of a capitalist world market, while obviously not wage labor, was a decidedly capitalist labor system. It is no irony that the New York Stock Exchange stands today at a site originally haunted by slave traders and their pirate cohorts. Designed for the forced production of a cash crop, the slave labor system was one that bound people to owners, not to land. In many ways more akin to a factory work force than a peasantry, slaves embodied transportable and exchangeable labor; they had in fact been transported to the production site, the plantation. There people were mobilized by systems of discipline and observation that are more familiar in the industrial factory than to those that prevailed on the feudal lands of Europe.

Similarly, the rise of great portions of the United States as a grain belt, a "bread basket" for the world, by the end of the nineteenth century, was not the result of an initiative by small, independent, "Yankee" farmers, as is the myth. Rather it was the result of a governmentally enforced integration of large-scale capitalist agriculture with highly industrialized networks of transportation (railroads, which were granted vast farmlands on both sides of the tracks) and communications (telegraphy). The American environment to which many Europeans came in the years at the turn of the twentieth century, even in its agriculture, was at sharp variance from their own historical experience, and the social forms that had shaped that experience.[4]

the abstraction of money (*false estate*) provided the basis of "value" or of "worth." Born of the land, many of these people held on to a notion of value bound to the tangible utility of the land (*real estate*) and the knowledge that it was the land—ultimately—that supports life.

Indeed, many saw money as a device, something to be saved and consolidated to replenish and revitalize their connection to a customary means of survival, while those who paid these immigrants their wages were merely concerned with sustaining them as laborers in the here-and-now. The immigrants themselves often hoped to bankroll a return to their roots. Many saw migration as but a temporary foray, one that would allow for a prosperous reunification with an old and more familiar way of life.[5]

Such hopes persist today among people who, over a lifetime, are caught in the dynamics of an unequally developed world; "guest workers," migrant, industrial laborers in Europe flock to industrial centers with the hope of returning home to enjoy a new prosperity. But now that the return home is systematically enforced at the completion of one's contracted work, it is a return more likely to be accompanied by impoverishment and extreme alienation. Such alienation is rooted in the unclouded recognition of oneself as a movable and malleable object in the design of others.[6]

In the United States, even at the turn of the century, this sense of alienation was widely expressed among the millions who made the journey. In Mike Gold's autobiographical immigrant novel, *Jews Without Money,* the author's father put this sense of cultural disruption succinctly when he called America "the thief." Initially interpreted as a vehicle for replenishing a familiar way of life, wage labor and the practice of selling time were soon revealed as a new structure of domination.[7] Wages did not behave like capital. Capital behaved a little like land; it was a form of wealth that sustained those who owned it; it replenished itself. Wages, on the other hand, were different. The little money that working people gathered in America was something to be spent, to be used up. It involved no posterity, held out little hope. Among people whose agrarian and handicraft backgrounds taught them that consumption was anathema, consumption was being proferred as a necessary definition of citizenship in the new world. Each day they *used up* the means to survive.

This new physics of survival, and the cultural trans- formation it entailed, can be seen in language itself. In Raymond Williams' historical etymology of the word "consumer," the alteration of meanings reflects altera- tions in the way of life.[8] In its original usage (rooted in French) to *consume* was an act of pillage. It meant to "take up completely, devour, waste, spend." "In almost all its early English uses," Williams contends, "*con- sume* had an unfavorable sense; it meant to destroy, to use up, to waste, to exhaust." It is the meaning ex- pressed in the old term for tuberculosis: "consumption." The implication was clearly that using up such a basic resource as land was contrary to the interests of survival. The negative connotation remained dominant in English through the sixteenth century. In the seventeenth cen- tury, as a world market economy grew, based on the new media of exchange, "using up" and the demand it cre- ated became increasingly linked to prosperity; as ex- change left the ancient sense of natural propriety behind, the term "consumer" took on a neutral, then a self- congratulatory meaning. Today, in the United States, people unselfconsciously refer to themselves as *con- sumers.**

* In the last ten years the words "consumer" and "consumerism" have taken on a new meaning connoting the advocacy of consumer rights. In popular terminology and in the mass media, being a "consumer" now refers to people or organizations seeking legal and social protection from the more overt abuses of the marketplace. Here, however, we mean a historically defined social relationship in which people's needs are increasingly encompassed by the mass production and distribution of goods and services.

In a context where value and survival were evidently and directly derived from the land, or from the direct appropriation of nature, consumption on a mass scale would have meant suicide. For the agrarian and handicraft people who came to populate industrial America, the wage system represented an intrinsic violation of a basic assumption, derived from a sensuous proximity to nature, now increasingly hidden in the mire of industrial production, marketing, and urban life. Even here there was a common compulsion to try to *save*; an often futile attempt among immigrants to appropriate their money *as if it were land*. In a world increasingly marked by mass industrialism and a nascent consumer market, the separation of people from nature was becoming axiomatic, entailing what Raymond Williams has called "a triumphalist version of 'man's conquest of nature.' "[9]

In the society to which immigrants came, waste and exhaustion were already the keys to the creation of new, industrial markets. In the cases of those people who made steerage to Gotham, the consumption of their traditional understanding of nature, the destruction of skills coming from that way of life, and the exhaustion of the familiar social patterns of customary life (family, community) were primary elements of American mass industrialism as it took shape in the early years of this century. Repeated calls for the "Americanization" of these immigrants. came from many decisive and decision-making sectors of American society. In 1925, Edgar Furniss, a social scientist at Yale, expressed an American conviction that was held by many in business and politics, in service bureaucracies, and by academic intellectuals.

"Americanization," Furniss implored, "is the paramount need, not only for the immigrant, but for the very existence of the Republic. Unless the millions of immigrants present and future are made an integral part of the population, understanding our institutions, sharing the standards and ideals of the democracy, the Nation itself is imperiled.''[10] While the call for "Americanization" was couched in the terms of eighteenth-century nationalism, immigrants were hardly being invited to join the ruling Yankee-Calvinist brotherhood. Rather, the "American nation" that was raised before them as a social standard was a nation in the process of taking form, becoming standardized and mass-marketed. It was a nation that not only called out to the newly arrived from southern and eastern Europe, but also to an increasingly large, increasingly mobile domestic population. "Americanization" was a process by which a cultural transformation was enacted, a process by which memory came under assault as people were encouraged and/or coerced into equating consumption with survival.

A more biting and satiric definition of "Americanization"—one that spoke eloquently to the pains of this transformation—came from two American social workers, Simon Lubin and Christina Krysto, at the height of a massive "Americanization" campaign in 1919. Offended by the barrage of propaganda that assaulted recently arrived immigrants, Lubin and Krysto insisted that "Americanization" was aimed at the obliteration of traditional culture and its substitution by new, marketplace values:

> Come on all you foreigners, and jump into this magic kettle. You are colored and discolored with things that do not fit in well with affairs here. . . . In fact to speak frankly, there is a certain taint about you, a stain brought by the old world . . .
>
> Your clothes are ill-fitting and ugly. Your language is barbaric. Of course, we do not hold you personally responsible; for you have come from backward and antiquated civilizations, relics of the dark ages. . . . Jump into the cauldron and behold! You emerge new creatures, up to date with new customs, habits, traditions, ideals. Immediately you will become like us; the taint will disappear. Your sacks will be exchanged for

the latest Fifth Avenue styles. Your old-fogey notions will give way to the most modern and new-fangled ideas. You will be reborn. In short, you will become full-fledged Americans. The magic process is certain. Your money back if we fail.[11]

The promise of the "melting pot" was inextricably tied to the consumption of American goods. It equated the utilization of consumer products not only with citizenship, but with a demonstrable and necessary transformation of the self. To be "reborn" meant a profound metamorphosis in the culture of daily life: a change in habits and understandings demanded by the new, unfolding agencies of consumption. The message leveled at immigrants found its corollary aimed at vast sectors of the domestic population as well. "Americanization" was a process through which all Americans had to pass, whether they were greenhorns from the old country or rural "hicks" from the new; it was a metaphor for the transition from the age-old logic of agriculture and handicraft to the logic of consumption.

The first stage was the integration of migrants into the wage system of labor, which created enormous fissures in people's comprehension of the material world. Money was an abstract system of value which was necessary to life, yet it seemed to operate according to an autonomous and lifeless code. It rendered useless much of the way in which agricultural and handicraft peoples understood themselves and daily life. The money system itself functioned as a *mass medium* that restructured people's needs, transplanting these into a soil nourished by the "rationality" of corporate industry and the retail marketplace. Robert Park, Chicago School sociologist, was one of the most ardent chroniclers of this transplanting and a vocal champion of "Americanization." In an enthusiastic, typically progressive discussion of the transformative powers of money in 1925, Park described what must have been for immigrant people a wrenching experience:

Money is the cardinal device by which values have become rationalized and sentiments have been replaced by interests. It is just because we feel no personal and no sentimental attitude toward our money, such as we do toward, for example, our home, that money becomes a valuable means of exchange. We will be interested in acquiring a certain amount of money in order to achieve a certain purpose, but provided that purpose may be achieved in any other way we are likely to be just as well satisfied. It is only the miser who becomes sentimental about money.[12]

Like many developments that are forged in the heat of historical transformation, the purge of the "sentiments" by modern "rationality" was a double-edged sword. As mass production and the wage system uprooted people from traditional world-views, they undermined traditional seats of local authority. For women and children this subversion involved something new—the possibility of freedom from the formerly unassailable power of patriarchy. Similarly, the idea of rationality at the heart of the new society undermined the sometimes unjust power of religion. Equally important, the money economy and industrial production raised the historically elusive possibility of material abundance, a development that has had a resounding appeal worldwide.

But what Robert Park celebrated as the eradication of sentiment meant—for most people entering the metropolis—the experience of a social fabric torn asunder. Bonds of family and community, traditions of mutual dependency, customary patterns of work, all of these were jeopardized by a world whose self-proclaimed destiny was the transcendence of nature itself. The results of this process were often devastating and continue to be so, decades after the "Americanization" of the great waves of European immigrants was completed.

In the Canadian Northwest Territories live twenty-three thousand Eskimos—"Inuit," they call themselves—who only recently have experienced the process of cultural transformation. Conventionally hunters and handicraft producers, the area in which they live—Frobisher Bay in Canada—has, since the late 1970s, become an area of massive industrial development, centering around oil exploration and production. Their traditional nomadic existence disrupted, the Inuits have been forced into permanent settlements with the trappings of modern life: "medical care, schools, telecommunications and a range of Government services." All of these, argued an article in the *New York Times*, were "designed to give them a decent living and the ability to cope in a modern waste economy."[13]

For the people, however, the results have been disastrous. John Amagoalik, an Inuit rights leader, reports that he has seen his father transformed from "a proud and independent hunter, the master of his own destiny," into a man ravaged by alcoholism. "Proud people" have been reduced to "beggars outside a bar." Violence consumes a society of people whose traditions were rooted in the "primary responsibility" of survival. Another *Times* article, a few months later, reported that "the Inupiat Eskimos of Alaska's North Slope, whose culture has been overwhelmed by energy development activities, are 'practically committing suicide' by mass alcoholism . . . violence is becoming the most frequent cause of death as a result of the 'explosive and self-destructive abuse of alcohol.' " Dr. Samuel Z. Klausner, a researcher from the University of Pennsylvania who has studied the development, commented—with little apparent sense of irony—that "their culture cannot contain the sudden enrichment."[14] While the severity of this instance is extreme, the cultural crisis of these Eskimo people throws light on the experience of Americanization among immigrants at the turn of the century. The magnetism of a consumer culture so eloquently recalled by Anna Kuthan meant a disruption of momentous proportions.

3 / "The Magic of the Marketplace"

IF ENTRY into the modern metropolis posed a social crisis to newly industrialized people, key aspects of this new world generated a powerful appeal. Modern consumerism presented new arrivals with new kinds of institutions and a compelling ideological panorama. Something about the failure of traditional cultural modes and the unraveling of customary human bonds made people particularly receptive to the lure of the new.* It is no accident that a *mass culture*—a social landscape marked by consumer industries, mass media, and merchandising—developed just when a formerly rural or otherwise non-industrial people were being transformed into a permanent, mass industrial population. The panorama of a mass culture was a bridge between the aspirations of an old culture and the priorities of a new one.

On a narrowly economic level, the origin of mass culture can be seen as an extension of the necessity to generate and maintain an industrial labor force and expand markets. Yet both of these imperatives were inextricably linked to cultural and perceptual processes of

* By *customary,* we mean the varied and intricate patterns of life and survival that predominated among people in pre-consumerist societies. These patterns varied, but often combined small-scale agriculture and goods production; the production of vital necessities in the home; and word-of-mouth networks of information through which skills, techniques, and knowledge of survival were exchanged and passed on as a regular part of the culture of daily life.

change. The creation of an industrial labor force and of markets necessitated an abolition of social memories that militated against consumption. A consumptionist ideology required a world-view in which people and nature were not merely separate, but at odds with one another. Consumerism posed *nature* as an inhospitable force, a hopeless anachronism. Industrial production and enterprising imaginations claimed for themselves the rights and powers of creation. Though the question of how such a momentous upheaval in perception could have taken hold cannot be fully answered here, it is clear that, by the early twentieth century, the double-prong of "Americanization"—mass production and mass consumption—had dramatically altered the social landscape of American life. The Jeffersonian ideal of a country of self-producing farmers was receding in the dim twilight of American consciousness, even if poets, sociologists, and ordinary folk each in their own idiom bemoaned the ways by which industry and its products had stepped between farm and home, country and city, people and their habits of survival. Edward Devine, a social worker and editor of the *Survey* magazine, distilled these feelings in 1907 when he exclaimed that the "home has ceased to be the glowing center of production from which radiates all desirable goods and has become a pool towards which products made in other places flow—a place of consumption, not of production."[15]

What Devine and others saw was the result of a historical redefinition of the nature of daily life. By 1900, in many critical arenas of life, the home had ceased production; the factory had taken its place. People now purchased what they had once produced for themselves. Production and consumption had become distinct activities, a fundamental rearrangement in the way people apprehended their material world. More and more, it was the *wage* that determined how well people could satisfy needs and desires. In large cities this relationship between people and survival was accentuated, but even small towns and farms were drawn into the network of influence. The elaboration of this network was a process that had unfolded in the preceding century; its story was the evolution of the modern, American consumer market.

In the late eighteenth and early nineteenth centuries, such a market was inconceivable to most people. As the continent was being settled, the maintenance of home and/or farm was a formidable and diversified project. Most goods were produced in the home. The demands of farm work and home production encouraged large families with many children. Women were the fountain from which many basic necessities flowed. As a source of survival, an inclusive arena of existence, the home was, in a sense, rooted. Even if families moved, over a lifetime, the arrangement of the home itself reflected its productive and sustaining nature. Alongside such a pattern of sufficiency, the consumer market—insofar as one existed—was an itinerant and picaresque phenomenon. It provided those few items home production could not; it existed on the fringes of necessity. Individual peddlers plodded the country roads of rural America, making house calls. Poorer peddlers trudged the byways with tin boxes on their backs; a prosperous peddler had his horse and wagon. Loaded down with "city" goods—nails, wood plates, tinware, a shovel or two, buttons, and so on—these nomads traveled the length and breadth of settlement, establishing a mobile marketplace of goods and notions. Here was the consumer society in its primitive essence, still operating often by barter, dealing in whatever goods were on hand—straight pins, combs, eyeglasses, musical instruments, clocks, shoelaces, window glass, and farm tools. Some combined their traffic in goods with artisan craftwork: carpentry, shoemaking, portrait-painting. Others provided what today might be called "professional" services, as legal advisors, doctors, preachers.[16]

Although in embryonic form, these traveling salesmen also dealt in images and desire for the unknown. They were forerunners of modern advertising and public relations. As people in motion, commercial adventurers, peddlers brought the world of the city to country people, employing the language of allure, glamor, and spectacle. Women whose hands had spun drab, homemade cloth were treated to the attractive promise of gaily colored calico and gingham, which showed no trace of the working conditions in the early textile mills from which they came. For those exhausted by the deadly routines of rural life, peddlers brought tonics and pills designed to alleviate or distract from the cares of everyday life. Other items—clocks, for example—offered *status* to those who made the purchase. Though relatively insignificant as a source of basic survival, the peddler offered the allure of that which might be had in another way of life.

By the mid-nineteenth century, the once itinerant market had gained a more stable place within rural and small-town life, in the form of local general stores, which eclipsed the peddler as the herald of the marketplace. The appeal of the general store to rural Americans was twofold: It centralized goods under one roof; and it was run by "trusted" people, who lived in the area and sought to maintain the goodwill of their neighbors. Familiarity and convenience were the hallmarks of the general store, and with them community life was increasingly touched by the channels of an emerging industrial commerce. Anxious to establish a monopoly over local trade, local store owners branded the peddler as an unscrupulous stranger, shrewd, morally questionable, greedy. Playing upon common distrust of the commercial world, general stores brought it closer. Store owners drew upon vernacular notions of the virtues of rural simplicity, and altered the face of rural life, making consumption more a part of it.[17]

Meanwhile, peddlers developed techniques in response to this ethos of rural distrust. One notable example was Benjamin Babbitt, a peddler whose innovations in marketing and packaging contributed to the commercialization of what had, previously, been home-produced. Before Babbitt, soap was a common product of the home, made from the fat of animals. He began his commercialized soap business when he bought a large number of hog carcasses. Producing a batch of soap, Babbitt now traded soap for hog fat. Eventually, he made enough deals with farmers to form a specialty business in soap, setting up a factory in New York. With an eye to aesthetics, Babbitt produced soap and sold it not in long loafs, but in individual bars, which encouraged its greater use. He also wrapped his cakes, labeling them with an attractive trademark, a personal claim of quality. Such innovations made his soap far more costly than home-produced, but with the cost came the allure of the packaged product, the mundane surrounded by finery. To encourage customers to spend, Babbitt established a premium system: In return for a few wrappers, one might receive some inexpensive but useful item.

Besides becoming millionaires, Babbitt—and other innovators like him—wrought massive changes in the daily life of Americans. Taking a staple of home production and turning it into an attractive marketable commodity, he established a basic principle of American marketing—masking the ordinary in the dazzle of magic.[18]

Jim Fisk, known primarily as a railroad baron, was another trailblazer of the consumer culture. Born into a successful peddler family, Fisk was expected by his father to go into the family business. Before settling down, however, Jim ran away and joined a circus, serving a few apprenticeship years. When he returned to take on his father's wagon, his head was filled with the ideas of P. T. Barnum, the first great adman. Fisk had learned, for example, that towns would be receptive to the circus if they were properly seeded with publicity beforehand.

Aware of the distrust of rural folk for strangers, Fisk employed the technique of "advance billing." First he decorated his wagon according to circus conventions— brightly colored, hung with flags. He wore a black silk suit, boots to the knees, and a large-brimmed white hat. Before entering a town, he hired people to plaster it with handbills and posters, depicting him and his gaudy wagon. When he finally arrived, hired musicians greeted him ceremoniously. If not familiar in the sense of the general store, Fisk had assembled a familiarity out of spectacle. His approach has become a fundamental component of a consumer society; the proliferation of images makes things known in advance. The dull familiarities of daily life were now confronted by the dazzling familiarity of promise; the challenge was formidable. To people schooled in the ways of home production, the inventions of the marketplace appealed to magic and wish-fulfillment, altering the terms by which objects were to be understood. The techniques of Babbitt and Fisk anticipated Elmer Wheeler's First Commandment of Salesmanship: "Sell the sizzle, not the steak!"[19]

Although peddlers and local merchants broke the ground for consumerism, by the late nineteenth century the scope of their commerce was becoming "quaint" and outmoded. Only in immigrant ghettos, filled with new generations of people unused to modern consumption, did peddlers thrive. Even there, their success was to be short-lived, for in more general terms, capitalist industry had begun to complement mass production with systems of mass distribution. Railroads were national avenues of commercial goods; mass production was turning home production into a relic. Ready-made clothing, canned goods, store-bought bread, factory-produced furniture each made headway into a wide variety of homes. Price lines were established according to the structures of social class.

As rural and artisan people made the trek into cities,

they left much of the rootedness of the home behind them. In the city, life was more mobile, less predictable, and peopled with strangers. If the commercial world of the peddler had been itinerant and marginal, the new industrial city presented commerce as stable and entrenched. Campbell's soup, Heinz ketchup, Hecker's flour, Carnation milk . . . trademarks and brand names became the familiar: These were what began to make people feel at home. This familiarity became a bond between people who were otherwise culturally heterogeneous.

The cement of such familiarity was further strengthened by important innovations in retailing, increasing the presence and impact of the marketplace in day-to-day existence. In rural and small-town areas, and to some extent in cities, *mail-order merchandising* was a "natural" outcome of mass production, with a particular appeal to people who held on tenaciously to a pre-industrial way of life; a way of life dominated by land, nature, and home production. Among these people, mail-order companies helped to mold a large-scale consumer market where none had previously existed.

The success of mail-order was built on some of the weaknesses of the general store system. Widespread by the 1870s, these stores had become known for high prices and usurious credit practices. Goods, it was reported, were often misrepresented and/or shoddy.[20] As an expansive decade for mass production, the 1870s offered another retailing possibility, one that circumvented the general store. Eager to find outlets for their products, manufacturers were generally willing to offer low prices on large orders of goods. Such entrepreneurs as Montgomery Ward and Richard Sears (founder of Sears, Roebuck) built their empires on this premise. Buying large lots of merchandise, Ward and Sears distributed provocative and alluring picture books—catalogs—from which potential customers could order goods. Both Ward and

Sears understood that the penetration of local, rural markets depended on the ability to present new, often unfamiliar goods, in a vernacular of "trust" and "friendship." Ward initiated the idea of a catalog, filled with beguiling images and text, designed to appeal to current-day folk wisdom. He offered customers that which the general store would not: "Satisfaction guaranteed or your money back." Appointed the official supply house of the Grange, and using its membership to develop a market, Ward sent out a one-page catalog by 1873. Within ten years his annual sales exceeded a million dollars.

Writing the catalog copy himself, in an amateurish, folksy vernacular, Ward became a source of information, an advisor, a self-proclaimed "personal friend" to millions of anonymous customers. As a benign progenitor of consumerism, his money-back guarantee signaled the generosity of a benevolent, if unseen, patriarch. The catalog—which came to be known as "The Great Wish Book"—pushed the need and desire for mass-produced goods beyond the established limits of contemporary imagination. It inspired promising fantasies of consumption among its customers. To people with little to read, and a desire to transcend the limits of their immediate environment, the combination of image and text was compelling; whole families reached for finery previously beyond their grasp or imagination.

The success of this "Wish Book" was phenomenal, growing from a one-page sheet in 1873 to a 24-page booklet in 1874 to a 544-page catalog in 1893. By 1890, Ward's enterprise had authoritative legitimacy. His catalog was used in rural schools as a modern reference on the new, emerging material culture. People eagerly awaited the coming of the catalog; through this window on a world of apparently unlimited possibility people caught a glimpse of things to come and received advice on how to get these things in the here-and-now. Home producers of clothing were instructed on how to order the latest fashions, ready-to-wear, easily through the mails. "In ordering clothing please be particular to send your size. Measure for coat around the chest, just under the arms; for pants take size around waist and length of leg. . . . Give your age and general build, and we will nine times out of ten give you a fit!"

Ward's expanded its market among immigrants as well, providing instructions for ordering products in ten languages. Here was an American institution that seemed to reach out, to embrace new arrivals with a sympathy that was rare. Customers were urged to use their native tongues in ordering. The catalog was a perfect vehicle for "Americanization"; the pictorial images spoke an easily understood, universal language, demonstrating what an American appearance was all about; actual transactions could be performed in one's language of origin.*

With his Sears, Roebuck catalog, Richard Sears, known as the "Barnum of merchandising," a man who could "sell a breath of fresh air," built the largest retail institution in the United States. Sears, Roebuck & Company was an ingenious blend of evocative propaganda and superbly orchestrated distribution system. Sears' warehouse was so efficient that it was one of the models cited by Henry Ford for the development of his assembly line.

Sears called his catalog "The Farmer's Friend." Early catalogs were introduced by a personal letter, designed to allay fears people might have about writing letters to the big city. "Don't be afraid that you will make a mistake," he assured potential customers. "We receive hundreds of orders every day from young and old

---

* In 1946, the Grolier Club Book Society selected the Ward's Catalog as one of the hundred most influential books on American life—a catechism of "the standard of American middle-class living," an apostle of "creature comforts."[21]

who never sent away for goods. . . . Tell us what you want, in your own way, written in any language, no matter whether good or poor writing, and your goods will be promptly sent to you."

The symbiosis between new commercial channels and traditional community networks that fed them is manifest in Sears' "Iowaization" scheme of 1905. Sears improvised a plan, first implemented in Iowa, to distribute catalogs and recruit customers. The company wrote to all of its current customers in Iowa and asked each to pass on catalogs to friends and neighbors. The customers, in turn, sent the names of people given the catalog to the company. The company kept track of who was ordering, and gave each "distributor" premiums on the basis of the number of incoming orders from among the friends and relatives of each. Accepting the role of "distributor," participants implicitly presented themselves as satisfied customers among their peers. Sears was trading on mutual bonds established autonomously, but which now entered the market. "Iowaization" was the most successful word-of-mouth campaign in the company's history, because word-of-mouth had been commercially structured. Sales from Iowa soon outstripped all other states; Sears went on to "Iowaize" America.[22]

Customary rural networks became pathways along which modern channels of commerce were established. In the process, social relations themselves were metamorphosed. Originally built on patterns of mutual reliance and barter, now these relationships provided an arena within which people became individualized agents and consumers of goods. Utilizing the patterns of friendship, Sears altered community networks into new avenues for the distribution of goods, providing benefits to individuals at the expense (literally) of one's friends. Perhaps most important, people who had lived, to a large extent, apart from a money economy were now embroiled in it.

Another factor in the success of mail-order merchandising was the creation of Rural Free Delivery and the parcel post system. Prior to Rural Free Delivery (RFD), rural people had to travel to town to pick up mail and packages; once in town they frequented local merchants and general stores, and bantered with friends. Proposed in 1891 and endorsed by Postmaster General and Philadelphia department store magnate John Wanamaker, RFD was a system of direct-to-the-home mail delivery. Local merchants lobbied against it for years, to no avail. Eventually it was installed, converting the farmer into a modern consumer; it made the promise of mail-order merchandising all the more possible, as it eroded the turf of local, small-scale enterprise. Made from a catalog in the comfort of the home, each selection was a negotiation between customary life and the attractive network of an emerging national consumer market.

Such far-reaching innovations were not made without protest. Given smaller volume, higher costs, and limited stock, local merchants could not easily compete with the new, national marketplace. Often desperate in their responses, mid-western and southern store owners appealed to parochialism and xenophobia among their customers: fears of the big city; of foreigners; of blacks and Jews. Exploiting the distant anonymity of mail-order companies, local merchants peddled rumors that Sears and Ward were black men, or that Sears was a Jewish company. They argued that these companies used the mails because "these fellows could not afford to show their faces as retailers."

By the turn of the century, some local merchants were encouraging people to turn in catalogs for Saturday night bonfires. Prizes of up to fifty dollars were offered to those folks who collected the largest number of "Wish Books" for public immolation. For the most part, Sears and Ward responded with little concern; theirs was the conceit of an unfolding commercial power. Ward proclaimed assuredly, "We are honorable and we know we are. So do three million of our customers. Thus are curses turned to blessings." In response to racial innuendo, Sears published "photos of its founders to prove they weren't 'colored.' " Ward offered a hundred-dollar reward for the name of the person who had initiated the rumor that he was a mulatto.[23]

If mail-order merchandising was a spectacular refinement of a mobile market, reaching out to a rooted clientele, other institutions evolved in areas where the population itself had become itinerant. Filled with immigrants and migrants from another way of life, the cities became sites for massive, imposing structures of consumption, beginning in the mid-nineteenth century. The department store was the city equivalent of the mail-order catalog, employing compelling visual dramas within which mass-produced goods played the starring role. As forms of home production slipped from the hands of city women, the department store provided an evocative, image-laden context for industrial modes of survival. Not all city dwellers flocked to department stores. Immigrant women still purchased goods from itinerant street peddlers, thinking that the display of the department store only added to the price of goods. Yet while the initial clientele of the department store was largely middle class, its conspicuous presence as a new, urban institution gave consumable products the aura of modernity and gentility, while newspaper and display advertising spread the connotation even among people who could not afford the emporia.

The department store was more than a site for consumption, it was a *sight* of consumption; goods were graced in monumental splendor. Shopping was a perceptual adventure. In the department store, industrial retailing created a place where the ideologies of progress and magic encountered the manifold needs of everyday life. From their beginnings, department stores were publicized as "cathedrals" and "palaces." This mixing of sumptuous metaphors was revealing; the department store surrounded practical concerns with a religious intonation, a touch of royalty, the promise that the mundane could become glamorous.

Innovators in the retail trade, men such as R. H. Macy, Marshall Field, and John Wanamaker, built mammoth structures replete with rotundas, Grecian columns, and grandiose courts where elaborate balconies and gaslit chandeliers surrounded and dazzled their customers. As a theater of goods, the department store combined sheer immensity with regal forms of display. Wanamaker's, in Philadelphia, contained 129 counters totalling two-thirds of a mile in length, with fourteen hundred stools in front of them. Lighting was supplied by leaded glass skylights by day, gas chandeliers by night. In 1896, Wanamaker built a nearly life-sized replica of the Rue de la Paix in his store—"a consolation for Americans who could not go to Paris." In 1911, Wanamaker opened a new twelve-story structure featuring a Grand Court, and the second largest organ in the world, the latter punctuating the shopping day with sacredness.

In addition to lavish retailing, the department store offered itself as a castle away from home. For middle-class city women, the traditional needs of the household had been ministered to by servants and merchant callers; the home was a blend of productive and social activity. Daily life had revolved around the dinner meal, a family occurrence. With the separation of work life from home life, dinner meals began the long march toward the TV dinner; home preparations began to recede in importance. As the mass production of goods and external activities cut into duties of the customary home, department stores offered themselves as arenas for spending newfound "leisure" time. Myriad services were designed to lure women into the nest of the Big Store. Macy's, for example, housed elegant lounges and restrooms; special writing rooms supplied with paper and pens; an art gallery filled with oil paintings (historically the property of the wealthy); rooms for reading newspapers; restaurants for luncheon get-togethers. Other department stores had nurseries, beauty parlors, meeting rooms, live music, and post offices. Lecture halls and meeting rooms were also included in some stores' facilities. Shopping at Macy's, claimed one advertisement, would "yield you more than you dreamed possible."[24]

Along with mail-order merchandising, department stores helped shape consumption as a palpable system of belief by providing an institutional structure for mass marketing. Goods became actors in the pages of catalogs and in store displays. As customers, with free time from the activities of production, increasingly were invited to be admiring spectators, the social process of consumption drew upon the imagery of royalty, of religion, of magic to elaborate its atmosphere of promise. Things customarily defined in terms of the long labor of home production reappeared as primarily aesthetic objects. Beauty and ease were claims that spoke loudly to people schooled by historic denial, and these were the blandishments proffered by consumer marketing as it evolved.

By the turn of the twentieth century the marketplace had evolved from a local and itinerant structure, servicing a rooted economy of self-sufficiency, into a formidable and "permanent" institution. Against the disruptive changes experienced by people undergoing industrialization, apparent stability and aesthetic allure began to reorganize the structure and meaning of *need*. If consumption was alien to a customary way of life, the genesis of the national marketplace was the historic passageway for the transition. A new way of life did not arrive merely as a cold, economic structure—wage labor, factory production, corporate goods. Its evolution was wrapped in the history of mass imagery and need, a complex amalgam that made the experience of transformation so conflicted—a conflict giving rise to such tensions as those of Anna Kuthan, so bitter over the false promise of happy plantations, waxing eloquent over Hecker's flour. Within such ambivalence, the human and ecological contradictions of the rise of consumer culture are blurred.

4 / *Changing the Subject*

OUT OF the social pains of industrialization, its spiritual and material deprivations, a consumer culture was born. In its imagery and ideology were powerful appeals from hitherto denied realms of leisure, beauty, and pleasure. Mail-order catalogs and department stores were prime examples in an array of institutions that provided vehicles for this new way of seeing. In exchange for adopting a consumerized understanding of survival, people could hope to enjoy aesthetic pleasures traditionally the province of the very rich or even unimaginable in times past. This enrichment was not proffered as a quantitative change, however. In order for people to enjoy the pleasures of the new order they had to abandon many old expectations. Simon Patten, one of the most important and outspoken apostles of industrial consumerism, argued in 1892 that the leap from "scarcity" to "abundance" demanded a break with the past. The universe of nature would be transcended by one of artifice; the old, familiar world would recede; a new one would take its place: "It is the reduction of old pleasures that forces the consumer to resort to new pleasures to make up for the loss of old ones."[25]

Patten clearly perceived that the pleasures of a consumer society took root in a turbulent soil, a soil soaked in the blood of decimated traditional cultures. It was worth it, he argued: The benefits of this new culture justified its costs. Anticipating Walter Benjamin's insights into the mechanical reproduction of images, Patten understood the decisive appeal of these images in the new order. Mass imagery would bring what he termed "*the beautiful* within reach of all" [emphasis added]. Advocating the metamorphic and democratic powers of such images, Patten—by the 1890s—already knew the eventual magnetism that mass advertising would hold within American society.

> So cheap are many kinds of pictures that they are largely distributed as means of advertisement. Everywhere the homes of the poorest people are full of beautiful objects, many of which have no cost; and when their taste is improved by contact with these objects, others more suited to the new condition can be obtained at a slight increase in cost.[26]

According to Patten, imagery would infuse the mass production of products, and the logic of consumption—much in the terms outlined in Raymond Williams' etymology—would take over. Continual waste and spending would be elevated as a social good, driven by a cycle of continual dissatisfaction. Patten celebrated this eventuality, setting out its logic this way:

> The standard of life is determined, not so much by what a man has to enjoy, as by the rapidity with which he tires of the pleasure. To have a high standard means to enjoy a pleasure intensely and to tire of it quickly.[27]

Patten's vision provides a description of the ways in which the demands of the market were shaping a new national identity, a philosophy of life. Although still undeveloped in many ways in Patten's day, the following patterns of modern life were established:

- a powerful break with the past had taken place;
- the basic groundwork of a consumer culture had been laid;
- the tunnels of vision had been dug.

It is upon these that ultimately shopping centers and urban malls have been built. Under this order, we have come to live in a visual space consumed by the imagery of commerce, a society organized around the purchase.

From the vantage point of late-twentieth-century America, this existence is familiar to us; its alternatives are not. While Patten's enthusiasm for consumption seems blind to the spiritual and ecological drawbacks we have come equally to know, his explanation of the *American standard of living* and the logic of consumption hits the nail on the head. Recognizing that industrial capitalism had severed people from their roots, from customary relationships with one another and with the natural world, he sketched out the shape of new drives that propelled the activities of life. Implicitly, and unwittingly, Simon Patten provided a sketch of the antisocial and destructive premises of the consumption process: Life would be a competitive struggle, continually using up the *old,* seeking and anticipating the *new.* Replenishment and the preservation of resources, systems of mutual interdependence were part of the old patterns of survival; they were of no concern within his vision of progress.

Patten also understood the importance that the mass production and distribution of commercial imagery would have in American material culture. They would tap the wells of need and desire. Commodities would be wrapped in an aesthetic of seduction. If, as Freud argued, pre-civilized humanity was propelled by insatiable drives for immediate, inconsequential gratification, the consumer culture appealed to these repressed drives with abandon. Today, the promise of ecstatic delight permeates everything from floor wax to toothpaste to mechanical vibrators. It is the undifferentiated, universal promise of the marketplace. Utopia is spectacle! Pain is only a reminder to those who have not yet bought the right product.

The acceptable arena of human initiative is circumscribed by the act of purchasing, given the status of *consumer* or *audience*. Within the logic of consumer imagery, the source of creative power is the object world, invested with the subjective power of "personality." History itself takes the shape of a succession of technological and commodity forms, forms propelled by the exigencies of the market economy. "The new basis of civilization" that Patten saw at the turn of the century really amounts to one in which the human subject has been expelled from history. Progress was to be measured by the extent to which social life, relations between people, had become what has been termed a "mirror of production." A consumerist cosmos was taking shape.

Insofar as this consumption cosmos liberated people from certain forms of oppression of the past, it assumed a certain cachet. Were not new realms of possibility being explored? Yet at the same time, it was an exploration within the limited confines of new, industrial institutions with their unprecedented ability to diminish the activity and imagination of individual human beings. Consumerism engendered passivity and conformity within this supposedly ever-expanding realm of the *new,* which put leisure, beauty, and pleasure in the reach of all. Customary bonds of affection and interdependence, born of other circumstances, disintegrated. Most important, the old bond of humanity and nature collapsed. The new survivor was the "wise shopper."

Alongside the considerable achievements of industrial development, the logic of consumption has become increasingly universal in our way of life. It is embroiled in our intimacies; tattooed upon our hopes; demanding of our energies. The "constant rapidity" with which we are encouraged to tire of consumable objects, of our elusive pleasures, is generalized as an axiom for existence. To buy is to succeed. Soon, this success becomes failure. A recent song by the English rock group The Clash angrily laments the dissatisfaction that is simultaneously played upon and exacerbated by consumption:

> I'm all lost in the supermarket.
> I can no longer shop happily.
> I came in here for that special offer,
> Guaranteed Personality.[28]

In the areas of love and sexuality, consumptionism is rampant, signaling its grip on the reproduction of life itself. Divorce rates climb amid the clichéd "search for meaningful relationships." The insatiable urge for new things, a hallmark of Patten's definition of industrial progress, finds its painful corollary in the insatiable need for new and different love objects. The separation from nature is exacted at the expense of reliable social bonds. Within such a framework, sexuality among strangers becomes the logical ideal. No matter how shattering the experience, we are continually enticed toward more of the same. In a society with its social fabric shredded, the models of love and friendship are most conspicuous among the illusory propaganda of the consumer industries. Only goods and images seem really to be *there*. Political and religious leaders aggressively bemoan the moral crisis that has beset us, yet their criticisms steer clear of the commercial environment from which they themselves have often achieved their goals of power.

As we have seen in the United States, the adversarial interpretation of the relationship between people and the natural world is prominent in commercial ideology and production. Waste and *throw-away* are signatures of what is often termed "the American way of life." It is still a basic component of marketing, and of our expectations. An extreme expression of this philosophy can be found in the words of Reagan's Secretary of the Interior, James Watt. A man with the job of administering and protecting the natural environment, Watt was asked whether he "favored preserving the land for future generations.'' Expressing his unabashed commitment to consumerism as a way of life, and revealing the hopelessness of it, Watt replied: ''I do not know how many future generations we can count on before the Lord returns.''[29] In the name of God, pillage is performed on behalf of Mammon.

The politics of consumption must be understood as something more than what to buy, or even what to boycott. Consumption is a social relationship, the dominant relationship in our society—one that makes it harder and harder for people to hold together, to create community. At a time when for many of us the possibility of meaningful change seems to elude our grasp, it is a question of immense social and political proportions. To establish popular initiative, consumerism must be transcended—a difficult but central task facing all people who still seek a better way of life.

Part Three

City Lights: Immigrant Women and the Rise of the Movies

FROM 1890 to 1920, over twenty-three million people from eastern Europe and southern Italy came to the United States and settled in primarily urban centers. Though they were to labor in and populate a maturing industrial society, they emerged from semi-industrial peasant and artisan backgrounds where the social institutions of family and community organized and maintained a customary culture. For these people, the migration represented an unraveling of the fabric of their lives, felt most deeply in the home and the family, the customary realm of women. The new urban world undercut the basis of traditional womanhood, forcing women to look in two directions simultaneously: to the past for strength to sustain life in the present and to the future to find new means of survival. This split impinged directly on family life and created strains on the customary expectations of the mother-daughter relationship. One generation, the mothers, had grown to maturity in European society. Urban life challenged the sense of survival and perception they had brought with them when they migrated to the United States. The next generation, the daughters, although touched by the experience of the Old World, were much more the children of the metropolis. Their lives were caught up in social dynamics beyond the frame of old-world understandings.[1]

In the cities new cultural images—billboards, signs, advertising, the electric lights of Broadway—

pressed themselves on people's attention and created a new visual landscape of possibility. An urban and distinctly American culture proclaimed itself in image form, demanding response and notice, as strange to small-town Americans as it was to incoming immigrants. Viola Paradise of the Immigrant Protective League analyzed the social complexity of this new cultural formation:

> The very things which strike the native born [Americans] as foreign seem to her [the new immigrant] as distinctly American: the pretentiousness of signs and advertisements, the gaudy crowded shop windows, the frequency of fruit stands and meat markets, her own countrymen in American clothes . . . she sums it all up as "America."[2]

One of the most powerful components of this new urban culture was the development of moving pictures. For immigrants in a world of constant language barriers, the silent film was compelling and accessible. Silent pictures spoke primarily to urban immigrant audiences of women and children, themselves caught up in the social drama of transformation.

Like radio and television after them, the movies were an exemplary piece of a cultural environment that interacted, over time, with the social history of its audience, playing a crucial role as an "agency of mass impressions" in the large-scale displacement of people.[3] Changing demographic and industrial patterns created the context for an audiovisual culture designed to fill the gaps and fissures of experience. As an agency of mass impression, movies became a new electronic presence in the social landscape of everyday life, explaining away the past, preparing people for participation in a new present.

The world these movies addressed was in crisis. Adaptation to city life required a constant struggle. Old-world societies, whether in eastern Europe or southern Italy, were rooted still in resources drawn from nature:

gardens, home production, and systems of family and community support.[4] In the New World, wages and money were the key to survival. In the old cultures, the social labor of women had converted raw materials into household goods; new-world immigrant mothers had to confront the industrial marketplace to secure the goods necessary for their families' survival and well-being.

In order to make ends meet, immigrant families adopted a new division of labor. The facts of urban economic life made family cooperation essential. A study of wage earners' budgets in New York in 1909 reveals that

> . . . the number of families entirely dependent on the earnings of one person is small when compared with the numbers whose incomes include the earnings of husband, wife, several children, some boarders, gifts from relatives. . . . Several or all of these resources may enter into the total resources of that family in a year. Perhaps this income should more accurately be called the household income, for it represents the amount which comes into the family purse, of which the mother usually has the disbursement.[5]

While the father and older children worked for wages outside the home, the mother was central to the family's well-being, and in a certain respect, the customary pattern adapted itself to the new situation. As one social worker noted at the time:

> It is the mother around whom the whole machinery of family life revolves. The family economy depends on her interests, skills and sense of order. Her economic importance is far greater than that of her wealthier sisters for as income increases . . . the amount of it controlled by the wife diminishes. . . . But in her humble status, her position is thoroughly dignified.[6]

Robert Chapin concluded in his 1909 study of New York working-class life:

> While the personal factor does operate in the case of
> every family . . . the limits with which it may affect
> the actual sum total of material comforts that make up
> the living of the family are set by *social forces*. These
> social forces find expression on the one side in the
> income which the family receives—that is, in the rate
> of wages received by the father and others who are at
> work; on the other side, they are expressed in the
> prices that have to be paid to get housing, food and
> other means of subsistence.[7]

The common experience for immigrant women on arrival
was to "figure the dollar in their home money. They
thought they were rich until they had to pay rent, buy
groceries, clothing and shoes. Then, they knew they
were poor."[8] To maintain home and family in the urban
economy demanded a range of skills from the daily negotiations in the marketplace for basic needs, to the careful
accumulation of money for rent, to taking in boarders to
help make ends meet, to occasional finishing work
brought back from the garment shops. In addition, the
social demands were equally pressing: from the care of
young children, to the daily grind of housework, to the
care of the sick, to providing help to neighbors and
relatives.

In all of these activities, immigrant mothers faced
impossibly high rents, the fear of eviction, high prices for
food and clothing, sickness, noise, inferior housing, and
times of unemployment and poverty. Barred from access
by reasons of sex, class, nationality, language, and custom to most of the institutions of American society, most
mothers relied on those most familiar and immediate:
family and community. Many sought out relatives, neighbors, and other women of the same ethnicity to establish
networks of support and common concern. Within the
congested tenement districts of New York, new forms of
community developed in which women learned from
each other and shared the problems of urban life. Elsie

Clew Parsons, the well-known contemporary anthropologist, observed:

> One of the most noticeable traits in the life of the average tenement dweller . . . to the eyes . . . of the private visitor . . . is the more or less intimate and friendly intercourse of the families of the house. Washtubs and cooking dishes are borrowed from one another at any hour of the day; a mother leaves her child with a friend across the hall when she goes shopping . . . ; a kindly soul sits up all night with a sick child; yet, in spite of all the little individual acts of service, the whole round of economic activity is entirely independent of every other family.[9]

The borrowing of tools, the lending of service, the exchange of activity became a buffer against the isolation imposed on women as housewives and a mediation between an older, more familiar culture left behind and the chaotic individualizing forces of urban life.

While immigrant mothers were coping with the new realities, fathers and elder children were engaged in the outside world of wage labor and urban life. On the surface, there seemed to be a split between first-generation immigrant mothers and their daughters. The urban environment created a historic division in the customary expectations of the mother-daughter relationship. The industrial city separated the home-centered experience of mothers from the more social experience of daughters in ways that were painful and difficult to understand. New urban institutions such as the public school, the settlement house, the dance hall, and the diversions of the street made claims on the lives of some immigrant daughters, redirecting their activity. Unlike that of their mothers, the immigrant daughter's sense of self, although halting and incomplete, was directed outward. American society was based on a conception of family life that demanded that female adolescents identify with a social world outside the domain of family. Access to that world meant having time and money for it. The price of admission to the new culture was the negation of old-world notions of womanhood; "needs" arose for clothing, hairstyles, and cosmetics to create the external appearance of an "American" and for other forms of economic and sexual independence from maternal authority.

This, of course, put pressure on the immigrant mothers, who on the one hand needed their daughters' outside earnings to help maintain the fragile household economy, but on the other, felt threatened by the separate social life demanded by some daughters. Patriarchal culture had deemed the outside world the proper place for men and boys, while young women were expected to stay close to home by the side of their mothers. The struggle against family bonds was harder for daughters to win than for sons.[10] In general terms, the outside world of American culture was viewed with hostility by most immigrant mothers, who saw it as a direct threat to their ability to carry on cultural traditions and achieve economic viability.

However, one American institution was a realm of shared cultural experience for mothers and daughters: the movies. While immigrant parents resisted their daughters' participation in most of the recreational opportunities of the city, *everyone* went to the movies, which were the one American institution that had the possibility of uniting generations and was cross-generational in its appeal. Most film historians agree that the first audiences for motion pictures came primarily from the immigrant working-class neighborhoods of America's largest cities. The movies were a welcome diversion from the hardships of daily life in the communities. By 1909, New York City alone had over 340 movie houses and nickelodeons with a quarter of a million people in daily attendance and a half million on Sundays. *Survey* magazine, the journal of social work, observed that "in the tenement districts the motion picture has well nigh driven other forms of entertainment from the field" and that "it was the first cheap amusement to occupy the economic plane that the saloon [had] so exclusively controlled."[11] Like the saloon, it was cheap: a nickel per person, twenty-five cents for the whole family. Unlike the saloon, it was not sex-defined; anyone who had a nickel could enter. There, for a low price, families could be enveloped in a new world of perception, a magical universe of madness and motion.

The movies became for immigrants a powerful experience of the American culture otherwise denied to them, surrounding them with images, fantasies, and revelations about the New World: "More vividly than any other social agency, they revealed the social typography of America to the immigrant, to the poor. . . . From the outset, the movies were, besides a commodity and a developing craft, a social agency."[12] In *Sons of Italy,* Antonio Mangano described the effects of motion pictures on the typical recently arrived Italian: "Moving pictures were a great attraction, and he went every day to see what new pictures there were on the billboards. . . . Cold chills crept up and down his back as he witnessed thrilling scenes of what he thought was *really* American life."[13] The movies became a translator of the social codes of American society, which could now be unraveled, looked at, interpreted, made fun of, understood. They formed a bridge between an older form of culture inadequate to explain the present and a social world of new kinds of behavior, values, and possibilities; their images and fantasies were a text of explanation, a way of seeing. Like their audience, early movies had not yet found a voice. Silent movies spoke in a more comprehensible language of silence, image, sign, and gesture.

The movies also presented themselves as a release from daily troubles, a world where the realities of daily life were rendered empathetically in comedic or melodramatic form. Movie advertisements pitched themselves to working-class audiences in a tone of compassion:

> If you're tired of life, go to the movies
> If you're sick of trouble rife, go to the picture show
> You'll forget your unpaid bills, rheumatism and other ills
> If you'll stop your pills and go to the picture show.[14]

In a sense, movies were a form of community. Families went together; local merchants advertised on the screen; people sang along and read or translated captions out loud; the organ played. Moreover, as one observer commented: "Visit a motion picture show on a Saturday night below 14th Street when the house is full and you will soon be convinced of the real hold this new amusement has on its audience. Certain houses have become genuine social centers where neighborhood groups may be found . . . where regulars stroll up and down the aisles between acts and visit friends."[15] The *Jewish Daily Forward* in 1908 commented on the growing popularity of this medium for women and children during the day. "Hundreds of people wait on line. . . . A movie show lasts a half an hour. If it's not too busy you can see it several times. They open at one in the afternoon and customers, mainly women and children, gossip, eat fruit and nuts and have a good time."[16]

The content of some early films bore a direct relationship to the historical experience of its audience. Some films depicted a landscape outside of immigration; these brought American history and culture, in the form of westerns, news clips, and costume dramas, to ethnic eyes. Some movies were nativist, racist, and sexist. But many early movies showed the difficult and ambiguous realities of urban tenement life in an idiom that spoke directly to immigrant women. The new medium attracted many immigrant and working-class entrepreneurs into its ranks. Before Hollywood took center stage, the movies were created in primarily urban settings. As Lewis Jacobs, the film historian, observed, "The central figure of adventure comedies was always a common man or woman—the farmer, fireman, policeman, housewife, stenographer, clerk, servant, cook. . . . Such characters were selected because the audience and filmmakers alike were of this class and because of the growing popular interest in the everyday person."[17] From 1903 to 1915, he argues, poverty and the struggle for existence were "favorite dramatic themes." In films with such titles as *The Eviction, The Need for Gold, She Won't Pay Her Rent, Neighbors Who Borrow, The Miser's Hoard, Bertha, The Sewing Girl,* and *The Kleptomaniac,* everyday situations were depicted, the causes of poverty were held to be environmental, and economic injustice was deplored.[18]

More important, these films spoke directly to tensions and contradictions in the world of immigrant mothers. For example, Edwin S. Porter's 1905 film *The Kleptomaniac* treated justice in a class-defined society. The first sequence shows the arrest of a wealthy woman for shoplifting trinkets in a department store, the second that of a poor woman, on the brink of starvation, for stealing a loaf of bread. The third sequence brings both women to court, wherein the poor woman is jailed and the judge discharges the rich woman. An epilog sums up the three sequences; we see a figure of Justice blindfolded, holding up a scale. On one side of the scale is a bag of gold; on the other, the loaf of bread. The scale moves in favor of the gold. The blindfold is removed, and the figure of Justice has only one eye, which is fixed on the gold.[19] In *Eleventh Hour* (1911), the slum dwellers are Italian. The father, a street peddler, goes to jail for fighting with a bully who constantly harasses him. When the bully dies, the husband gets a life sentence. The wife pleads with the governor to no avail, as do the children. At the "eleventh hour," the father is released, the family reunited.[20] This film spoke clearly of the defense of the family against legal injustice and harassment.

Sometimes the immigrant experience itself was the subject, as in Chaplin's *The Immigrant*. In Thomas Ince and Gardner Sullivan's *The Italian* (1911), a series of dramatic contrasts is used to depict the social transformation and economic dislocation of immigrant families on New York's Lower East Side. It begins with a romanticized image of Italian life in Venice, where the audience is introduced to Beppo, a gondolier, and Gallia, a young peasant woman. The film develops images of a bounteous and festive Italy. The scene then shifts to the Lower East Side; the new landscape is framed by stark, bleak, realistic images. Beppo has become a poor bootblack, Gallia a housewife in a stifling tenement apartment. Aided by neighbor women, Gallia gives birth to a son, who rapidly becomes sickly. The doctor explains that the baby is sick from the heat and the impure milk he has been fed. In 1911, pasteurized milk was sold in bottles at high prices, but lower grades of unpasteurized milk were sold "loose" in tenement neighborhoods and carried home in glasses or pails. John Spargo, a well-known social reformer, argued in 1908 that in immigrant neighborhoods "one third of all babies die before five years old of diseases chiefly connected to the digestive tract and a considerable percent of these diseases are definitely known to be caused by milk."[21] In contrast to the bountiful imagery utilized to frame peasant life, the image of poisoned milk spoke to the inversion of nature and mothering in industrial America.

At this point in *The Italian,* a new level of contrast is presented. While Beppo and Gallia try to raise money for a supply of bottled, pasteurized milk, the baby languishes and dies. Beppo tries to raise money from "The Boss, The Wealthiest Man of the Slums." The Boss refuses him, throws him off his car, and has him arrested. Beppo is imprisoned. The Boss also has a sick child, so he uses his money and influence to rope off his elegant house from the public noise that would be fatal to his child. Beppo, out of prison and consumed with hate, sneaks into the Boss's house to harm the child, but he cannot bring himself to do it. While the Boss's child lives, Beppo and Gallia grieve. The contrasts between peasant and urban life, rich and poor, class and family, spoke directly to immigrant mothers: The maintenance of family and the care of children was a class question, since only through access to money could these conditions be transformed. This film provided a prism through which the audience could look at and recognize itself.

In *The Eviction* (1907, director unknown), a poor man, drunk with his friends, dreams that his wife has sold her wedding ring to save their home and furniture. On awakening, he hurries home to see the landlord removing the furniture from their tenement apartment. Passersby chip in to pay the rent, the husband repents, the wife forgives, and a new life begins for the family.[22] This movie would have made perfect sense to urban immigrant women. Maria Ganz, in her autobiography of New York tenement life, recounts a similar incident:

> The evicted woman kept staring at the litter of cheap things in which she must have taken no end of pride and pleasure while she had been gathering them one by one in the making of her home, now left in pieces on the street, a symbol of eviction and destitution. She brought out a china plate from the folds of her dress and placed it on one of the chairs. . . . People would drop pennies, perhaps even nickels and dimes into that plate—enough to save her from being wholly destitute.[23]

Mike Gold, in *Jews Without Money,* explained this system of community support: "This is an old custom on the East Side; whenever a family is to be evicted, the neighborhood women put on their shawls and beg from door to door."[24]

Early movies existed outside of the moral universe of correct and respectable middle-class society. Comedies also mocked respectable ruling elites and looked at authority, social conventions, and wealth with a jaundiced eye. In the Sennett and Chaplin comedies, the artifacts of the new consumer culture became objects of ridicule. Mack Sennett explained the attraction of his films:

> Their approach to life was earthy and understandable. They whaled the daylights out of pretension. . . . They reduced convention, dogma, stuffed shirts and Authority to nonsense and then blossomed into pandemonium. . . . I especially like the reduction of authority to absurdity, the notion that Sex could be funny, and the bold insults hurled at Pretension.[25]

Yet, despite the affinities between audience and early film, the movies were primarily an institution of the larger society, subject to its shifts and pulls. If some of the silent movies registered, to some degree, the social and economic problems of urban life, others spoke increasingly to the social and sexual dynamics, the ideological superstructure of an evolving consumer culture. The outlines of this development are to be seen in the contradictory experiences of immigrant daughters and their interaction with the silent screen. The concerns and experiences of immigrant daughters, as opposed to those of their more homebound mothers, led in some cases to active participation in the trade-union movement, political life, and involvement in the suffrage movement.[26] For others, contact with American culture was mainly involved with educational aspirations and cultural transformations.

For many, contact with American culture at work or at school created compelling new definitions of femininity, which spoke to a sense of independence from the constriction of family bonds; ready-made clothes, makeup, dance halls, amusement parks all symbolized a cultural environment that assumed greater individual freedom and less formal relations with the opposite sex. As one social worker noted at the time:

> Inevitably, the influences of her new work life, in which she spends nine hours a day, begin to tell on her. Each morning and evening as she covers her head with a crocheted shawl and walks to and from the factory, she passes the daughters of her Irish and American neighbors in their cheap waists in the latest smart styles, their tinsel ornaments and gay hair bows; a part of their pay envelopes go into the personal expenses of these girls. Nor do they hurry through the streets to their homes after working hours, but linger with a boy companion "making dates" for a movie or affair.[27]

While most immigrant mothers became reconciled to the fact that their daughters would leave home to go to work or school, they still expected their daughters to obey and adopt their own standards of sexual deportment. For the second generation, the gap between home life and work life was acute: "It wasn't that we [the younger generation] wanted to be Americans as much as we wanted to be like other people. . . . We gradually accepted the notion that we were Italians at home and Americans elsewhere. Instinctively, we all sensed the necessity of adapting ourselves to two different worlds."[28] A social worker noted: "The old standards can scarcely be maintained in a modern community where girls work in factories side by side with men. . . . It was impossible for the parents to supervise young women in school or at work . . . the girl naturally thinks that if she can take care of herself at work, she is equally well able to do so at play."[29]

Some immigrant daughters developed strategies for claiming a part of their income for themselves. Ruth S. True, in her study of working-class life, recorded this example:

Filomena Moresco, whose calm investment of $25 in a
pretty party dress, a beaver hat, and a willowed plume
was reported as little less than the act of a brigand. If
she had withheld twenty cents out of her pay envelope, she probably would have been beaten by her
mother. As it was, she appropriated $25 and her high-
handedness was her protection.[30]

On the one hand, adolescent daughters were reared in
the morality of family obligation; "good girls" returned
their unopened pay envelopes to their mothers and were
obedient to the needs of their families. "Bad girls" snuck
or took money out of their envelopes to spend on themselves and defied the wishes of their mothers. Having
money to spend on the self was intimately connected to
breaking out of the family circle; yet personal ideas of
independence were against the tradition of feminine
sacrifice. For example, Anges Mazza, an Italian garment
worker, was a good girl: "I gave my pay envelope to my
mother. I wouldn't dare open it up. I'd give it to my
mother because I knew she worked for us and I thought
this was her compensation. I always stayed close to my
mother." Her sister, however, was different.

She used to open the envelope and take a few dollars
for herself if she needed it. They [sister and friends]
would come home at twelve o'clock—this was terrible, especially for the Italian people. The neighbors
would gossip, would say "Look at that girl coming
home by herself." My mother would talk to her but it
did no good. And then one day, my sister wanted to
pay board. She was eighteen. My mother said, "What
do you mean, board?" She said, "I give you so much
and keep the rest." So my mother said, "Alright, do
what you please."[31]

Independence from the family obligation implied not
only the right to wages, a new physical appearance, and
a social life, but, most important, the right to a mate of
one's own choice. At issue were not ultimate goals, for

both the bad and the good girls had severely limited options, but the means to the future, the means to marriage. In a sense, the initial stages of the sexual revolution of the twentieth century can be identified with this desire for independence on the part of those daughters who broke with family tradition and control to marry men of their own choosing.

Despite the enormous energies and activities of some immigrant daughters in the trade-union and women's suffrage movements, the options open to most women at this time were limited to the appropriation of urban adolescent culture as a wedge against patriarchal forms of sexual control. New, often bewildering dating, courtship, and sexual patterns caused pain and anguish for mothers and daughters alike. While family-dominated culture was repressive, it did present a familiar form of courtship and sexual relations. The more anonymous nature of sexual relations in the city created traps for women, and immigrant women were often taken advantage of by strange and unscrupulous men.[32]

It was ironic that those immigrant daughters who worked in the ready-made clothing industry were not paid enough to purchase what they produced and, consequently, had to engage in a family battle for the right to the fruits of their labor. Their inability to purchase an American "appearance" led to anguish and frustration. This problem was not associated only with immigrant life; the conflict between family obligation and more individualized definitions of social life was also felt in the homes of the prosperous middle class.[33]

While the old family ways of understanding seemed inadequate as a guide to industrial culture, the movies seemed more shaped to the tempo of urban life. Increasingly, the social authority of the media of mass culture replaced older forms of family authority and behavior. The authority of this new culture organized itself around the premise of freedom from customary bonds as a way of turning people's attention to the consumer market-place as a source of self-definition. This new cultural thrust took on the culture of Victorian America as much as that of first-generation immigrant parents.

The movies became less identified with family enter-tainment as young people increasingly turned to them for a place away from family life, a place to escape, to use a hard-won allowance, to sneak a date. As True observed:

> There is a signal of restlessness beneath the sur-face. . . . Into her nature are surging for the first time the insistent needs and desires of her womanhood. She is the daughter of the people, the child of the masses. Athletics, sports, discussions, higher education will not be hers to divert this deep craving. . . . The city bristles with the chances she longs for—"to have fun and see the fellows."

Because of these needs and the limited options for their expression, "the control of a little money is far more essential to these girls in their search for enjoyment than to girls in another class. There are many doors which a very small coin will open for her."[34]

One of these doors was the movies, where "flashing gaudy posters lined the entrances. . . . These supply the girls with a 'craze.' These same needs send them . . . to the matinees. There pictures spread out showing adventure and melodrama which are soul-satisfying."[35] Filomena Ognibene, an Italian garment worker brought up by strict parents, claimed that "the one place I was allowed to go by myself was the movies. I went to the movies for fun. My parents wouldn't let me go out any-where else, even when I was twenty-four. I didn't care. I wasn't used to going out, going anywhere outside of going to the movies. I used to enjoy going to the movies two or three times a week. But I would always be home by nine o'clock."[36] Sometimes the movies were used to subvert the watchful eye of parental supervision. Grace

Gello recounted that she met her future husband in 1918 through her father. "We kept company for a year and a half. We weren't allowed to go out alone, even with groups of people. My father or mother always accompanied us. But we did meet on the sly. Occasionally, we would take the afternoon off to go to the movies. We didn't do this too much because we were afraid of my father. He would say, 'If I catch you, I'll break you neck.' "[37]

By 1915, the year of D. W. Griffith's *Birth of a Nation,* the movie industry had expanded its initial audience to include middle-class patrons, had moved to the remote environs of Hollywood, and had established the studio and star systems. The thematic content showed the transition; the earlier images depicting the urban housewife embattled by the economic forces of the New World were increasingly displaced by images of women in flight from or redefining the meaning of home, family, sexual behavior, and social codes. The first female "stars" of the industry were cast in new roles: the vamp, the gamine, and, of lesser significance, the virgin.[38] Through the creation of these feminine archetypes, the silent screen began to raise sexual issues and develop imagistic fantasies that spoke directly to the confusing sexual experiences of immigrant daughters.

The vamp was the symbol of the war between passion and respectability. Theda Bara, born Theodosia Goodman, daughter of a Jewish garment worker from Cincinnati, was created by Fox Studios as one of America's first movie stars. In over forty films from 1915 to 1919, she played the vamp, the woman who flaunts men and social convention to get what she wants. In the American lexicon, the archetype of the sexual woman was European, a woman who used her beauty and passion "to lure some helpless and completely dumb man to his ruin."[39] Underneath this image was a new consciousness about sexual relations. In Theda Bara's own words, "Believe me, for every woman vamp there are ten men of the same . . . men who take everything from women, love, devotion, youth, beauty and give nothing in return. *V* stands for Vampire and it stands for Vengeance too. The vampire that I play is the vengeance of my sex on its exploiters. You see . . . I have the face of a vampire, perhaps, but the heart of a 'feministe.' "[40] For example, in *A Fool There Was* (1914), Bara portrayed a woman who reduced respectable middle-class men to bumbling idiots, leaving a trail of madness and suicide along the way. Its imagery depicts a woman who has broken with social convention, who drinks and smokes with abandon, and who reverses the traditional assumptions of the male-female relationship. In doing so, her image points to a clear critique of the double standard.[41]

The gamine, epitomized by Mary Pickford, was an archetype of female adolescence whose pluck and determination allowed her to create a more independent future. Born Gladys Smith into a poor family and forced at an early age to become "father" to her family,[42] Mary Pickford often played a battling tomboy "provoked by a sense of injustice and motivated by the attempt to bring happiness to others."[43] In her many films, she took on repressive fathers, ministers, and moralistic community values and defined for herself her own space. While she was part sweetness, she was also part "hellion . . . morally and physically committed to all-out attacks against the forces of bigotry and malicious snobbery that sought to frustrate the proper denouement of a triumphant lovely girl."[44] Playing a spirited adolescent girl in such movies as *Rags* and *Little Annie Rooney,* she was an appealing example for women attempting their own fights against barriers. Although Mary Pickford occasionally played adult roles, her screen projection of independence was usually circumscribed by childhood. She herself stated the irony of her position. For Mary Pickford, "the longing for motherhood was to some extent filled by the little children I played on the screen. Through my professional creations, I became, in a sense, my own baby."[45]

While the vamp and the gamine projected images of sexual freedom and social independence, the virgin—the Griffith heroine—was, in many ways, the last holdout of the patriarchal tradition. The virgin, played by Lillian Gish, was the good woman firmly devoted to the protection of her virtue against the menace of male passion. While the virgin, as the male symbol of American womanhood, registered the existence of the new sexual wilderness, she recoiled against it, seeking protection from its claims through patriarchal solutions.[46]

The history of these transitional female archetypes parallels the social and sexual struggles of the immigrant daughters. If they were torn between fresh notions of sexuality and constricting family structures, the vamp and the gamine, who seemed to point the way to new definitions of femininity, were locked into a constricting star system, which severely limited their expression and development. Their images were used by the new studios as building blocks of an expanding industry. By 1919–20, the movie industry had become a major corporate enterprise, committed to a national rather than a class audience. To create this audience, some movies opted for images from the consumer marketplace. Some of the content and form of postwar movies revealed a new definition of "Americanization," the consumer society as an ideal way of life. Perhaps early movies had shown an ambivalence toward urban industrial society, but by 1920 American capitalism's consumer culture was in full force.[47]

By 1920, a new "formula" for movie making had been developed, most notably in the films of Cecil B. De Mille. Realizing that "a new generation of movie goers, not in sympathy with its elders,"[48] was growing up, De Mille redefined the subject matter of film. While the

De Mille films continued to explore the sexual dynamics of urban culture, they also began to demonstrate the maturation of a new sexual logic. Instead of the traditional settings of the prewar movies, De Mille ''withdrew the curtains that had veiled the rich and fashionable and exhibited them in all the lavish and intimate details of their private lives.''[49] The new De Mille movies created a fantasy world where sex, romance, marriage, and money were intertwined to create a new frame of reference. In such movies as *Old Wives for New* (1918), *Male and Female* (1919), *Why Change Your Wife?* (1920), and *Forbidden Fruit* (1920), De Mille gave voice to a crucial myth of modern culture: metamorphosis through consumption.

In the De Mille formula, the key to modern marriage lay in the ability of women to maintain a sexually attractive appearance. In *Old Wives for New,* the plot hinges around a slovenly, lazy wife in danger of losing her dapper husband. In *Why Change Your Wife?* a dowdy, modest woman interested in high culture is embarrassed by her husband's gift of a risqué negligée. The marriage breaks down. The wife then experiences a metamorphosis: She realizes that sexual appeal is crucial and thereafter transforms her appearance by purchasing new clothes. In brief, the vamp had become respectable.[50]

In *Male and Female* and *Forbidden Fruit,* De Mille explores class relations through the lens of sexuality and consumption. *Male and Female,* a satire of aristocratic manners, contrasts the exquisitely coiffured and well-mannered mistress (Gloria Swanson) with the sloppy and ill-mannered servant girl, Tweeney. For example, in the first part of the film, each of them eats breakfast. Edward Wagenknecht, a De Mille defender, argued that there was a social purpose to the scene: ''From Tweeney's eating habits in *Male and Female,* it is just possible that some of the comfortable gum chewers in our 'movie palaces' may have learned that it is not good form to leave your spoon standing in your cup or to cover a whole slice of bread with jelly and then bite into it."[51]

In *Forbidden Fruit,* De Mille gave the Cinderella myth a modern twist. The heroine, Mary Maddock, is the wife of a lazy, working-class husband who lives off her earnings. In contrast to a film like *The Italian,* the depiction of working-class marriage here assumes that husbands live off the labor of their wives. Mary is asked by the oil magnate for whom she works to help him and his wife "vamp" another oil magnate in order to close a business deal. They offer her twenty dollars, and she agrees. Replete with Cinderella fantasies, the film details her transformation. The wealthy wife phones for "jewels from Tiffany, gowns from Poiret, and perfumes from Coty." The servants dress her, and a hairdresser does her hair; she has become an object subject to the manipulation of experts. Her new appearance is quite convincing: She has transcended her class. The only obstacle to her success now is her manners. In a key scene, Mary, through cues and imitation, triumphs by choosing the correct fork. The rest of the film revolves around her duty to her husband versus her newly found life and "love" in the upper classes. Ultimately, "Cinderella" wins her love choice and escapes her husband and her class.

In contrast to the earlier movies, the De Mille films demonstrate the new logic of consumption as a way of presenting the self in the urban world, as the essence of the promise of modern life for women. In doing so, these films openly attack the customary assumptions, behavior, and style of the audience and point the way to a new self-definition. In this sense, they became an agency of Americanization. After the success of *Why Change Your Wife?* and *Forbidden Fruit,* many producers "turned their studios into fashion shops and the screen was flooded with imitations. . . . Wise wives, foolish wives, clever and stupid wives were portrayed in every variety of domestic situation that gave an opportunity for displays of wealth, money getting, money making, smart clothes and romance."[52] In imitation, movies with such titles as *The Amateur Wife, The Misfit Wife, Poor Men's Wives,* and *Behold My Wife* "all lectured to the frump who learns that it is important to remain stylish and good looking after marriage."[53] They emphasized that the metamorphosis of the female self was the new condition for securing the means of survival in modern society—getting and keeping a husband.[54]

For second-generation immigrant women, one step away from arranged marriage and family obligation, these new movies were manuals of desire, wishes, and dreams. What was remarkable about them was the combination of new ideas of romance and sexuality with practical guidelines for change. Out of De Mille's movies came a visual textbook to American culture, a blend of romantic ideology and practical tips for the presentation of self in the new marriage market of urban life. Here was guidance their mothers could not offer. By presenting an illusory world where "a shop girl can marry a millionaire,"[55] these movies evoked a vision of the American dream for women and the means to its feminine realization.

The appropriation of Americanized styles of dress, manners, and relations to the opposite sex were experienced as a gap between immigrant mothers and their daughters. In this sense, the imagery in the films—supported by the rapid growth of the ready-made clothing industries, the cosmetics industry, and new forms of advertising and display—made possible the liquidation of traditional culture. Maria Zambiello, who migrated here in 1903 and was the mother of three children, explained:

> I don't feel as good as the American women because I am old-fashioned, from the other side. . . . When I am with American women, I am afraid I don't talk good enough for them. Then sometimes they serve tea

or coffee in nice cups and napkins—I feel ashamed
. . . and they got different manners. We put the hands
on the table, they don't. That's why I don't feel so
good. But the young Italian girls, my daughters,
they're up to date, just as good, just as polite like the
Americans. They were born here, they go to school
together, they see the same movies, *they know*.[56]

In other cases, an uneasy compromise between cultures developed. Maria Frazaetti articulated this possibility:

There are no old-country customs prevailing in our
house. My children follow the American customs. I
would like them to remember that the parents must be
considered as an authority. I approve of allowing my
children the freedom they desire; by doing so, they
learn for themselves. My children misunderstand me
when I advise them what style clothes they should
wear. I blame styles and clothes on some of the stuff in
magazines and the movies of this country. If I had my
way, I would like my children to follow some of the old
disciplinary laws of the old country.[57]

Filomena Ognibene measured her distance from
American culture by contrasting her real life and style of
dress with those she saw in the movies:

We dressed plainly. We wore long dresses that were
different than the styles in the movies. I knew about
flappers from the movies, but I never dressed that
way. None of my friends dressed that way. There was
a flapper in my building. I guess . . . it was her nature.
She was Italian and went to speakeasies. Her mother
was upset at her daughter's behavior, but she didn't
bother anybody.[58]

With the change in content came a dramatic change in
form. The nickelodeons gave way to movie houses designed to win over "the steady patronage of a new
class"[59] and to hold their audiences in the dark somnam-
bulism of celluloid fantasy. Starting with the construc-

tion of the Strand Theatre in New York in 1914, these palaces, in the words of one of their architects, were designed as "social safety valves in that the public can partake of the same luxuries as the rich."[60] Another critic commented that "the differences of cunning . . . and wealth that determine our outside lives are forgotten. . . . Our democratic nation reserves its new democracy for the temple of daydreams."[61] The form itself was a demonstration of new content. If the old noisy neighborhood nickelodeons were an experience of community, the new palaces were a reprieve from community, a vision of wealth, a touch of royalty. If there were sexuality and romance inside the frame, the dark interiors, away from the watchful eyes of parents and neighbors, encouraged sexuality outside the frame, creating a new definition of a participatory audience. One critic observed:

> In the dim auditorium which seems to float on the world of dreams . . . an American woman may spend her afternoon alone. . . . She can let her fantasies slip through the darkened atmosphere to the screen where they drift in rhapsodic amours with handsome stars. In the isolation of this twilight palace . . . the blue dusk of the deluxe house has dissolved the Puritan strictures she had absorbed as a child.[62]

Some early films spoke sympathetically to the confused cultural experience of uprooted women—to the tasks of maintaining home and community in a world threatening to tear them apart. They helped to unify generations caught up in the divisive experiences of urban life. To the daughters, also the children of cultural transformation, film spoke differently. As themes of traditional family and community began to fade, the cinema spoke increasingly in the idiom of an urban, individualized culture. At first, these films briefly revealed new archetypes of feminine possibility that bore a relationship to the dynamics of cultural change. Yet in affirming the daughters' break from the traditions of family life, these films also pointed, as teachers and guides, to a mode of existence predicated on a commitment to individual survival and satisfaction within the social relationships defined by the consumer marketplace.

The ability of film to speak, in various ways, to the experience of its audience provides us with a key to understanding its appeal and power. In the first instance, film as a component of mass culture became a mediation between a historic uprooting and an unknown and threatening urban society. In the second instance, it was a mediation between traditional culture and the emergent terms of modern life. Film as a part of mass culture has the power to act as a force of unity as well as becoming an aspect of "the liquidation of the traditional value of the cultural heritage."[63]

While some of the contents of early films reflected a trend toward the liberation of women from patriarchal constraints, the social order was able to utilize this new release for the construction of a new form of domination. As women moved from the constricted family-dominated culture to the more individualized values of modern urban society, the form and content of domination changed, but new authorities replaced the old. In the name of freedom from tradition, women were trapped anew in fresh forms of sexual objectification and bound to the consumerized and sexualized household.

Nonetheless, moving pictures were the most universal form of cheap and satisfying entertainment in urban immigrant communities. As escape, education, or pleasure, they constituted a major source of new ideas and social experience. For immigrant women, motion pictures were a community-sanctioned form of urban mass culture, beguiling in its presentation of dress, manners, freedom, and sexual imagery. They provided an escape, but they also extended the world as a visual universe of magic and illusion.

Part Four

Fashion and Democracy

1 / "The Ends Justify the Jeans"

*Have we worked out our democracy
further in regard to clothes than
anything else?*
— *Jane Addams (1902)*

JULY 14, 1980. Bastille Day. On Broadway, at Seventy-second, a bus rattles to its stop. Above, a blur of color—bright red, orange, shocking saffron, lavender blue, marine, livid, purplescent, raven—invades the corridor of vision. Looking up, we see a poster ad that, running along the entire roof of the bus, offers an outrageous display: an assembly line of female backsides, pressed emphatically into their designer jeans. On the right hip pocket of each, the signature of an heiress.

We see the figures from waist to mid-thigh, yet we *know* they are women. We have seen it before. These buttocks greet us from a rakish angle, a posture widely cultivated in women from time to time, in place to place. What was termed in nineteenth-century America the *Grecian Bend*. The bustle. Foot-bound women of China. Corsets. High heels. Hobble-skirts. Here it is, women hobbled in the finery of freedom.

The bus moves along. Pinned to its rear, we see its final reminder: "The *Ends* Justify the Jeans . . . Gloria Vanderbilt for Murjani." Today's freedom is molded and taut. An animal in perpetual heat. Individuals are identical, but come in colors. Over *this* rainbow lies the promise of perpetual pleasure.

109

Calvin Klein makes a similar promise. These jeans are blue; their double-stitched seams mottled by the *image* of wear. But there all evidence of toil evaporates. The shirt—white, casual, rolled at the sleeves—is satin. His model stands locked at the knees, flexed in a paroxysm of ecstasy. She too assumes the Grecian Bend; a moment of submission, captured for you, by a pair of pants. She purrs; she growls—restrained by the cloth, caressed by the seams. Calvin Klein has done this for her. He will do it for you.

Bon Jour blue jeans are "Built to look like you're moving even when you're idle." The Protestant ethic creeps in. Ben Franklin would have loved it.

A simple pair of pants is infused with a multiplicity of meanings. In the 1850s, denims were the unemotional, durable garb of miners and others among a newly mobile work force that came to California in the aftermath of the Gold Strike. Seams were riveted to make them hold, a technology borrowed from the construction of horse blankets.[1] Cloth for beasts of burden was translated to the needs of men of burden. These were the clothes of hard laboring people. Loose and ill-fitting, these pants were mass-produced for men separated from their homes, and from the clothing those homes had customarily produced. These pants held little promise for the men who wore them, save the promise that they would be ready for the next day's labors.

For others during the same decade, horse blankets were hardly enough. In the court of Empress Eugénie, "the dress worn by a fashionable lady in attendance contained 1,100 yards of material used in the construction of flounces and worked into tucks, folds and various trimmings."[2] American women of means were also wrapped in an abundance of cloth. While such makers of overalls as Levi Strauss and John H. Browning worried over how many men could be fitted into a given yardage of cloth, for women of wealth the concern was with how many yards of cloth could be pleasingly draped upon a given individual. This was the mark of prosperity: to wear enough material on one's back to clothe many of a more common caste.

"Three-flounce skirts were commonly seen" on women of property:

> Full sleeves were split in front revealing the white sleeves of the soft blouse underneath. . . . The skirt and bodice were often separate because of the immense weight of the full skirt with the stiffly boned point of the bodice coming over the fullness to flatten it. . . . Braid trims the skirt flounces, split sleeves, and bodice. It covers the curved bodice side-front and dropped-shoulder armhole seams too. Wide grosgrain ribbon sashes, caught up in poufs, decorate the skirt. Sometimes flowers were added to them.[3]

While merchant burghers in America were not as fancily dressed as were the women of their estate, neither did they wear horse blankets. Box coats, edges "trimmed with dark braid accenting the lapels and cuffs," provided a sporty prototype for today's "business suit." For those more tied to an elegant past, the "double-breasted coat has a fitted bodice and flared skirt with a split. . . . This man wears a black satin vest with a collar and a black cravat on his high shirt collar."[4] The display of cloth was the mark of substance and, most certainly, profit.

In the 1850s, the *fashionable* rich could not imagine themselves wearing the dungaree pants of proletarians and "peasants."* Neither could working-class people realistically imagine themselves in the finery of wealth and power. The only fashion link between them—subtle at best—was the austere, coal-black stovepipe hat of capitalist wealth, symbolizing the factory smokestacks

---

* The term "dungaree," although it sounds as though it may derive from a close proximity to dung, is, instead, of Hindi origin; a reference to a rough cotton fabric imported from India, commonly worn by sailors.

that brought profit to one, toil to the other. Blue jeans wore the signature of deprivation and sweat.

Success in that world required a dramatic change of clothes. In Horatio Alger's *Ragged Dick* (1866), it is a neat gray suit of clothes, a gift from a fortuitous benefactor, that signals Dick's impending metamorphosis from a ragged bootblack to "Richard Hunter, Esq.," a gentleman of substance:

> When Dick was dressed in his new attire, with his face and hands clean, and his hair brushed, it was difficult to imagine that he was the same boy. . . . He now looked quite handsome, and might readily have been taken for a young gentlemen, except that his hands were red and grimy.[5]

Years later, the clothing of nineteenth-century laborers would assume new and different meanings. Functional beginnings became increasingly obscure within unfolding imagery. In the movies, the range hands of the early cattle industry were reborn as icons of a noble, rural simplicity; rugged individualism; primal morality and law. Blue jeans were conspicuous within the moral landscape of media Americana. On the screen these pants taunted the imaginations of city folk as emblems of a simpler and uncorrupted life. While laborers would continue to wear them at work, now the well-heeled might don a pair—a symbolic escape from the regimen of the marketplace, at home or in the garden. Democracy in action!

In the fifties, blue denim became part of a statement, a rejection of postwar suburban society; of the tyrannies of the fashion-conscious consumerism that gave that society its definition. In James Dean's *Rebel Without a Cause,* or Marlon Brando's *Wild One,* dungarees provided a channel of contempt toward the empty and conformist quietude of cold-war suburbia, and for the "rural idiocy" of small-town life. The affirmative images of

American consumer capitalism were under cultural siege. What had been a piece of Americana—blue jeans—became a rejection of Americana. These images found a responsive audience among those for whom gray flannel suits and crinoline shirtwaist dresses had been elevated as ideals of the age. In blue jeans, men and boys found relief from the priorities of the business world. Women and girls found relief from the Grecian Bend. Even some suburban gardeners slipped into their Levis for their moments of casual comfort, for a nap on the porch.

By the mid-sixties, blue jeans were part of an essential ensemble within an emerging commitment to social struggle. In the Deep South, where tenant farmers and sharecroppers, grandchildren of slaves, continued to wear denim in its mid–nineteenth-century sense, they were joined by college student activists—black and white—in a battle to overturn the deeply embedded centuries of segregation and race hatred. Blue denim—pants, jackets, overalls—became a sacred bond between them. The garb of toil was sanctified by the dignity of struggle. The blue *image* moved north with the song:

> *We've been 'buked, and we've been scorned.*
> *We've been talked about, sure as you're born.*
> *But we'll never turn back.*
> *No we'll never turn back*
> *Until we've all been freed,*
> *And we've got e-qual-i-ty.*

In the student rebellion and the antiwar movement that followed, blue jeans and work shirts provided a counterpoint to the uniforms of the dominant culture, whether fatigue-green in Southeast Asia, or police blue in Chicago, or gray flannel on Madison Avenue. Denim provided an anti-fashion, an anti-uniform.

With the rekindling of a long-dormant feminism in the late 1960s, the political configurations of dress became

increasingly explicit. Rejecting the sex roles of convention, blue jeans were a feminist weapon against restrictive fashion, sexual objectification, passive femininity.
This was the cloth of action, a challenge to the social
fabric of sexuality. The cloth of labor became the emblem of liberation.

If blue jeans were renegade in the 1960s and early
'70s, by the 1980s they had become the mainstay of
fashion—available in a variety of colors, textures, fabrics, and fit. These simple pants have made the long trek
"from workers' garb to counter culture revolt to status
symbol." According to a newspaper article:

> As American families back away from having their
> used-to-be requisite 2.3 children, they're snapping up
> jeans at a rate of 2.3 pair per person *per year*. That's 16
> pairs of jeans bought per second, or 50,000 pairs per
> hour. Annually, that adds up to a cool $5 billion indus-
> try figure.[6]

On television, in magazine advertising, on the sides
of buildings and buses, jeans and backsides call out to us.
Their humble past is obscured in the imagery. In ads,
"horse blankets" are infused with "a surrealistic, new-
wave flavor." Functional roots are rendered aesthetic;
corporate sources are hidden. Dan Carroll, advertising
director for Bon Jour Jeans, explains his task simply.
"We try to stay away from commercial-looking ads. . . .
We try to make advertising artistic."[7] The exploitative
labor system that underwrites these fantasies of freedom
in capitalist America is nowhere in evidence. The image
is seductive; the name is French; the signature is personal; the cotton is American; the weavers and dyers and
cutters and sewers and finishers toil in the sweatshops of
Hong Kong.[8]

The contradiction between promise and production
resides in the image itself. Jeans are the facsimile of
freedom; brought to us by models who are tucked—
painfully—into a skin-tight fit. They are the universal

symbol of individualism and western democracy; mass-produced clothing of workers, embellished by the imprimatur of Paris, the home of *haute couture* since the time of Louis XIV. They are the vestments of liberated women, cut to impose the postures of Victorianism: corsets with the *look* of freedom and motion.

Their allure is compelling. A student writes to the Soviet youth newspaper, *Komsomolskaya Pravda*. He explains that when he went to a dance wearing the clothing available in the Russian stores, "Nothing happened." He continues:

> The next night I dressed entirely in foreign clothes and brought some Western records with me as well. You should see what happened. Invitations and telephone numbers came raining down on me. Now I have jeans, good suits, records and all that sort of junk. I have plenty of friends who can get me anything I want. I have gone into business, but now I dictate my own conditions.[9]

The ideological attraction is international in scope; fashion is the "bounty" of capitalist culture. Growing up in the cold war of the fifties, fashion was the dividing line between friends and enemies. Russians and Chinese could be known by the uniformity of their dress; Americans were brightly packaged.

In blue jeans, the most functional and least ritualistic of clothes, fashion reveals itself as a complex world of history, promise, and change; as a capturing of continual "truths." Opposite worlds collide violently and then mesh in fashion. Social conflict and contradiction are displayed . . . and diffused. Resistance and conformity coexist within "the mirror of fashion."

What are we to make of all this? Do we dismiss it as a meaningless frivolity, irrelevant and immaterial? Paul Nystrom, a writer on fashion and economics in the 1920s and '30s, and a father of modern mass-merchandising techniques, contended that it was "foolish and shallow-minded people" who refuse to take fashion seriously. "The wiser ones," he said, "have tried to find explanations and to understand."[10] Yet looking at fashions, in and of themselves, provides explanations that often defy understanding. Our ability to interpret a specific fashion—the current one of jeans, for example—shows us that as we try to make sense of it, our confusion intensifies. It is a fashion whose very essence is contradiction and confusion.

To pursue the goal of understanding is to move beyond the artifact of cloth itself, toward the more general phenomenon of fashion and the world in which it has risen to prominence. It is a piece in the political discourse of consent, and of revolution. It is a keystone in the shifting architectures of class, sexuality, national identity. Fashion is situated within the framework of industrial development; it interacts with the rise of consumer capitalism and mass-media imagery. It is a way in which people identify themselves as individuals and collectively.

What events, what developments, what forces proceeded to make *fashion* a more considerable concern than *function* among increasing numbers of people? In what ways have fashion and sexuality coincided, particularly in the context of palpable transformations in the structure, ceremony, and economy of family life? How does fashion provide a social language that infuses the historic emergence of women's liberation?

Exploring the role of fashion within the social and political configuration of industrial America helps to reveal the parameters and possibilities, the fantasies of freedom, the industrial democracy of American capitalism. Blue jeans alone suggest that politics and fashion may be the warp and woof of American culture in an era of mass production and mass merchandising. The ultimate question is whether the incorporation of images of rebellion into mass-produced fashions has been a meaningful component of social change.

2 / In the Beginning . . .

> *And when the woman saw that the tree*
> *was good for food, and that it was pleasant*
> *to the eyes, and a tree to be desired to make*
> *one wise, she took of the fruit thereof, and*
> *did eat, and gave also unto her husband with*
> *her; and he did eat. And the eyes of them*
> *both were opened, and they knew that they*
> *were naked; and they sewed fig leaves to-*
> *gether, and made themselves aprons. . . .*
> *And the Lord God said unto the woman,*
> *"What is this that thou hast done?"*
>
> *—Genesis 3:6–13*

WITHIN THE biblical account of creation, the first appearance of clothing was the mark of sin. Adam and Eve, born naked into Paradise, get dressed at the threshold of perdition. With the putting on of clothes, the future life of humanity is cursed. In the leaves of the fig tree, standing before God, man and woman received the dire sentence of "The Fall."

For these "sinners in the hands of an angry God," the penalty was monumental. Once a garden of universal bounty and reciprocity, the earth was now bounded by hierarchy, scarcity, and denial. As the most cursed of all the animals, the serpent was relegated to eat dust all the days of its life, crawling upon its belly; yet the curse on humanity was also severe.

For woman, who bears primary guilt in this venerable tale, the judgment carried sorrow and pain in the bringing forth of children. It also established her subjugation as a class. From that time forward, she was destined—so generations have been told—to submit willingly to the desire and the rule of her husband. The prototype of domination, one human over another, was inscribed upon history.

With sin, and with the assumption of clothing, Adam's sufferings were likewise multiplied. Sorrow would pursue him all the days of his life. Labor and toil were his miserable inheritance. So, too, was death: "For dust thou art, and unto dust shalt thou return." For each person, the miracle of creation would be ceremonially and inevitably undone.

As the trappings of sin, clothing is infused with these wretched conditions of existence. Hierarchy and domination are elevated as the way of God on earth. The common lot of humanity is to persevere under the constant reminder that we are essentially scorned, sinful. The sexual divisions of labor and of power are also established concurrently with the assumption of clothes. Clothing bore witness to this world-historic, tragic moment, and would continue to do so in the millennia to follow. It was the word of God, emblazoned upon the very surface of humanity.

This injunction informed and permeated the structure of European feudalism. Within this static and landed society, hierarchy and caste had the underpinning of religion. The social world was cut deep with the imprint of power and inequality. The prerogatives of nobility and clergy were seen as God-given, as was the subordination of the peasantry. Obedience to God, to an eternal law, was defined by an unhesitating acceptance of one's station within the existent hierarchy. Salvation itself was predicated on compliance.

As in the realm of *the word,* in the decisive arena of clothing, the dominant biblical interpretation was one that perpetuated the rule of landed nobility and Church.

Among a degraded peasantry, historically bound to the land and wedged at the bottom of an immobile social order, the curse of Adam was the characteristic definition for life. Labor and sorrow were a continual plight, and the dominant interpretation of the Bible offered no possibility of escape. In the lives of those who worked the land, the wages of sin were exacted perpetually.

The structure of material life in general, and clothing in particular, was sustained by this presupposition. Scarcity and abundance coexisted as in a great chain of being. While evidence is slim regarding the clothing worn by poor people in that era, certain general parameters can be deduced. The social misery of peasant life was embodied in the inelegance of their clothes. Peasant clothing was simply made and rough of cut and cloth. The phenomenon of "fashion," whereby clothing design undergoes a general and discernable process of change, was unknown among the poor.

> For 1,500 years the essential lines of dress had hardly changed . . . a shepherd of the Fourteenth Century might have inherited his garments from his great, great, great grandfather many times removed. The usual attire was a coarse gray smock, trousers, leg wrappings and shoes.[11]

Needless to say, such garments were a part of the broad home production of the peasantry. This was a society of self-sufficiency, and needs were addressed within the immediacy of the locale. Weaving and sewing were performed at home, as was dyeing where it was employed.[12]

Against this rustic backdrop of peasant simplicity, the clothing of the feudal landowner was something to behold. If the shabby togs of plowmen betrayed a kinship to fallen man, a life defined by labors of the soil, the vestments of clergy and of nobility bore no such shame.

While those at the bottom of the feudal hierarchy bore the weight of sin most heavily, those at the top acknowledged a servitude only to God. Otherwise they bore the weight of life with little difficulty. Within the structure of feudalism, the nobility was—it would seem—largely immune from Adam's curse. While others' God-given station required a commitment to the invocation "*In the sweat of thy face shalt thou eat bread,*" the stature of the nobility and priesthood was defined by a life of consummate leisure.

"The nobleman, like the lady, was a creature incapable of useful work," argues Quentin Bell in his evocative study of fashion, *On Human Finery*. Idleness, within the prevalent reading of the Bible, was a mark of favor in the eyes of God, insofar as it exempted the nobility from the judgment of labor. For the nobility, stewardship over cursed humanity defined them, along with clergy, as agencies of the Lord. This role was imprinted upon the practices and material conditions of their lives. Bell continues on the life of the nobleman:

> A high degree of conspicuous leisure was expected of him. Equally, it was important that he should be a consumer; if he had relied simply upon the vicarious consumption of his household, it would have appeared that he was working to support them. He had to establish the fact that he was a rentier (which until the eighteenth century almost implied the ownership of land).[13]

Idleness and waste were symbolic of a God-given freedom from the ecological terms of common life.

Clothing was an essential part of this conspicuous display of sloth and needless expenditure of resources. It was the material embodiment of what Thorstein Veblen called "conspicuous leisure" and "conspicuous consumption."[14] Clothing was a palpable and powerful expression of a social relationship. Among men and women of nobility, cloth—in abundance—was an achievement of their prosperity. The immense amount of labor and intricate needlework required in assembling and embellishing their clothing was testimony to the immense amount of labor that was held under the sway of their domain. In a world of general scarcity, their birthright was a surplus. Cloth was worn in billows and tucks. The God-given powers they claimed were underwritten by a visually tangible differentiation between themselves and the common lot of humanity. Their clothing was cut and arranged to reveal the depth of its sumptuosity. These clothes had no functional association with work. Indeed, their function was largely to convey the message that their owners lived beyond work. Freed from the biblical inscription to labor, they stood within their world, somewhere between God and humanity. Sartorial aesthetics, clothing imagery was their province and their prerogative. To violate this prerogative was to violate not only the dominant structure of power, but also the dominant structure of religious belief.

As in the Bible, where the assumption of clothing immediately precedes the demarcation of gender, there was some distinction between the clothing of men and of women. If noblemen were immune from the curse of Adam, Eve's sin was not so easily expiated. By recent standards, however, these distinctions were minimal.[15] Among peasant folk, the distinction was almost nonexistent. In the clothing of the rich, a sexual division is evident, yet in both men's and women's clothing, leisure and consumption are dramatically proclaimed. Within the order of feudalism, such a claim was an essential component of inequity. In their clothes, and—as Anne Hollander has pointed out—in their portraits, "cloudlike, flame-like rivers of cloth" were the honoraria of a religiously ordained status over society.[16]

With the development of a "democratic" challenge to this structure, among peasants and among an incipient bourgeoisie, the prerogatives of nobility took on an increasingly legalistic character—an attempt to stem the tide of history. Elaborate systems of "sumptuary law," governing consumption along class and caste lines, developed in Europe in the Middle Ages, and continued to be established—in certain places—into the twentieth century. According to Frances Elizabeth Baldwin, a scholar of sumptuary legislation in England, the enactment of such laws between 1327 and the early seventeenth century—when they begin to disappear from English canon—was motivated by three general concerns. First, and foremost, was to "preserve class distinctions, so that any stranger could tell by merely looking at a man's dress to what rank in society he belonged."

Second, sumptuary legislation was designed to "check practices which were regarded as deleterious in their effects, due to the feeling that luxury and extravagance were in themselves wicked and harmful to people." Initially, this concern was leveled by the upper echelons against the lower, and applied selectively throughout society. Only later, with the rise of new forms of mobile wealth and the ascendency of Puritanism and other Protestant sects, were such invocations directed at the sumptuary practices of the church or the nobility, *per se*.

The third concern was economic. Laws were designed to promote home industries, as in the case of late eighteenth-century America where homespun was seen as a patriotic resistance to British domination over the American market. It could also mean that consumption was restricted to "encourage savings," for the purposes, often, of supporting the political, military, or sumptuary demands of a sovereign.[17]

It is clear that the first concern—that of maintaining hierarchy and convention—was the pre-eminent impetus behind the enactment of such statutes. "Sumptuary laws," argues clothing historian Pearl Binder, "constituted a means of enforcing class privilege in a regimented social structure. . . . In the Middle Ages, both Church and State rigorously enforced social distinctions. 'Men may be equal in the sight of God, but on earth they are commanded to stay in that status of life into which they are born.' "[18]

Under the broad canopy of sumptuary law, "men and women, in literal truth, were regulated from the part in their hair to the soles of their feet."[19] Behind these laws lay the word of God.

> Each man's place was appointed to him in a common scheme; he must, in general, be content to live in that state of life unto which it had pleased God to call him at his birth. . . . Since each man's place in life was thus fixed by social custom, it was heresy for him to attempt to rise above his class either in his manner of living or in his dress.[20]

Such laws were overwhelming in their detail, and categorized according to the lines of social power. An English law, enacted under the reign of Elizabeth I (1582), gave specific directions to apprentices regarding their acceptable mode of dress. "No apprentice whatsoever should presume," it began, "to wear (1) any clothing except what he received from his master; (2) a hat, or anything except a woollen cap . . . ; (3) ruffles, cuffs, loose collars . . . ; (4) anything except canvas, fustian [a stout fabric of cotton and flax], sack cloth, English leather, or woollen doublets, without any silver or silk trimming." Punishment for violation of the statute was at the discretion of the master for a first offense; a public whipping for a second offense; and six months added to the period of indenture for the third offense.[21] Likewise, a proclamation of July 6, 1597, lists a vast array of cloth and accessories which "none shall wear," save those of high rank. In an elaborately drawn document, indicating what is forbidden and who is exempted, we discover that

"Cloth of gold, sylver tissued," and "Silke of purple color" are forbidden in garments, save those of "Earls and above that rank and Knights of the Garter in their purple mantles." Among ladies of nobility, only "Knights' wives and all above that rank" might wear velvet in their upper garments. In "Kirtles [a skirt or outer petticoat] and Petticoats, however," velvet was permissible for "Wives of knights' eldest sons, and all above that rank."[22] Within that same statute we see the arrival of another significant realm of status within the arena of hierarchical dress codes: *money*. While the highest levels of sumptuary practice are still reserved for those landed lords of inherited lineage, we see that "those with net income of 500 marks per year for life" share the same level of exception as "Barons' sons and all above that rank," as well as "Gentlemen attending upon the queen in house or chamber," and "those who have been employed in embassies" as emissaries of a monarch.[23] As the ranks of nobility are solidified within the structure of law, the law itself betrays a portentous vulnerability to a class of people whose wealth is defined not in the static tenure over land, but in the mobile negotiations of a money economy.

In Augsburg, somewhat earlier, in 1530:

> Only princes, knights and their ladies were permitted to wear brocade, velvet garments were for patricians. The upper bourgeoisie were allowed three ellens of velvet to decorate their headdresses. Those dedicated to learning wore silk, damast* or satin, whereas wool and homespun materials were for simple folk. Furs were regulated in the same manner: ermine and sables for princes and aristocrats; fox and polecat for simple townspeople; goat and lamb skins for the peasant.[24]

---

* *damast:* probably *damask,* a silk imported from Damascus, woven with patterns. The appearance of this and other luxury items is an indication of mercantile trade, and gives some inkling as to the heightened status and power of an emergent bourgeoisie.

Sources indicate that while sumptuary law became increasingly prevalent at the dawn of the modern era, it was rarely imposed and almost impossible to enforce. In England, the reign of Elizabeth I saw the most vigorous development of sumptuary legislation in British history, yet only a short time after her death, early in the reign of James I, sumptuary legislation was altogether abolished.[25]

Like censorship, which arose rapidly in the aftermath of the European development of the printing press, sumptuary law may be seen—in part—as a desperate gesture to maintain entitlements of customary power in the face of mounting pressures. Clothing, like *the word,* was essential to the mediation of feudal powers. Control of both *the word* and the sartorial image was the province of elites. The possibility of diffusion of these media to those previously excluded threatened social revolution and gave rise to state-sanctioned regulation.

Particularly in the arena of clothing, the development of mercantile wealth posed a serious challenge. Regardless of law, it was unlikely that a peasant or an apprentice would have the resources available to violate the code surrounding "cloth of gold." Occasionally, the idiom of rebellion would assume a sartorial component, as in sixteenth-century Germany, where "rebellious peasants . . . demanded the right to wear red cloaks like their masters," but—for most—the garb of wealth was forbidden by economic rather than legalistic circumstances.[26]

In reality, it was from an emerging mobile class of monetary wealth that the greatest threat to social prerogative was perceived. Merchant trade, often feeding the luxurious practices of the nobility, elevated an embryonic bourgeoisie to circumstances of prosperity, if not political franchise.[27]

Over time, with the ascendency of a mercantile and later an industrial bourgeoisie, exclusive possession of a sartorial eloquence eroded as an aristocratic privilege. Initially, incipient capitalists had access to the material comforts born of the purse. Eventually, their successors in mass industry, and then in merchandising, would transform that eloquence into the profitable terms of mass production, establishing a vernacular imagery of consumption. Insofar as clothing constitutes a generally understood language of society, however, the categories of adornment, dating to the aristocratic tradition, still hold sway. The great difference, as will be discussed later, is that this continuity of meaning has persisted more in the clothing of women than of men in the era of capitalism.

While significantly diminished from the standards of the past, even today the signs of aristocracy assert a considerable—if now mass-produced—presence. Much of this persistence is rooted in the particular history of France, as is, ironically, its renunciation. During the reign of Louis XIV, a pregnant admixture of absolute monarchy and mercantile capitalism produced an economy geared toward the fabrication of luxuries. The Sun King's principal financial advisor, Jean-Baptiste Colbert, happened to be the son of a cloth merchant in Reims. Colbert bound his mercantile roots to the splendor of the court and "gathered together all the plans and expedients of his predecessors for a prolonged attempt to establish an entirely self-sufficing national economy." At the heart of this enterprise lay Colbert's particular strategy: "With our taste," he proclaimed, "let us make war on Europe and through fashion conquer the world."[28] A central part of the program was the promotion of French luxury industries and their products.

Colbert "used many methods: encouragement through the giving of honours and monetary rewards; regulation through the *Code de Commerce* which set forth exactly what was to be produced and by which methods it was to be manufactured."[29] In addition, import tariffs, state subsidies, and relaxed guild regulations contributed to the realization of this economic program, and since that time, the predominance of French *haute couture* has been unchallenged. Expressing perhaps Colbert's own mercantile roots, the continuity of aristocratic influence has been dependent on the growth and success of the bourgeoisie, and the mobile market economy.

Alongside this tendency, the bourgeois revolutions altered the terms of politics and ushered in a whole new mode of life. A broad alliance of classes assembled around the explosive banner of "natural rights." One aspect of this revolutionary process played itself out in the area of fashion. Against the aristocratic clothing customs that accentuated social inequality, a new, egalitarian fashion developed. We can see this in the rise of Puritanism, where a "plain style" of dress was a mark of opposition to feudal waste and privilege, paralleling the rise of a "plain style" in language as Latin texts were replaced by vernacular ones and popular access to Scripture became key to the Protestant notion of salvation. A Puritan could be known by the simplicity of his garb, and by the Bible carried under his arm.[30]

The renunciation of aristocratic modes crested dramatically, and prophetically, with the French Revolution. Before the revolution, the conventions of clothing were deeply entrenched along lines of class. In the *ancien régime,* men and women of nobility wore the conspicuous apparel of their caste. Ladies of the court were decked in elaborate gowns, deeply layered, and inscribed with labor and lace. Their waists were constricted by corsets, driving powdered breasts upward beyond the frontiers of a plunging neckline, and pushing faint sighs from their lips. While the hobbled habit accentuated a demeanor of erotic availability, it also asserted a leisurely existence.

Men, too, were marked by privilege: *culottes* (knee breeches); silk stockings; the *justaucorps,* an ornate body coat, close fitting and reaching to the knees. Men and women alike wore elaborate wigs upon their aristocratic heads. In a society sharply divided by broad restrictions on social and political rights, these garments were notorious as symbols of domination, just as motor cars would be viewed in urban working-class neighborhoods in the early years of the twentieth century, before the mass production and merchandising of auto-mobility.[31]

In contrast to this splendor, the laboring poor of Paris were known, simply, as *sans-culottes;* they wore ankle-length trousers or rough smocks. With the revolution and its egalitarian idiom, *culottes* fell into disrepute, as did silk stockings and *justaucorps*. Wigs disappeared in the spirit of democracy and emancipation. Breaking with the aristocratic past, and adapting the public images of popular sovereignty, fashion and democracy were symbolically fused. Asserting solidarity with the Parisian masses, the dress of middle-class men adapted a vernacular cut, the cut of modern-day trousers. For a time, women of means also took on the garb of social equality, wearing simple and flimsy shifts.[32] If France would be the fountain for the continuation of aristocratic elegance in fashion, so too was it a source for the revolutionary imagery of emancipation.

3 / *The Cloak of Morality*

CLOTH STANDS prominently at the heart of capitalism's development from the sixteenth century to the present. It is woven deeply into the massive social transformations wrought by capitalism. In England and northwestern France, the shift from crop production to the raising of sheep for wool irrevocably altered the course of world history. Cloth was conspicuous in the *sinews* of trade by which a world-market economy was created and mobilized. The isolation of local self-sufficiency gave way to a "modern world system."

Dealings in cloth were essential to the development and prosperity of an urban bourgeoisie. From the end of the eighteenth century, the city as a social and economic network, the bourgeoisie, and the growth of technology coalesced to define the contours of modern commerce.

If laborers in agriculture and industry were not at first motivated by the impetus of "fashion," they were decisively affected by it. After initial inroads established by the cash crops of sugar and tobacco, the plantation system of slavery—particularly in the southern United States—was driven forward by seemingly insatiable markets for cotton. The industrial factory system, in England and America, was likewise propelled by textile production. Factory labor had its harsh birthplace at the side of a loom.

Cloth provoked a horrific uprooting of peoples, across frontiers and oceans. While a handful prospered in trade, the vast majority of the rest labored out of necessity, often against their will. Factory production of textiles moved women from the arena of home production and engaged them in the public spheres of modernity as mill workers. Customary definitions of womanhood and of family life were shattered in the process.

Over the course of the nineteenth century, the development of the ready-made clothing industry began to alter the very terms of popular survival, signaling a shift from home production of goods to the general consumption of factory-made products. With the input of emerging structures of mass merchandising, around the turn of the twentieth century, and urged on by the burgeoning agencies of mass impression, clothing and fashion began to take their central place in the popular imagination.

For an urban bourgeoisie, at the beginning of the nineteenth century, clothing was a matter of principle, a statement of purpose. If the Protestant Reformation had split sumptuosity from the realm of the sacred, mercantile capitalism had erected a bastion of power and wealth whose emblem was diligence, not idleness.[33] In his *Autobiography,* Benjamin Franklin—Max Weber's archetype of the "protestant ethic and the spirit of capitalism"— presented a clear picture of the importance of surface appearance:

> In order to secure my credit and character as a tradesman, I took care not only to be in *reality* industrious and frugal, but to avoid all appearances to the contrary. I drest plainly; I was seen at no places of idle diversion. . . . To show that I was not above my business, I sometimes brought home the paper I purchas'd at the stores thro' the streets on a wheelbarrow. Thus being esteem'd an industrious, thriving young man, and paying duly for what I bought . . . I went on swimmingly.[34]

In this late-eighteenth-century account, the man of business is engaged, morally, in the world. Simplicity of attire was a hallmark of that morality. In violent juxtaposition to the customs of the landed aristocracy, a secular saintliness was inscribed, proudly, with the mark of one's worldly activity. In Franklin's Philadelphia, where Quaker businessmen forged a powerful unity between commerce and Christianity, the "plain style" of dress was a visible sign of their commitment to hard work and simple justice. Under no circumstances did this mean that their garments were cheap or inelegant. The "plain style" was, indeed, a style. While simply cut coats signified a break from the visual language of sumptuosity, they were at the same time made of the finest cloth, and employed a time-consuming artisan dexterity in their creation.[35]

The "plain style" was also not totally plain. Like the business suit of today, which derives from this shift, it had vestigial remnants of the sumptuous mode. Coats and vests were cut to reveal the layers of linen beneath them—tangible evidence of prosperity, although understated in comparison with the tradition they rejected. Surely a man of means could still be known by the clothes he wore, but the image conveyed had changed from one of idleness, waiting to be served, to one mobile and self-serving.

In certain areas, the "rich but grave" aura of the commercial garb did not take hold, even within the capitalist epoch. Ceremonial garments continued to betray a commitment to sumptuosity, as is still in evidence in formal academic attire. In a world of mundane commitments, the doctoral hood allows for the mystification of unearthliness. In military attire, as well, epaulets, braids, and other ornamental flourishes functioned to ennoble the practice of war.[36] Perhaps, as Quentin Bell suggests, this is rooted in war itself: giving symbolic legitimacy to the conspicuous consumption of human life. The separation of business from evening or leisure dress, as well, left certain areas of masculine bourgeois life more ornamental or languid than others.

Overall, however, the trend was toward the tangibility of industry, thrift, and action. Even such figures as Beau Brummel or Beau Nash, whose names come to us with the reputations of archetypal dandies, stood in stark contrast to the dash of courtly splendor. They were exemplars of the elevation of the "plain style" to the height of fashion around the turn of the nineteenth century. Both avoided what Victorian writer and critic John Ruskin was to call "that flabby flutter, wrinkled swelling, and puffed pomp of infinite disorder."[37]

The elegance of their garb was a costly investment in "simplicity, good fit and cleanliness." This fixation with cleanliness was a characteristic development of the capitalist ethic; set against the unbathed—if perfumed—bodies of the nobility.

> Beau Brummel hated dirt and was meticulously tidy. . . . His clothing was distinguished by its perfect fit and extreme cleanliness. He changed his linen three times a day, and he had the soles of his boots polished like the upper part. . . . He wore a cambric shirt with valuable buttons and an immaculate white cravat, which he spent three hours tying every day. Beau Brummel usually wore black or navy blue, the garments fitting so well that not a single crease was ever formed.[38]

Brummel was an architect of a simple, unflamboyant form of ostentation, where fit and workmanship began to replace the weighty display of cloth in the perfection of "elegance."

As industrial capitalism developed in the nineteenth century, bourgeois men's clothing continued to develop in a mode of fastidious austerity. As the wealth of industrialists grew, "an industrious life no longer implied a poor or laborious existence. . . . Masculine dress betokened a complete abstention from industrial labour, but that was all; it was not 'highly sumptuous.' "[39] Immense power, even, was understated. Dark colors were both resistant to the dirt of the industrial landscape and consistent with the democratic ideology of enlightenment.[40] Black coats and cylindrical "smokestack" hats betrayed a sartorial commitment to a new, industrial aesthetic. In industrial areas of the United States, this mutation was fairly complete by about 1830, while among the landed wealth of the plantation South, an aristocratic motif persevered.[41]

While men of capitalist wealth employed highly skilled tailors, and demanded fine, if substantial, fabrics for their clothes, the idiom of their garments was one of engagement and social ethics. An emanation of precisionism was implicit in the fit. A suggestion of asceticism was projected by the dark gravity of the cloth. In the midst of these vestments, men of extreme wealth claimed a moral penance, a righteous place in the world. Capitalist fashion had freed men from the evidence of rapacity and waste, from the guilt and conceit of gluttony that marked the aristocratic tradition.

Yet if capitalists, merchants, and somber professionals made sartorial claims of self-denial and egalitarianism, the social world they forged and administered offered a very different picture. Those who stood outside the stewardship of capital did not have access to the conspicuous symbols, these finely tailored emblems of austerity and moral purpose. The cloak of morality was not available to those who labored beneath its threads. The hypocrisy of capitalist wealth was revealed—most glaringly—in the lives of those who stood in the shadow of its righteous image.

4 / The Three Faces of Eve

IN 1868, an eight-year-old girl named Jane Addams prepared herself for a weekly trip to the Union Sunday School in Cedarville, Illinois. Dressed proudly in a beautiful new cloak—"gorgeous beyond anything I had ever worn before"—she stood before her father for his approval. The owner of a sawmill and a flour mill, Mr. Addams was the epitome of middle-class substance. Himself a teacher of a large Bible class at the Union Sunday School, Jane's father cut "a most imposing figure in his Sunday frock coat, a fine head rising high above all the others." He wore the cloak of morality with pious pride.

His Quaker eyes looking sternly down at his daughter, Mr. Addams suggested that Jane forego her illustrious garment in favor of more humble garb.

> I was much chagrined by his remark that it was a very pretty cloak—in fact so much prettier than any cloak the other little girls in the Sunday School had, that he would advise me to wear my old cloak, which would keep me quite as warm, with the added advantage of not making the other little girls feel badly. I complied with the request but I fear without inner consent, and I certainly was quite without joy of self-sacrifice as I walked soberly through the village street by the side of my counselor.

Yet after moving beyond an initial response of confused reluctance, the event proved to be a moral lesson:

> My mind was busy . . . with the old question eternally suggested by the inequalities of the human lot. Only as we neared the church door did I venture to ask what could be done about it, receiving the reply that it might never be righted so far as clothes went, but that people might be equal in things that mattered much more than clothes . . . and that it was very stupid to wear the sort of clothes that made it harder to have equality even there.[42]

Whereas for Benjamin Franklin the appearance of diligent piety was essential in the carrying on of business, for Jane Addams appearances provided an external symbol, a visible testimony of social morality. In a world that said that clothes shouldn't matter very much, the one thing that was clear was that they mattered completely. "Above everything else," her father's message conveyed the admonition that "mental integrity" should be there to be seen. Sumptuous dress, in a world of inequality, was a manifest mark of greed.

In her life in social work, Addams kept to the lesson, and to the faith. She appropriated the "plain style" not for business, but in the name of community service. A worldly calling in the thoroughfares of commerce was the province of men. The general morality of the time instructed bourgeois women to dedicate themselves, unswervingly, to what Jane Addams referred to as "the family claim." Yet this was not for her. As one of an early but significant band of "educated" women, she perceived the family as a trap, one that would deny her outlets or activities in which she could adhere to the social morality inherited from her father.

Caught between the masculine principle of social engagement and the stark inequity of feminine reality, she translated the Protestant ethic into the terms of nurturance and service, rather than productivity and industry. In the early 1880s, while a junior at Rockford seminary, Addams proclaimed her calling, prophetically setting the terms for a life's work:

> As young women of the 19th century, we . . . proudly assert our independence, on the other hand we still retain the old ideal of womanhood—the saxon lady whose mission it was to give bread unto her household. So we have planned to be "Breadgivers" throughout our lives, believing that in labor alone is happiness, and that the only true and honorable life is one filled with good works and honest toil.[43]

Despite her hopeful claims for a generation, Jane Addams stood prominently as a heretic to the Victorian standards of femininity. Her "plain style" of dress and her blunt commitment to a social world placed her outside of the conventions of womanhood. Her transgression—unwittingly encouraged by her father's stern morality—must be placed against the panorama of a more dominant social tradition. To a large extent, Addams' embracing of social works, and of a "plain" attire, was at the same time a rejection of *woman* as "a family possession, whose delicacy and polish are but outward symbols" of subservience to male prosperity.

For most wealthy women in nineteenth-century America, social engagement was relatively minimal. Their dress was not as "plain," nor did it evince the moral claims borne by the somber clothing of men. If men of money scorned sumptuous claims for themselves, the ideals propagated for women of their class were far less economical. Similarly, while the social language of men's clothing tended to denote activity and industriousness, the idiom of women's clothing was fragility, idleness, and the conspicuous consumption of cloth.

In the United States, as in much of Western Europe, most nineteenth-century middle- and upper-class women dressed in sharp contrast to men of their economic position. If austerity was a component of feminine attire, its social message was sexual rather than economic. These were times when in the name of good taste, legs were referred to as "limbs"—if it was necessary to mention them at all. While men of wealth exuded the worldliness of the marketplace, women were the keepers of a higher morality, limited to the confines of the home. The sexual shame of "the Fall" was woman's to bear: A proper bourgeois wife and mother was covered from the nape of her neck to the tips of her toes. The display of skin was inappropriate. The ostensible morality of men in business was underwritten by the keepers of the home, untouched by the tarnished activities of commerce and isolated from an increasingly mobile and social world.

Within this bulwark of bourgeois morality, women were idealized icons, worshipped in a cult of purity and placed on a spiritual pedestal. If bourgeois men were actively consumed by the symbolism of industry, bourgeois women were symbols of virtue and decorum. This predominant social pattern, according to French historian Theodore Zeldin, effected an increasingly broad social distance between the realms of men and women. For women, "the cult of their purity made them inaccessible." Particularly, "pleasures in sexual intercourse could not in such circumstances be sought with them, who were dedicated to motherhood."[44] Childbearing defined the proper limits of married women's sexual horizon. Socially and emotionally, the nineteenth-century institution of bourgeois marriage was a barrier rather than a bond between men and women. For women, the ideological baggage that informed this separation was nothing less than disastrous. By pious definition, women were unable to fend for themselves. In the words of the feminist theoretician Charlotte Perkins Gilman, women were imprisoned within a "sexuo-economic" relation; one in which their moralistic and childrearing functions, their "home service," was exchanged for economic survival, provided by men. Their femininity became paramount as their social definition.[45]

This configuration, precisely as it claimed to elevate women to a higher purity, above worldly and carnal concerns, only served to accentuate their carnality. To clarify this point, let us take an example from another time and place. In China, over a period of ten centuries and into the very recent past, the practice of foot-binding was customarily enforced on women over a broad range of social class. From an early age—usually about seven years—little girls would have their toes pulled back under the soles of their feet and bound in that position. Over years the feet became deformed and misshapen. Effectively, foot-bound women of China were systematically crippled by this custom. In order to walk, they had to take slow, mincing steps, painfully executed with the help of a walking stick.

Clearly, this example of hobbling, one of a variety of ornamental body practices that severely incapacitate the individual, functioned to limit women's mobility in an environment that designated women as a form of property. Yet within the context of Chinese culture, foot-binding was not conceived of as restrictive. Rather it was considered as an aspect of eroticism. The grossly transfigured foot was termed, poetically, "lily foot" or "lotus foot." A broad liturgy of sexual practices focused on the feet, and in its metamorphosis, the foot became known as a sexual organ, an additional genital. In addition to the use of botanical terminology, the institution of foot-binding was founded on horticultural theory. In plants, restricting the development of one branch tends to accentuate the development of another. Similarly, it was believed that by constricting the mobility of women, their sexuality would flourish. As one student of the foot has put it, by atrophying the foot, the genitals would undergo hypertrophy. Our reason tells us that this is absurd and physiologically unfounded as a theory. Yet in certain ways, the theory became a self-fulfilling prophecy. By limiting the ability of women to function in the broad range of human activities, foot-binding did—in effect—accentuate the primacy of their sexual function. Sexuality became an expanded definition of womanhood, as other definitions were culturally and physically eclipsed.[46]

The equivalent of the "lily foot" in nineteenth-century American and European middle-class culture was the commonly worn corset, which restricted not only the mobility but even the breathing of women who wore them. The romantic stereotype of women continually fainting was a common occurrence, a result of the restriction and the debilitating pressure on internal organs from wearing corsets.[47] As a form of bodily restriction, the corset accentuated carnal concerns precisely as its wearer was expected to transcend them. The very practice of restraining the body of a woman implied that this model of chastity stood at the frontiers of abandon. Along these lines, Havelock Ellis wrote that corsets tended to make "breathing thoracic instead of abdominal, thereby keeping the bosom in a constant, and presumably sexually attractive, state of movement."[48]

At the same time, tight body lacing around the waist produced what was idealized as a proper feminine bearing. The narrow waist indicated minimal consumption of food, an imagistic representation of self-denial. The broad expanses of bosom and hip, accentuating the reproductive roles of women, provided an image of bounty in childbearing and nurturance.

The bustle, a fixture of women's fashion for about twenty years in the latter half of the nineteenth century, added to the general broadness of the hips and to the imagery of reproductive bounty. Bustles worn in conjunction with corsets effected the posture known as the "Grecian Bend," or the "S-curve." With the buttocks pushed up and back, and the back driven forward, the bend approximated the posture of a female animal in heat, anticipating rear penetration by the male. In the midst of restrictive purity, the implication was of a continual sexual readiness.

The question of women's wearing underpants is another example of this ambiguity and tension between chastity and carnality. Up until the 1850s, proper middle-class women wore no underpants. Only those females who enjoyed some degree of mobility wore them. Little girls, up until the age of propriety, wore drawers under their skirts, as a concession to the irrepressibility of youth. Upon maturation, drawers were abandoned, and the genital area remained uncovered save by the layers of skirts and underskirts. Occasionally, underskirts would be gartered around the knee, but the general convention presumed the combination of immobility and male protection. Oddly, underpants were perceived as male clothing, and the only women who wore them were those who enjoyed a greater degree of worldliness and mobility than proper wives and mothers—courtesans, coquettes, demimondaines. In a world of severely restricted womanhood, these were among the most visible models of a liberated womanhood, unifying sexuality and pleasure, worldliness, mobility, and education. Standing outside the highly delimiting kinship system of patrilineage, these women had rights and privileges unavailable to those of a "higher" morality and purpose. Wearing the pants of men, trimmed often with the lace reminiscent of the late-eighteenth-century French court, these women wore the garb of an erotic transvestitism.

Good women, in their frail and housebound immobility, would never think of wearing underpants. Yet here too, the signal of virtue is also one of continual availability. One's sexuality became paramount within an ethic that countenanced no sexuality. The restrictive foundation of a female bearing, accentuating the body at the cost of mobility and health, established the terms of feminine existence for many women. Insofar as fragile health was a mark of purity, social and dress restrictions resulted in a broad epidemic of female "troubles," specific to middle-class women. Corsetry produced a female population perpetually short of breath. Disease became part and parcel of the cult of proper womanhood. According to Paul Nystrom, "paleness, frequent fainting and ailing bodies were prized as desirable features of fashionable life. Medicine and therapy enjoyed an enormous boom. Patent medicines came into wide use." So general was this fetish of frailty that during the 1830s and '40s in the United States, "customary greetings changed from 'Good morning' to 'How is your health?' "[49] This convention survives today in the form of "How are you?". Corsets also tended to cramp the stomach, thereby nullifying the appetite—consistent with the ideology of womanhood, which saw an appetite as vulgar. "It was much better to go into a decline," notes clothing historian Pearl Binder, "than to confess to an appetite for earthly food."[50]

While self-denial permeated the ornamentation of femininity, the resulting emotional and biological constraints produced a severe delicacy. By the latter part of the nineteenth century, the health of middle-class women was so debilitated that the corset became the target of increasing medical attack. In 1885 in Lyons, France, Dr. Frantz Gerard argued that corsets were "causing *enteroptose*, dropping of the female abdominal organs," in a number of women patients. So alarming was Gerard's assertion that the House of Worth, a leading fashion establishment in Paris, designed a corset specifically to correct this condition—one that pushed up instead of down. By 1904, however, the new design had taken its toll, reaching "so far in the opposite direction that it was pushing the bowels out of place upward instead of downward."[51] In 1904, another doctor, Arabella Kenealy, published a paper in London entitled "The Curse of Corsets." Based on experimental research, the article noted that if monkeys were put into corsets, so as to approximate the official posture of contemporaneous womanhood, they died within a matter of days. These were among a significant range of medical literature of the late nineteenth century calling for reform in women's dress.[52]

The enfeeblement of women was a crucial aspect of nineteenth-century middle-class fashion. The restrictive practices placed women on a pedestal, above concerns of trade and carnality, yet it produced generations of women whose concerns were mobilized around issues of the body. As the predominant ideology denied women any pleasures of the flesh, it simultaneously fixated on female flesh, molding it and restricting it. On the one hand women were the embodiment of spiritual purity; on the other, the purity was not intrinsic and had to be imposed. Like the foot-bound women of China, whose crippling was supposed to enhance their sexual role, the corseted women of the nineteenth century embodied the Victorian ideal: frail, self-denying, incapable of worldly pursuits, yet essentially carnal. Within the framework of dress restraint, women combined the reciprocal categories of purity and sin. Purity was, in effect, payment for sin. Physical restraint, essential to the structure of feminine attire, re-enacted the Biblical interpretation of the Fall. Because of Eve's transgression, humankind is destined to a life of work, a life of burden. In the bourgeois cosmology of the nineteenth century, man assumed the burden with a pious willingness, exploiting the marketplace with religious fervor. His clothing bore witness to his piety. Woman bore the guilt of sin while man pursued its world-historic implications. She was bound, restrained. The heights of her molded purity were only testimony to a sinfulness that demanded shaping and restraint. Among women, this restraint was monitored and enacted through the medium of clothing, the biblical mark of sin.

This imputation of female guilt through fashion continues today. Two recent ads supply us with a telling example. One is for women's lingerie (*Vogue*, October 1979). Three women, presumably prostitutes, are shown, backs against the wall in a police lineup. Dispensing with frills, these three stand in their underwear, bare and sexy: lace bras with deep *décolletage*, bikini underpants cut high on the thigh. The woman at the right stands with hand on hip, pelvis thrust forward, sporting a white lace garter belt and stockings. All three are in spiked heels and dripping with jewels; the accoutrements of "kept" women surround them. Even here, apprehended in the police station, their faces wear the complacent look of willful and casual seduction. They know that "sometimes innocence is no virtue." Beneath them, in the shadows, two men look up at them, inspecting the lineup. Which of them is guilty? All of them! "The new French connection of Lily of France," says the caption. "Once you've worn it you can never plead innocent." The women appear in the filmy trappings of male pleasure; even as they await their punishment, it is men who get to enjoy their display. Yet while the pleasures they serve are those of men, it is men who make the judgment, women who wear the guilt. Adorned for the interests of men, these women bear the guilt of those interests, graphically reinforced in the context of a police station.

The above ad is clearly not intended to promote garments of purity and virtue; these are clearly ladies of the world, blatantly sinful. Nevertheless, the same context of sin and judgment can be applied equally to demure fashions. An advertisement for "Act I" dresses (*New York Times Magazine*, January 27, 1980) conforms more closely to the nineteenth-century ideal of proper womanhood. Here again are three women, but they wear modest shifts, and their pose betrays a girlish decorum and

The new French Connection by Lily of France.
Once you've worn it you can never plead innocent.

Midnight lace. Morning-after satin. And lingerie so sexy, it's meant for women who know that sometimes innocence is no virtue. Experience the French Connection and you'll discover the secret pleasures of French-inspired lingerie. Bras that are little more than a bare hug of shimmering color and revealing lace. Panties cut higher on the thigh, so you look leggier. And garter belts that do more than just hold up silk stockings.

Shimmering nylon in a line-up of arresting colors like champagne, raisin, dusty rose, peach, navy and red. Demi-underwire bra, $8.50; garter belt, $6.00. Underwire front hook bra, $8.00. D cup $9.00; bikini, $4.50. Soft cup front hook bra, $6.00; hipster, $5.00. Soft cup front hook bra with light fiberfill, $7.00.

LILY OF FRANCE

For the Lily of France store near you, please write to Lily of France, 90 Park Avenue, N.Y. N.Y. 10016.

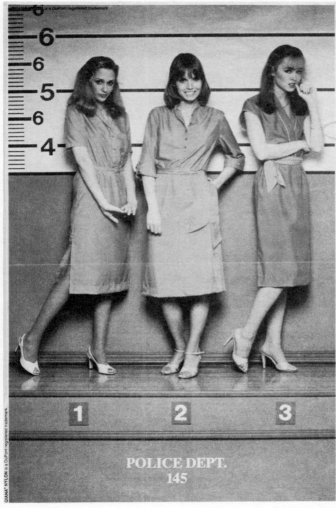

Act Romantic
Act Natural
Act Sensual
Act Guilty
Act Crazy
Act Smart
Act Darling
Act Sexy
Act Chic
Act Elusive
Act Dangerous
Act Glamourous
Act Devilish
Act Innocent
Act Sly
Act Lovable
Act Elegant
Act Silly
Act Haughty
Act Sophisticated
Act Casual
Act Worldly
Act Naughty
Act Happy
Act Vivacious
Act Coy
Act Cool
Act Sporty
Act Decadent
Act Luminous
Act Right
Act Mysterious
Act Precocious
Act Elegant...

POLICE DEPT.
145

reticence. The woman at the left assumes a posture of quiet retreat, while the woman at the right pensively sucks her thumb. The woman in the center strikes a somewhat more suggestive pose, but her toothsome smile assures us of a wholesome honesty. While in the lingerie ad the three women stood arrogantly, legs astride, these three stand knock-kneed with thighs held protectively closed. Yet here too, these paragons of virtue stand in a police lineup. Even in innocence there is guilt. Under the assumption of purity lies the premise of judgment; the sin of Eve is a universal component of decorative womanhood, whether that decoration is openly seductive or passively restrained. Woman, in the logic of the ad, is essentially sinful. Innocence is but an act, and this is borne out in the accompanying text—a list of prescriptions for feminine behavior: "Act Romantic . . . Act Sensual . . . Act Sexy . . . Act Dangerous . . . Act Devilish . . . Act Innocent . . . Act Sly . . . Act Lovable . . . Act Elegant . . . Act Worldly . . . Act Naughty . . . Act Happy . . . Act Coy . . . Act Decadent . . . Act Right . . . Act Mysterious . . . Act Precocious." Amid this bevy of behavioral choices, "Act Innocent" is circled. It is a choice, along with the others, and as a choice for self-presentation it is marked by mendacity. Even innocence is a pose. As women conform to the cult of purity they receive the same judgment as those who assume "Naughty" or "Decadent." If men's clothing, in its sobriety and fit, reflects purposeful commitment, women's clothing, even in the display of virtue, demands judgment. Once again, women are apprehended. They assume the passivity of a restrictive sexual code, are policed by the eyes of men, yet their guilt is still unmitigated. Acceding to the terms of innocence, they continue to bear the burden of guilt. In the arena of masculine scrutiny, one's femininity, one's sexuality can never step down from the lineup. Whether flagrant or suppressed, sexuality perseveres as the primary acceptable social definition of womanhood.

If nineteenth-century middle-class women bore the guilt of sin, they also assumed the guilt of class, of wealth. The conventions of women's clothing were, to a large extent, the antithesis of men's. While men's clothing displayed an imagistic presentation of economy and purpose, women's fashions were the repository of bourgeois conspicuous consumption. If it was immoral for the capitalist man to adorn himself in the sumptuosity of wealth, there was still need to display prosperity and success, the visible results of his industrious and worldly efforts. Even as men dressed in the "plain style," the *ability* to consume stood as testimony to their commercial morality. Thus it is that within the bourgeois tradition, as it evolved in the nineteenth century, women become the visible evidence of this ability. Their dresses were full, spread out by numerous layers of skirts, or given a full appearance by crinolines and hoops. Here in women's clothing was the idiom of aristocracy that had been moralistically rejected in the fervor of bourgeois revolution. Women, and also servants, carried tangible proof of commercial success. They became, to use Veblen's terminology, "vicarious consumers" for men of wealth. Like the herd of cattle or the chests of gold in antiquity, women—through their fashions and forced exclusion from the productive world—entered the state as a generally understood form of social capital. For a man of property, a woman assumed the leisure and waste that only money and power could buy. As Quentin Bell has argued, "The demands of conspicuous consumption remain. Men might escape them, but women could not. Attached to each industrial breadwinner was his vicarious consumer; on all public and social occasions it was her task to demonstrate his ability to pay."[53]

Much of this demonstration was enacted on the level of the sheer expanse and weight of cloth. An 1891 medical study that sought to determine how much extra weight the "well-dressed" woman was required to carry "found that on the average . . . indoor clothing weighed seventeen pounds, while in many cases it far exceeded that amount.'' With outdoor clothing added, the average weight reached twenty-five to thirty pounds.[54] Clothing tended to consolidate the female body into bountiful masses, weighty and ponderous symbols of success. Breasts were unified, not separately defined, into what Bernard Rudofsky has termed the ''monobosom.''[55] Bustles exaggerated the storage of fat deposits in the rump, palpable evidence of a massive surplus. Within these garments, physical activity was not only proscribed, but virtually impossible. Women's clothing, insofar as it subscribed to fashion, was a representation of wealth, a bauble by which men could display their plunder without assuming any of the guilt associated with it. Once again, in a society that had designated the sumptuous practices of the nobility as marks of indolence and greed, the male cloak of morality was posed against the evidence of avarice, worn by the woman. To a large extent the lifestyles and vestments of bourgeois womanhood became the imagistic repository of masculine, commercial transgressions. Men assumed the pose of virtue, while women bore the ornamentation of sin—even the commercial sin, which was the exclusive prerogative of men. It is not surprising that in the nineteenth century when the moral separation of gender enters the world of fashion to an extreme, we find that men begin to enter, and then dominate, the world of high-fashion design for women. The sins of wealth, like those of sexuality, were forged and articulated by men, as they were worn and displayed by women.[56] Once more, sexual politics ran true to the biblical inscription.

This tendency to define women as part of a male-controlled livestock is ancient, and continues today. While much of the extreme distinction between the morality of women's clothing versus that of men has receded, the construct that assumes a simple and austere man and a highly sumptuous woman still stands to underwrite masculine morality, feminine guilt. It is re-enacted in the buying of furs and jewelry; excessive investments, given by men, worn by women. A recent article about Ronald Reagan underwrites the perseverance of this logic. As reported by *Time* magazine, Reagan is presented as an archetype of capitalist ethics. Although he is worth "as much as $4 million," Reagan is a Protestant paragon. "The GOP presidential candidate has simple tastes, carries little cash and doesn't like spending even at that. Reagan once flew to Paris with only $5 in his pocket—and then was annoyed when he had to part with it for a tip." Yet this man of austere morality, we discover, "spends lavishly only on his wife. . . . Nancy Reagan wears $5,000 designer dresses, collects fine jewelry, paintings and antiques, and keeps her hairdresser and an interior decorator on call."[57] Reagan adorns himself in the garb of moral simplicity; his abilities for careful and sensible leadership are, literally, worn on his sleeve. All evidence of rapacity or self-aggrandizement is worn, conveniently, by his wife. Even the home in which Reagan lives, filled as it is with paintings and decorated with antiques, is her cross to bear. As Ronald Reagan takes on the visage of austere simplicity, Nancy Reagan undertakes the trappings of excess. A moral lesson is inscribed in the choreography of daily life; the man of wealth displays the rigors of thrift while his wife assumes the guilt of leisure, consumption, and the tangible symbols of an "upper class." The display of capitalist morality depended dearly upon those willing to bear the sumptuous evidence of guilt, of sin. For women, the enticing rewards of service were, and to some extent still are, the symbolic harness of elegance and the guilt that that entails. The cost of those rewards is to wear the signature of uncontrollable consumption, and to be seen as one who bewitches and plays on the benevolent weaknesses of a man who—in terms of his own patterns of consumption—remains uncorrupted. To paraphrase a line from a recent song, *the very thing that makes her rich, makes him poor*.[58] The image is a continual fixture within our culture: Women arrive home with vast quantities of department store boxes, containing new dresses and outrageous hats; men wear the mantle of patient victimization and benevolent chagrin.

The dominant trend in bourgeois women's fashions of the nineteenth century perpetuated a moral defense of wealth through the delineation of gender. The spoils of power were borne, most conspicuously, by those who enjoyed little power themselves. Both ideologically and physiologically, the double burden of purity and elegance immobilized women within the idiom of guilt. Yet as we have seen before, fashion is not a phenomenon of historical stasis. Beyond providing a language of social caste and power, fashion is an arena in which social struggles are enacted and, perhaps, pre-figured. While the predominant middle-class mode placed women in a position and symbolism of immobility and guilt, devoid of desires and appetites yet suffering for them, by the latter half of the nineteenth century, women's fashions begin to incorporate the language of transformation. Coinciding with the rise of a politics of female emancipation, two distinct trends emanated from the realm of feminine fashion that were expressions of a move toward greater mobility and worldliness, toward a goal of equal social possibilities for women.

To a large extent, these two trends offered a vestmental response to the idealized prescriptions of womanhood. If the proper Victorian was fragile and immobile, a stranger to the world and to pleasures of the flesh, these two developments—seemingly at odds with each other—provided a sartorial language of revolt. One development was the entry of certain styles of clothing—formerly associated with courtesans—into the fashionable attire of middle-class women in general. This development, emanating from the high-fashion houses of Paris, included the wearing of lace underwear, rouge, silk stockings, and the halting but increased display of flesh. By no means universal among middle-class women, this development was viewed by some as a mark of immorality and decadence. Yet so widespread was its impact that by the turn of the century, Edward Bok, editor of the *Ladies' Home Journal*, despaired that it was becoming difficult to tell the prostitute from the lady.[59] The interaction of prostitute and lady was enacted along the circuitous routes of fashion. Among Paris designers, great efforts were expended in dressing the *demimondaines*— the "half-worldly" courtesans with whom French gentlemen could engage in sensual and other worldly pleasures, unknown to their wives. Pictorial representations, fashion books and plates, "fashion babies," pasteboard dolls dressed in the latest fashions, were shipped from France throughout Europe and America.[60] These sartorial images began to enter the vernacular of middle-class existence.

While these fashion influences may be seen as exploitative to women, insofar as they still countenanced the primacy of masculine concerns, they were also an emancipatory assault on the canons of Victorian womanhood. The conventions of proper womanhood had denied worldly access to those women whose offspring would assume the name and the inheritance of the father. Wives and mothers were, as we have seen, dressed in the attire of isolation and infirmity. On the other hand, even within the strict moral structures of the nineteenth-century bourgeois sexuality, there were some women who stood outside the confines of patriarchal lineage. Insofar as their offspring stood beyond the boundaries of inheritance, limitations on the mobility of these women were less severe; issues of paternity were of less significance. Thus while moral invocations placed the *demimondaine* in an inferior position to that of the proper middle-class woman, her reality was far freer and bore a broader range of worldly experience and possibility. Salons were not merely arenas of a sexuality that transcended the functional definitions of procreation, but were also establishments of culture. The courtesan was likely to be more educated and more worldly, more self-reliant than the wife. Degraded by moral sanction, she was at the same time more engaged and viable within the terms of society. The lace garters of the prostitute, standing as marks of Eve's unbridled passion, were also the trappings of a more active and less self-effacing womanhood.

If appetites were considered vulgar among women of the home, they were not only permissible, but encouraged, among women of the world. Erotic satisfaction, and power—albeit limited to arenas of sexuality—proscribed by propriety, found fulfillment in the wombs of impropriety. Similarly, as *demimondaine* and gentleman shared a worldly sphere of commercial exchange, it is not unlikely that illicit relationships provided a more fertile soil for equitable and textured involvements between men and women than did the moral strictures of bourgeois marriage.

Clearly, this relative freedom must be understood within the restrictive framework of patriarchy, but it was within that framework that the proper wife was ensconced. The entry of courtesanal influences in the realm of an "acceptable" fashion was a suggestion of greater mobility, worldliness; an acknowledgement of the possibility for erotic fulfillment for women. In an evocative way, this shift of fashion was implicitly an attack on the patriarchal ideal of a confined womanhood. The putting on of such garments as panties was infused—given their connotations—with a map of cultural meanings. In custom these were the garments of prostitutes, and of women whose mobility presumed boundaries beyond the constant yoke of male protection. Underpants on women sounded a strong erotic intonation—far greater than the absence of them. According to Anne Hollander, a historian of fashion and art, the French "Can Can" was invented to display the lacy drawers of the abandoned dancers, as was a good deal of Victorian pornography fixated on displays of lace ornamentation.[61] This was an eroticism of female sexual power and arrogance that stood as a thrilling and "perverse" counterpoint to the frail and lethargic dependency that marked the horizons of wifely ethics.

The assumption of panties in the general realm of women's fashion, from the 1850s onward, was no less than a statement of desire for greater worldliness, a concession to the legitimacy of the "temptations" and vestments of a female carnality and pleasure.

There is an ahistorical temptation to moralistically understand the accoutrements of coquetry as flatly committed to the oppressive project of female objectification; to reject the devices of allurement as the shackles of bondage. Yet the arrival of this mode within the general theater of middle-class fashion carried another facet of connotation. Breaking through the social imagery of confinement and passive weakness, this progression empowered a larger population of women with the tools of secular activity and passionate love. Unquestionably, as is evident in the advertisement for Lily of France lingerie, the implication of guilt and sin was still judgmentally present, but now a woman might more justifiably enjoy pleasure and power within the ambit of her alleged transgressions. If carnality stood at the heart of the objective definition of bourgeois womanhood beforehand, now it was becoming a piece within a female subjectivity.

The vestments of passion and love provided one vector of resistance to the conventions of nineteenth-century middle-class life. An alternative vector was drawn from the masculine realm of moral diligence and work. Initiated not by Paris designers, but by women who were attempting to escape what Jane Addams called "the snare of preparation," this second tactic of sartorial resistance found its roots in a small but strident move toward dress reform.

"Dress reform" had various embodiments, yet a common thread was the rejection of restrictive garments, often in favor of a more *mannish* costume. The simplicity of male tailoring provided a model for this development. From the rise of the bourgeois style, the evolution of men's suits had been a renunciation of conspicuous consumption and waste, a statement of motion and of industriousness of purpose. The "plain style" suggested a similar weapon to women, one by which they could break through the confined lethargies of middle-class feminine existence. If some women sought expanded social possibilities and activities, the clothing that relegated them to an immobile existence needed to be transcended. Insofar as it provided the most widely understood model of action and social purpose, the more comfortable "plain style" pointed the way for feminine dress reform. Consistent with the bourgeois-Protestant ethic of a purposeful "calling," these clothes were conceived within an earnest and programmatic appeal to "rational dress."

In the latter half of the nineteenth century, in the United States, Germany, and England, proponents of dress reforms stood largely within circumscribed subcultures of social experimentation. Reform dress was a part of the experimental communalism of John Humphrey Noyes' Oneida Community, where plainly cut garments encouraged the group's commitment to a sexual politics—to greater equality between men and women in love and in work. Amelia Bloomer, an American feminist who in the 1850s promoted a costume consisting of a short, understated frock—with no petticoats—worn over billowing "Turkish" trousers, found support from Elizabeth Cady Stanton, and drew most of her comrades and adherents from among the early movement for women's rights.

The taking on of clothing conventions previously defined as "male" challenged the basic social tenets of gender among the middle class. These had posited a rational piety and worldly engagement for men, while the feminine essence was understood to be dangerously passionate—to be restricted in the uniform of purity, or to be enjoyed away from home. Unlike the erotic inversion implied by the wearing of lace panties, this style broke from a fundamental equation of women with carnality. It sought to exemplify a more integrated, more totalistic vision of womanhood.

Insofar as the proponents of dress reform challenged the basic legacy of gender differentiation—essential to the physics of bourgeois morality—they were in large degree outcast and ridiculed, characterized and taunted as strange and fanatical. Yet their impulse toward a freer, less constricting garb evolved within a broader social environment that was pregnant with the possibilities of a burgeoning female mobility. By the last years of the nineteenth century, these tendencies had escaped the terminology of "reform" and entered the vocabulary of "fashion." Within that framework of propriety, they began to be adopted on an increasingly wide scale.

Beyond being ideological emblems of limited and sometimes idiosyncratic movements, mannish clothes pre-figured the irreversible opening up of the public sphere to women that had been endemic to the rise of industrial capitalism. First and foremost, bourgeois gentlemen had demanded a virginal isolation for women of their own families. Yet against this stern demand stood an obvious and hypocritical double standard. Men, who insisted that one class of women conform to the social categories of a supposedly fragile and weaker sex, presided over an expanding industrial world that increasingly drew another class of women away from the confines of the home and into the degraded context of industrial production. Indeed, within the textile industry itself, the first factory force was drawn from farm girls of the New England countryside. For middle-class women, while confinement persevered as a basic principle within the cult of prescribed purity, the industrial era created contexts that made such confinement increasingly difficult to maintain. The modern city was a magnetic arena of motion and diverting display. Activity was its conspicuous spectacle, and the city made the insularity of the home ideal more and more anachronistic. Against the sensate allurements and attractions of urban pageantry, the notion of the home as an unsullied fortress became harder and harder to justify to its appointed keepers. Motion was the social language of a cosmopolitan tableau, and that language began to leave its explosive charge within female activity and dress. By the 1890s, the bicycle, for example, had become a vehicle of diversion and purpose for both men and women; altered styles of female adornment became not only statements of politics, but functionally requisite.

When the bicycle emerged as an acceptable device of female mobility, the weighty excessiveness of dress conventions had to be abandoned. Bicycles, and other mechanisms of urban transport, signaled a breakdown in the sartorial designations of gender. Massive skirts and their mountainous underpinnings of petticoats, crinolines, and bustles began to crumble in their aesthetic monopoly over ladylike propriety. As women entered the restless environs of urban desire and diversion—parks and kinetic boulevards—appropriate garments entered the borderland of fashion. Bicycles in particular required a simpler and lighter garb; trousers made a telling and prophetic incursion into the outposts of female respectability in the form of the divided skirt. Sports in general, which combined the conventional equation of middle-class *women* and *leisure* with the energetic choreography of city life, became a prime arena of transformation and synthesis. The "masculinization" of female clothing—

the permissibility of trousers and other garments that allowed for the comforts of motion—made its first conquests of gentility in the garments of sport.

Increasingly, the allure of the social world stood at the gates of the bourgeois home, and this potent proximity imposed itself not only on the perceptions of women, but visibly on "the glass of fashion and the mould of form." Not all breaks from the nineteenth-century attire of confinement spelled liberation. Paul Poiret, the "King of Fashion" who took personal credit for leading Parisian designers in a war against the corset around 1910, replaced it with the "hobble skirt," which only altered the anatomy of constriction, tightly encircling the lower legs.[62] To a large extent, the move was toward an enhanced mobility for women of the middle class. The interplay between women and society, however, asserted itself not merely within the material presentation of self. For a growing number of women, the isolation of the home was rejected in favor of greater social engagement and commitment. Within this development, the *mannish* look made a dramatic leap from the particularity of sports clothing to the more general wardrobe. Throughout much of her active life, Jane Addams, who had learned the lessons of sartorial morality from her unwitting father—on the way to Sunday School—wore the "plain style" as an emblem of honor, and a statement of worldly dedication. "Dressed down" in austere threads, Addams pursued her earthly calling of social work, attempting, along the way, to shatter the mark of Eve, which had hobbled women of her estate throughout much of the nineteenth century.

The sartorial models of middle-class female emancipation derived from two distinct arenas: *honorable work* and *shameful love*. In distinctly different ways, the imagery of the Puritan and of the prostitute conspired to offer a way out of the ennui of "home service." Neither, unfortunately, offered the idiom for an integrated solution. One promised the possibilities of pleasure and of power, but confined both within a primarily sexual ghetto of self-definition. The other intoned the honors of worldly labors, often at the expense of acknowledging, openly, one's sensual self. In the name of purpose, one was forced—if one was a woman—to take flight from the pitfalls of the body. The mark of Eve presided over the terms of female existence, as it still does today; although lessened, the burdens of sexual inequality remained.

Social power and social transformation mark the history of bourgeois women's clothing in the nineteenth century, and much of today's fashion bears the imprint of this turmoil. Yet it would be misleading to assume that the roots of contemporary fashion can be understood only through the glass of nineteenth-century middle-class life. While conflicts and interactions of imagery are highly visible within the context of this existence, other forces were also at work. The clothing we have described was the province of an elite few, limited to those with access to the resources and skilled labor necessary to partake in the privilege of fashionability. To pursue the magnitude of fashion in our current world, we must look elsewhere, toward other changes that broadened and massified the social terms of fashion. These changes were experienced most dramatically, at first, not within the arena of the middle class, but of working-class life; it is these general developments to which we must turn.

5 / *Labor and Cloth*

TODAY, in the United States, as throughout much of the industrialized world, most people buy their clothing "off the rack." Like almost all of the goods by which we supply our needs, clothing comes to us ready-made. Through the prism of a consumer culture, these are the terms of survival; our experience within the world of merchandise is one where goods mysteriously appear. Their source is unknown. The people who produced them are unseen. Their presence in our lives, as a historical phenomenon, is generally unexamined. Fashion images abound, and their lure touches the lives of multitudes. What once was a concern of privilege is now known and consumed by almost everyone; it is the hallmark of a "democracy."

Yet the current ubiquity of ready-made clothing, and of fashion in general, has a relatively short history. Before the nineteenth century, ready-made was virtually unknown. For people of means, clothing was produced by skilled artisans of cloth: tailors and seamstresses. The opportunity to wear a skillfully crafted garment symbolized a status within society—the status of one able to afford the employment of those whose long labors and intricate touch could be mobilized to construct an appropriate public or private image.

For the majority of people, the wearing of clothes did not employ the capacities of seamstresses or tailors. Routinely, clothing was produced in the home, and bore the functional mark of many of the products that—in a pre-industrial world—were produced within the broad scope of household activity. Alexander Hamilton, in his *Report on Manufactures*, noted that in 1791, "two-thirds, three-fourths, and even four-fifths of all the clothing of the inhabitants" of many districts of the United States, "are made by themselves."[63] A government report issued twenty years later reaffirmed Hamilton's contention, indicating that "⅔ of all garments worn by inhabitants of the United States" were made within the confines of the homes in which they lived. While men's tailored clothing and dresses sewn by seamstresses had a notable presence within the above percentages, for most people—particularly the poor—home production clearly predominated.

In the context of the late eighteenth and nineteenth centuries, the primacy of home-produced clothing was consistent with the more general terms of material life. The home was still a major center of production. The modern idea of a home as a receptacle of consumer goods was virtually unknown, unimaginable, save for those few whose wealth allowed them to attend to an aristocratic pursuit of luxury. Most of the accoutrements of life were produced by people for themselves. Self-sufficiency was not just a moral invocation; it was a necessity of survival. Women would take a wide spread of homespun "linsey-woolsey," lay it upon the family table, "mark it, and . . . cut out the article desired."[64] The cut of the resulting clothes was loose and, often, imprecise. Not elaborate in their conception, execution, or purpose, these clothes bore little trace of sumptuosity or elegance. If gracefully worked cloth was a mark of social exception, these simple clothes marked the common lot.

By the early twentieth century, clothing would undergo dramatic change in its production, distribution, and meaning. Clothes would increasingly be *bought*, not *made*, by the wearer. Moreover, fashion—long the symbolic preserve of wealth—would enter, more and more, the symbolic vernacular of common people. By 1913, home economist Bertha June Richardson noted that even poor shop girls of New York City, earning no more than five or six dollars a week, were able to dress "beyond their station." In tenement neighborhoods, she saw women with "plumes on their hats, a rustle of silk petticoats, everything about them in the latest style."[65]

In Robert and Helen Lynd's classic study of *Middletown* (Muncie, Indiana) in the 1920s, an employer mused, "I used to be able to tell something of the background of the girl applying for a job" by the clothes that she wore. "Now," he complained, "I have to wait until she speaks, shows a gold tooth, or otherwise gives me a second clue."[66] Class distinctions remained, to be sure, but surface evidence pointed, increasingly, to a democracy of the image; a stylistic equality was unfolding.

The history of these developments is somewhat more complex than is generally conceded. The ideology of *progress* tends to encapsulate explanations for such evolutions within the framework of a triumphal, technological determinism. *Modernity brought science; science brought the machine; the machine brought a better life; it continues to do so!* So goes the argument. The historical rendition of the rise of mass fashion tends to follow this mechanical rationale: 1733 brought the flying shuttle, which allowed broad pieces of cloth to be woven at a quicker rate than ever before; 1764 brought the spinning jenny, improving production of yarn and thread. Late eighteenth-century developments included the power loom—which replaced the old weaving frame—and the famous/infamous cotton gin, which separated cotton seeds from bolls at a rate that allowed for the mass production of cotton cloth. The list continues with only cursory mention of the Lowell System of factory producton; the "dark Satanic mills" of Manchester in England;

or the slave system of plantation labor that produced the vast quantities of raw material upon which the American industrial system of textiles and clothing was erected. We move to the first U.S. patented sewing machine in 1846; machinery for riveting boots and sewing leather, and so on. Late nineteenth-century developments included lace-making machines, which made the *imago* of the eighteenth-century duchess and the nineteenth-century courtesan available to more and more women. With synthetic, chemically produced fabrics listed high among twentieth-century achievements, the look and texture of royalty—silk, velvet, fur—became replicable, available to almost anyone who had a yen for fashion. Each invention has its inventor, its "great man." Each has its corporate promoter, beneficently bringing "progress" as its "most important product," or "better living through chemistry."

Yet these technologies did not appear in a vacuum. The development of ready-to-wear clothes cannot be understood solely as an offshoot of technological advancement. The rise of the ready-made clothing industries found its roots, to a large extent, in new forms of social and economic life that were intrinsic to capitalist development, and to the emergence of a world-market economy. The first markets for ready-to-wear clothing were among people who experienced the new mobile forms of social and economic life.

For the most part, ready-made clothes did not come about—initially—to serve the desires of an urban middle class with a taste for fashion. These people were still generally committed to hand-crafting by tailors or seamstresses. The greatest part of early ready-to-wear clothing served a clientele who—caught within the historical maelstrom—were unable to supply clothing for themselves through customary home production. Ready-to-wear clothing came into being alongside the phenomena of increasing mobility, increasingly specialized forms of labor, and the evolution of an individualistic mode of life. Its roots were crude and functional. Rather than signs of egalitarianism, these clothes stood testimony to the broad chasm between laboring and propertied lives in the nineteenth century. They were a piece of the oppression that shaped working-class existence, and outrage.

The first ready-made establishments, mostly situated on streets adjoining wharfs, appeared around the turn of the nineteenth century, in Boston, New York, Philadelphia, Baltimore, and in smaller cities with whaling or fishing trades. In Boston, the first of these shops appeared on Fish and Ann Streets, later, on North. New York's first clothing shops were on Water and Front Streets; then on Cherry Street and Maiden Lane. Philadelphia's ready-made shops were on Front Street; Baltimore's could be found on Calvert and Water Streets.[67]

The initial customers were sailors who required clothing when they came into port. Ready-to-wear emerged as a service industry, supplying the needs of a work force in the varied seabound trades. Clothing sold in these shops stood in stark contrast to the tailored garments of gentlemen; it was woefully crude in terms of both workmanship and materials used. Clothing was generally produced in only one size, to be tied, tucked, or cut by its wearer to achieve the approximation of comfort, if not of "fit." From the early 1800s, when the first such shop opened its doors in New Bedford, Massachusetts, until the 1870s, when industrial clothing began to undergo significant changes, ready-to-wear establishments were known, simply, as "slop shops." The clothing they sold was called "slop clothes."[68] Like the "slops" for animals from which they got their name, these clothes denoted degraded and minimal terms of subsistence. Their presence was hardly glamorous. It served the functional requirements of clothing a work force that—due to the force of circumstance—was unable to produce clothing for itself, much less afford to have clothing tailored to order. One of America's most illustrious haberdashers, Brooks Brothers, began as a "slop shop" around 1810.

Slop shops would purchase rough material—often of English or East Indian origin—to cut on the premises. Cut cloth would then be sent out to women who, working at home, would hand-sew the "slops." Most of these were farm women, living in regions adjacent to big coastal cities. Long winter evenings were spent by the fire, bringing cash into the realm of the farm, dispensing goods for a mercantile trade.[69] This is worth mentioning, not merely as another fact within the history of ready-made clothing, but to indicate that the lives of women were, from the beginning of the industrial era, deeply affected and transformed. Farm girls had provided America's first factory force within New England's incipient textile industry, only later to be displaced by entire families of immigrants. Far more than is evidenced among women adhering to the doctrines of the middle class, these early industrial women's lives reveal—even as they sat beside the homefire of the farm—the inexorable tendency of the tendrils of capitalist enterprise to draw increasing numbers of people into the marketplace. With the taking-in of slop work, the very meaning of home production was immeasurably altered.

Sailors ambled along portside alleys and streets wearing the fruit of these women's home enterprises. New patterns of production were linked to embryonic contours of consumption, the beginnings of a mass-produced clothing industry, geared to the needs of anonymous consumers—initially produced to clothe laboring men, a configuration that would continue throughout much of the nineteenth century. Fashion imagery was not discernible, nor an issue. Functional uniformity was the paramount characteristic of slop clothing.

The factory production of clothing proceeded hesitantly in the 1830s, turning out a humble product for wearers at the bottom levels of society. Then, following the Gold Rush in 1849, the market for ready-to-wear moved west. Dealers on the East Coast and in the Mississippi Valley responded to the demand for large amounts of ready-made, shipping goods westward. Such manufacturing and merchandising pioneers as Levi Strauss and John H. Browning began producing ready-mades in San Francisco to outfit hordes of gold diggers, miners, and lumbermen arriving in search of work or fortune. Again, the market for ready-made was built on the foundation of a mobile labor force, separated from the customary arenas of home production. Overalls and trousers, made from hearty sailcloth or the somewhat lighter—but still rugged—blue denim, were designed for long and continuous wear.[70] Against the sweat of a hard, laboring existence, the primary demand upon clothing was durability. The adoption of rivets from horse blankets and the multiple stitching along seams were not elements of style, but tactics of construction. While today Levi Strauss advertising may claim that "a legend doesn't come apart at the seams," legendary considerations were the last things on the minds of western miners as they pulled on their dungarees. The seams didn't contain legends, but tired bodies whose meager wages ruled out products that were ornately sewn, or had to be cared for or frequently replaced.

Aside from sailors and forty-niners, the biggest early market for ready-made clothing—the market that dramatically expanded the scope of the industry—was provided by the Southern system of plantation slavery. In many ways, the idea of "ready-to-wear" as an "intrinsic outcome"—to borrow a phrase from Raymond Williams—of capitalist development is illustrated most graphically here. The archetype for the modern industrial labor system, slaves were a population of forced, migrant labor. With the rise of the British textile industry, and then that of New England, cotton was a lucrative source of America's merchant and landed wealth. A cash crop of burgeoning magnitude, cotton—particularly in the middle states of the Deep South—mobilized black labor in increasingly large-scale patterns of production. While some plantations continued to produce their own supplies, employing a small number of slaves to produce clothing for the general population, the period 1840–60 brought profound changes. As cotton production grew to the exclusion of other plantation activity, a large sector of the American ready-to-wear clothing industry took up the slack, and "the business of supplying rough working clothing for the slave laborers of the South grew to large proportions."[71] Trade routes between an incipient garment industry in New York and other Eastern cities and the port of New Orleans were established, supplying the clothing needs of large plantations. Among British ready-made exports as well, "a good portion of the shipments went under the heading of 'slops and Negro clothing.' " Dealers in New Orleans, such as Folger and Blake Company of Magazine Street, advertised to planters that they would "find it greatly to their advantage to purchase their clothing ready-made" for slaves.[72] Drawing the greatest part of their fortunes from cotton sold to industries in the North and in Britain, Southern planters welcomed the opportunity of purchasing cheap, mass-produced provisions, rather than divert valuable slave labor toward these unprofitable handicraft activities.

Slavery, thus, was a prime impetus to the U.S. garment industry. Numerous firms in New York were organized specifically around the production of what was designated as "Negro clothing." These clothes were made of cheap, coarse fabric. Despite the low price these firms received for their goods, oppressive conditions of high productivity and low pay for factory or home workers maintained high levels of profit. Even technology was geared to the task. In the 1850s, the I. M. Singer (sewing machine) Company advertised the development of a "new, improved sewing machine especially adapted to the making up of Negro clothing."[73]

Even outside New York, a garment industry grew to cash in on the plantation market. The Louisiana Plantation Clothing Manufactory produced—during the 1850s—clothing on a large scale, "with ready-made Negro clothing" offered at low cost.[74] In Cincinnati, Ohio, "the growing demand for cheap clothing to supply farm hands and Negro Slaves" was cited by the Commissioner of Statistics as the prime reason for the development of the clothing industry in that city.[75]

Throughout the South, stores advertised "slop clothing" for black slaves, in the pattern such clothing was marketed to "free" labor forces of the Eastern seaboard and the West Coast. Developments in large-scale production (industrial and agricultural) and in trade brought about new demands for a clothing industry to supply those laboring within the expanding social orbit of slavery and capitalism. By the time of the Civil War, the idea of clothing produced for an impersonal audience of wearers was beginning to take hold as an American institution; within a few decades, hand tailoring and the work of seamstresses would be eclipsed.

With the advent of the Civil War, the ready-made clothing industry suffered somewhat on a localized level. The end of economic relations between North and South proved calamitous to several companies whose viability depended on open routes of trade, and over a period of time, some bankruptcies were filed.[76] Overall, however, the Civil War provided boom conditions for the garment industry, primarily in New York. Another form of mobile activity provided a new market for mass-produced clothes—military uniforms—and the ready-made industry grew, sprouting important refinements in production and distribution. Whereas "slop clothes" had been produced with no regard for the size or shape of the wearer, the military market gave rise to the development of size standards and distributions. Conscripts were measured, and a range of sizes was established. A broad variety of physiques could now be clothed in a manner approximating "reasonable fit."[77] The Grim Reaper now fetched his crop from among a more regular bunch of irregulars than ever before: an industrially fitted army. A key aspect of a modern, mass-produced clothing industry—diverse sizing—was established adjacent to the field of battle. Later, the Spanish-American War and then the First World War provided sanguine opportunities for additional refinement and clarity in the designation of fit.

By the end of the 1860s, the sizing of garments—if not splendidly accurate in each individual's case—was generally adopted in the production of ready-to-wear. The human body was submitted to a mechanical/industrial categorization, subdivided into species of standardized body types. Civilian ready-made clothing, and even paper patterns for homemade clothing, followed the military initiative. The production and design of shoes was likewise refined and industrialized in the years of battle.

The Civil War provided an explosive catalyst for a general industrial development. In its aftermath, American industry grew to monumental proportions; vast armies of laborers made the journey into industrial cities; robber barons and finance capitalists reaped incomprehensible fortunes and amassed the tools of modern political power. Though "free" in the years following the war, labor enjoyed little freedom. "Wage-slavery," it was called, and it meant long and hard toil and miserable dependency. The urban, industrial poor became a massive market for clothes poor in quality, cheap in price. Coming out of the war, the industry grew by leaps and bounds, a massive supply industry for those who had no choice but to consume its wares.

While today's ready-made clothing industry is enveloped by the propaganda of aesthetic transcendence, its roots were neither aesthetic nor transcendent, but a part of the banal misery of nineteenth-century working-class life.

6 / *Images of Democracy*

WHILE the industrialization of America deepened the divisions of caste and class, other developments in the mechanical age offered a new, leveling language of democracy and social promise. If the machine represented a modern basis for misery and domination, it also contained an ability to reproduce—on a massive scale—the images and symbols of luxury and abundance, of privilege and franchise. Things theretofore limited to the province of an upper class now became reproducible, if only as surface images.

This capability had been pre-figured in the development of printing four hundred years before. While the printing press presented new modes of establishing power and authority, it was also intrinsically democratic. Little by little, over centuries, the written word spread to the masses, and reading and writing became aspirations of common folk. The very existence of a mechanically reproduced text, multiplying what had previously been a hand-inscribed treasure, was a palpably democratizing development. For those intent on maintaining or protecting their traditional prerogatives and power, this trend was viewed—rightly, from their vantage point—with foreboding. Censorship was established to assert control over what had, before printing, been controlled by virtue of its rarity and the small number of those with access to its cipher. In England, as a mobile working class emerged out of a landed peasantry, print and literacy became symbols of common aspirations, of democratic goals. During the Puritan Revolution of the 1640s, mobile masses of Englishmen carried printing presses to the field of battle, asserting in pamphlets and proclamations their "freeborn" rights.[78] Printing was democratic not only for what it could say, but for *what it was*. Given a common memory of exclusion from *the word*, the very presence of a machinery that spread the word embodied the promise of a "world turned upside down."

By the mid-nineteenth century, in the United States, the horizons of printed matter were wide. A mass-circulation, commercial press, read by factory operatives and mechanics, stood as evidence of an American democracy, even as its editorial pages defended the privileges of landed or monied wealth. Literacy and social possibility went hand-in-hand, and the press pointed to itself as a democratic institution, regardless of its outlook.

Within this proliferation of printed matter, there was a particularly significant development, perhaps as significant as the development of printing itself. *This was the enhanced ability, from the 1840s onward, to mass-produce not only words, but images*. The elegant tokens of wealth and high culture now became reproducible. The impact of this enterprise was staggering.

Previously, most artistic imagery was a guarded possession, limited to those few who could afford it. Original oil paintings, most prominently, were a holding of wealth; moreover, they were—as they are today—a *form* of wealth. John Berger has argued that the European tradition of oil painting evolved "in order to express a particular view of life," a view predicated on possession. As landed wealth gave way to the abstraction of money, *representations* became—little by little—the accouterments of wealth and power. If money represented the ability to buy, oil paintings represented what could be bought. To the art collector, paintings "show him sights: sights of what he may possess." Oil painting, according

to Berger, was particularly suited to this task of repre-
senting things to be possessed.

> What distinguishes oil painting from any other form of
> painting is its special ability to render the tangibility,
> the texture, the lustre, the solidity of what it depicts. It
> defines the real as that which you can put your hands
> on. Although its painted images are two-dimensional,
> its potential of illusionism is far greater than that of
> sculpture, for it can suggest objects possessing colour,
> texture and temperature, filling a space and, by impli-
> cation, filling the entire world.[79]

Within the framework of the bourgeois epoch, oil
paintings, like luxurious clothing, were designations of
status: of wealth and social power. Their absence from
the lives of common people were part of the fact of class,
as much as was their presence on the walls of those who
displayed them as property. Access to the image was
limited to those able to enjoy what Berger calls "the
special relation between oil painting and property."[80]

These patterns, regarding images, conveyed a social
language—one that divided rich from poor, the haves
from the have-nots. A power relation was embedded in
the history of the painting, and of its possession. When,
beginning in the 1840s, printers—mostly German immigrants—began producing "chromolithographs" in the
United States, the monopoly over the image began to
crumble. While original oil paintings continued as an
expensive investment and diversion of the wealthy, the
new technique of chromolithography was able to capture
and replicate much of their aura. The image was concrete
and lustrous—and available. The symbolic province of
the image had been invaded.

Between 1840 and 1900, a mass market in imagery
developed. "Original paintings were being reproduced
lithographically in color and sold in America by the millions." What came to be "the public's voracious hunger

for images in color" was "marked by a faith in fine art, a belief in the power of art to enrich the life of anyone."[81] If art was an enjoyment of privilege and abundance, its dissemination was perceived as the spread not only of rare images, but of the social conditions those images invoked. The market in "chromos" was broad and expansive; they were merchandised by mail, through advertising, and as premiums, as well as being sold in galleries. Amid the gray din of industrial development, here was a tangible rupture in the customary inequities of class. Chromos were a dramatic display of democracy; their spread broke through the symbolic boundaries of an old and hierarchical order.

Many chromolithographs were brilliant reproductions of paintings, previously unknown and unseen by their now-broad audience. In addition, chromos spurred an evocative impetus to the embryonic field of advertising. Billboards reached out to command the attention of passersby; advertising cards gave the goods of the industrial age the aura of sumptuosity and the magic of allegory. Goods and alluring images were linked, forging one of the most basic and prophetic alliances of contemporary capitalist culture. A world of symbolic promise was emerging; the mass dissemination of this promise made for a conspicuous and mesmerizing gesture toward a more equitable world.

The printers who produced these wonders saw themselves as the authors of a new and democratic world, and, to a limited extent, they were right. Chromos represented a flourishing democracy of the image as it had never before existed. Few chromolithographers were native born; most came from European societies, schooled by hierarchies of class and opportunity. Lithographically produced images were understood as emblems of privilege; their dissemination throughout American society appeared as nothing less than a social revolution of giant consequence. By 1893, a spokesman for the National

Lithographers' Association hailed the rise of chromolithography as a monument to improved and egalitarian social conditions:

> Within a few decades, public taste has been lifted out of the sluggish disregard for the beautiful . . . and now seeks to adopt the decorative accessories, which beneficent enterprise has so cheapened as to place them within reach of all, to the ornamentation of its homes. . . . The depressing monotony of plain walls are [sic] now relieved by bright touches of color . . . awakening in some degree, however faint, the innate love of beauty which marks the scale of aspiration in the human soul. There is no place, high or low, where pictures are not now seen, for the campaign of popular education in art has been carried to the very utmost boundaries of ignorance, and the cost of reaping its advantages is next to nothing.[82]

It was argued that life now could be enhanced by a "beneficent enterprise," an industrialism of image production, offsetting the "depressing monotony" of industrial life, spreading the surface impression of a better life at a relatively low cost. While the disparities of society remained, and industrial conditions worsened, a democracy of surfaces was being born.

For people coming out of a history of deprivation, the power of these images cannot be underestimated. European immigrants, coming to labor in America, confronted a free-flow of words and images unimaginable in the old world. Brightly colored labels, an offspring of chromolithography, transformed industrial swill into icons of a better life. Images, deriving their power by association with the historic freedoms of upper-class life, proliferated in America by the end of the nineteenth century. Cruel capitalism was assuming a generous face, countering the scorn and rebelliousness of working people. Urban life was now graced by the imagery of nature and bounty, even if these only colored its facade. The chromo took the lustrous symbols of privilege and generalized them across the visible skin of industrial society.

Frederick Douglass saw the spread of chromos as a tangible transcendence of oppression. Coming out of the harsh and unadorned experience of slavery, he interpreted the dispersal of beautiful images as proof of concrete, material improvement of social conditions. Speaking particularly of the availability of chromos to black Americans, Douglass placed these bright images against the grim backdrop of slavery:

> Heretofore, colored Americans have thought little of adorning their parlors with pictures. . . . Pictures come not with slavery and oppression and destitution, but with liberty, fair play, leisure, and refinement. These conditions are now possible to colored American citizens, and I think the walls of their houses will soon begin to bear evidence of their altered relations to the people about them.[83]

By the turn of the twentieth century, these images could be widely seen in the homes of the urban poor. Social worker Elsa G. Herzfeld, whose *Family Monographs* surveyed the tenement homes of New York City in 1905, noted the presence of chromos in abundance. Chromos would be given as cheap but luminous presents for weddings and other occasions. Peddlers sold them throughout tenement districts; they were distributed as cigar coupons and premiums; Sunday papers occasionally included them as a bonus. Offering themes of sentiment, heroism, drama, and religion, these were the graven images of American industrialism. Soap coupons presented devotional pictures of American presidents: Lincoln, Washington, and a recent "martyr," William McKinley. The female characterization of "Liberty" was likewise available as a soap coupon. Chromos comprised part of the political education of immigrants into Americanization. Buying soap was tantamount to a patriotic experience; an American past was here available to all, in brilliant color, to be consumed. A heritage, a culture was being erected, in the form of cheap and consumable merchandise.[84]

Protectors of "culture," as an elite province, spoke disparagingly of the newly emergent "chromo-civilization." To it they attributed a decline in morality, in commerce, in political life. Edwin Godkin, editor of *Nation* magazine, expressed the feeling that chromos brought art to those who were unable to appreciate it. Within this democratization, he felt, lay grave dangers:

> A society of ignoramuses who know they are ignoramuses, might lead a tolerably happy and useful existence, but a society of ignoramuses each of whom thinks he is a Solon, would be an approach to Bedlam let loose. . . . The result is a kind of mental and moral chaos.[85]

Yet in the imagination of those entrepreneurs who produced and disseminated them, chromos appeared more as a social palliative than something that would engender chaos and class upheaval. Amid the widespread hostility to the social conditions of capitalist America, chromos could help achieve a harmonious peace. Understanding fantasy and inner desire as a realm to be exploited by enterprise, a writer in the *Lithographer's Journal* (September 1893) noted chromos' ability to turn the mind away from immediate conditions.

> The love for the beautiful . . . acts upon the individual and forces him to unconsciously idealize the scenes of his daily life. So habitual does this become . . . that new avenues of refinement and true culture are continually being opened by its unseen activity. The individual thus becomes an added power to the nation.[86]

Slowly, desperately, perhaps unconsciously, a social strategy was beginning to coalesce. While the basic relations of social power would remain intact, the "democracy" of the image would act as a fundamental prop of capitalist American society. Beneficence and opportunity were being codified, not in an expansion of social power and rights, but in the widely extended availability of images *associated* with the prerogatives of power. If mounting working-class demands expressed the imperative of an industrial democracy, chromos and other images offered a superficial alternative to genuine democracy. Broadened access to lustrous imagery was an inexpensive, purchasable response; a lucrative response to potentially subversive demands for a better life.

As chromolithography made deep inroads into popular consciousness, the spread of the image took many additional forms. Photography, stereopticons, public expositions, a popular press all contributed their visionary output to the popular perception of the world. Greater access to the material world, if only through pictures, expanded the sensual parameters of popular experience. A consumer culture, in which apparitions of a better life were appended to the surface of manufactured goods, was assuming a primitive yet premonitory form.

Concommitant with the rise of popular images, an important change took place in the second wave of ready-made clothing after the Civil War. Goods that had, in the first wave of their production, expressed the modern terms of social stigma and degradation—first as "slops," then as "standardized" military garb[87]—now in the second wave took on the *look* of improved conditions. Insofar as fashion had existed for centuries as a franchise of wealth, the mass production of clothing implied a rising egalitarianism within American industrial society, paralleling the proliferation of chromolithographs. By the 1920s, this development had left its mark on the surface of American culture. Social critic Stuart Chase, writing in 1929, mused that "the function of clothing as a protection against the weather is certainly declining for both men and women.'' Noting the cohabitation of social inequality and egalitarian symbolism, Chase commented on the cunning capacities of fashion.

> The function of clothes as a badge of social rank is enormously expanding over all classes in America for both sexes, but particularly for women. Only a connoisseur can distinguish Miss Astorbilt on Fifth Avenue from her father's stenographer or secretary. An immigrant arriving on the Avenue from the Polish plain described all American women as countesses. So eager are the lower income groups to dress as well in style, if not in quality, as their economic superiors, that class distinctions have all but disappeared. To the casual observer all American women dress alike. The movement to cut down the margin of class distinction . . . has made great headway since [World War I].[88]

This ability to erect a unity of opposites, social and economic disparity along with a mask of parity, is part of the genius and achievement of American capitalism.

As early as the 1900s, poverty and finery no longer inhabited entirely separate worlds. The look of fashion was everywhere: on Fifth Avenue and Orchard Street, among ''swells'' and slumdwellers simultaneously. Layered cloth, once worn primarily for warmth by the poor, now conveyed some of the symbolism historically preserved for the rich. Layers were cut, slashed, and tucked, even in mass-produced garments, diminishing their ''value as insulation'' but implying a ''conspicuously expensive character . . . cut away so as to show how many things are being worn and what expensive things they are.''[89] What fashion merchandising expert Paul Nystrom referred to as the ''effective and cheap reproduction of style goods'' gave impetus to the spread of fashion, and the concern for fashion, among an ever-broadening swatch of the American social fabric.[90]

With the rise of mass fashion, the language of elegance and luxury entered the common vernacular of perception and expression. The garment industry, initially a supplier of clothes designed explicitly for workers, and *for work*, now began to dress its public in wares that suggested the common accessibility of prosperity and leisure. The infrastructure of a consumer democracy was taking hold; demands and desires for equality, self-determination, and individual diversity amidst standardized tedium were being codified within the range of industrially produced goods.

In the garment industry, the first step in this direction was taken in the arena of men's clothes. Factories originally producing uniforms for the Civil War began producing men's suits at low prices. Wholesalers, such as Julius Rosenwald—who eventually became president of Sears, Roebuck & Company—were middlemen who ordered suits from sweatshop owners, focusing most of their energies on marketing and distribution. Tailor-made was replicated, at some cost to quality and fit, and reproduced on a grand scale.[91] The display of linen, once a prerogative of gentlemen in daycoats and vests, was now available to all. A generation whose first encounter with "ready-made" came on the battlefield gave to their sons and grandsons the legacy of civilian uniformity: the suit.

During the 1880s, as the men's garment industry expanded its product, labor force, and market, women's clothing also began to be mass-produced. The rise of a large-scale women's garment industry meant more than a new and decorative product; it signaled a profound alteration in the daily lives of women. As the rise of "ready-made" clothing had had its early origins in the provision of a primarily masculine, mobile work force, the mass production of "ladies' garments" was a response to the increased mobility of women in an urban, industrial world. Ironically, if women's moving out of the home established them as consumers of mass-produced fashions, they were likely to be working within the garment industry itself. As home producers became garment workers, they also became a market for the fruit of their new labor.

It began with cloaks, modeled after those worn by European women of rank, emanating from factories and sweatshops in New York and Chicago. Within a decade, bustles, corsets, crinolines, and other tributes to the delicacy of Victorian upper- and middle-class women were being sold cheaply to the millions. Elaborate dresses, with flounced skirts and decorative folds, were topped off by ornamented hats, turbans, and bonnets, once exclusive signs of upper-class majesty. Even as women's clothing evolved in response to conditions of greater mobility, such styles as the popular shirtwaist of the early 1900s were fronted by folds of lace and ruffles. Marks of "distinction" were appended to the garb of mobile labor.

While for two decades into the twentieth century, the stockings and undergarments of common girls were made from cotton lisle, in the 1920s silk began gracing the thighs of more and more women. If late-nineteenth-century women of wealth had sought the mobility of "shameful love" by embracing the silken sensuality of courtesans, by the 1920s this mark of independence was broadly marketed. Women increasingly moved from the dreary utilitarianism of cotton underwear toward the implied glossy leisure of silk. With the development of rayon, a lower-priced imitation of silk, the trend spread. Legs, also, were increasingly displayed through sleek transparency. A sartorial idiom, once the risqué accent of class distinction, was entering the common parlance.[92]

In the sphere of cosmetics, certain "society" women had, by the late nineteenth century, taken on the "unrespectable" practice of making up their faces with powders, paints, and rouge. Borrowing once again from the theatrical world of the *demimondaine*, such women were chided by *true* Victorians as "painted ladies," seduced from nature by "artificiality," shamefully "blind of the spectacle they present to the world." Similar to the proliferation of silk (later, rayon) stockings and drawers, this "tawdry" presentation of female independence was widely available across store counters, and from mail-order catalogs, by 1905. David Cohn, a historian of Sears, Roebuck, and a former Sears employee, wrote that "by 1905, rouge in limited quantities was demanded and used by simple housewives throughout the country," sold to them as "Rouge de Théâtre." Such a designation indicated the mass appeal of the *demimondaine* motif: "To say, in 1905, that rouge, a then morally dubious product, is being used by the theatrical profession, a then morally dubious profession, is the equivalent of recommending a bed today because it is the kind used in some bawdyhouse."[93]

Today, although clothing and cosmetics are marked by clear distinctions of quality, style, and pricing, the impact of these developments is unmistakable. Clothes consciousness and the attention to fashion constitute near-universal elements within American culture; their lure and mystique are worldwide. Beginning in the 1880s, the look of fashion attached to industrially produced clothing did more than alter the character of economic life. It offered an essential channel of popular desire, which has left its mark on the world ever since. The tracks still had two sides, but they were linked by a mesmerizing, symbolic bridge. This bridge asserted itself as visible evidence of increased social equality; for people who over millennia had lived beneath the symbols of its absence, its appeal should not be underestimated. The idea of "democracy" was assuming its modern, consumerist dimensions. Writing in 1925, a social prognosticator, Allen Devere, articulated this development in strident ideological terms:

> Progress toward democracy has made amazing strides in this matter of personal decoration. Formerly it was

the ladies of the court who used it most. Today it is the serious concern and dearest pastime of all three estates. . . . And nowadays no one can tell . . . whether a given person lives on Riverside Drive or East 4th Street.[94]

Devere's proclamation is certainly an overstatement. It cannot be assumed that personal decoration was not an element in the home production of poor people's clothes. While little evidence remains as to the dress of common people in pre-industrial times, it may be assumed that homespun crafts evinced a popular, sartorial vernacular, marked surely by the limits of scarcity, yet embroidered by desire as well. Neither can we accept Devere's claims about the leveling capacities of fashion uncritically. Despite his literary linkage between the avenues of wealth and the alleys of deprivation—a device common in writing about clothing from the 1920s—there were sharp gradations in quality and fit, as there are today. The hidden secret of fashion democracy was the class dimension, demarcating differences between hand-sewn originals and the cavalry of often shoddy copies that followed with varying degrees of loyalty—pregnant blind spots in his statement.

Be that as it may, the most telling point within Devere's rhapsody is the existence of a marketplace that gave some support to his claims. Clothing was emerging as a vehicle of presentability, of self-realization, of distinction for an increasingly large purchasing public. For more and more people, "fashion" was now available as a device of outward appearance.

Yet surface features are—by definition—potentially deceptive. Social history cannot be divined merely by looking at its objects. To understand the development of mass fashion, we must look more closely at the fateful interaction between it and its public. The labor process by which these potent channels of desire were produced—and are still, for the most part, produced—laid bare the painful contradictions of an industrial culture itself: economic exploitation; monotony and boredom; crowded and miserable working conditions; "work and work without end"; all within a machinery of "plenty."

The fashion industry, in its genesis, offers a revealing lens for examining some of the cultural collisions of modern life. Through it can be seen both the bold promise of social transformation, of "freedom," and the conditions of purgatory to which that promise addressed itself so loudly, as *a way out*. In purgatory we find not only those whose laboring lives were spent inside the machinery of fashion, but also those who were among its most conspicuous early consumers.

7 / The Backrooms of Fashion

IT WAS in the decades following the Civil War, beginning with the production of men's suits, that the mass production of fashionable goods began to take hold. By the 1880s women's clothing was also entering the modern networks of production and distribution. Organized initially by German-Jewish immigrants, the mass market in styled clothing represented a dual, often contradictory, reality. While the market offered goods that broke through the class monopoly on fashionable imagery, so too did it breed conditions that exacerbated the sting of social disparity.

The rise of fashion goods was led by German Jews who had entered the men's clothing industry during the 1850s. The Rosenwald family offers us an illustrative example. The father, Samuel Rosenwald, came to the United States in 1854, an immigrant from Bünde, Westphalia, in Germany. Beginning here as a peddler— first on foot, then by horse and wagon—the elder Rosenwald was, by 1856, employed by the Hammerslough brothers' Baltimore clothing firm. Marrying into the family, Samuel migrated to Springfield, Illinois, to run the family outlet there. During the Civil War his business grew, selling large shipments of uniforms to the Union.[95]

The son, Julius Rosenwald (born in 1862), carried his father's trade into the civilian market. With a cousin, Julius Weil, the younger Rosenwald built a successful business, selling men's ready-made suits. After early troubles in New York, the business moved to Chicago with much success. So effective was Julius Rosenwald in the wholesale men's garment industry that his father soon sold the business in Springfield and joined his son's firm in Chicago. During a period of general economic difficulty and of depression (1893), Rosenwald and Weil flourished, wholesaling the first generation of inexpensive, ready-to-wear men's suits. Business boomed as Rosenwald and Weil began to sell suits to the new and promising mail-order firm of Sears, Roebuck & Company. By the turn of the century, Rosenwald had moved into management at Sears itself, beginning with the clothing department, later becoming president of the company.[96] Within a period of three decades, this family had moved from peddler, to the selling of military uniforms—"shoddy" clothes—to large-scale men's fashion merchandising.

Like most of his generation of clothiers, Julius Rosenwald conformed to a pattern within the industry. He was not a producer of merchandise, nor a factory owner. He was a *jobber*. Selling clothes at wholesale, jobbers would farm production out to people who ran sweatshops, employing immigrant workers at low wages.

Dramatically divorcing clothing production from its domestic traditions, fashion jobbers altered patterns of work, and of dress as well. Before the 1870s, for example, "women's cloaks and jackets were little known in the United States. Shawls were worn by the masses. What few cloaks were seen were on women of means and fashion . . . imported from Germany."[97] With the massive migration of Russian Jews, beginning early in the 1880s, a labor force was mobilized that gave a tremendous impetus to the American women's cloak business. Jobbers organized this development.

Copying and counterfeiting the look of fashion, jobbers sent patterns out for production. Insofar as the business was dominated by these wholesale merchandisers and distributors, sweatshop owners and labor contractors competed for their patronage. Jobbers sought to farm out production as cheaply as possible. Factory owners and subcontractors were pushed to drive their own costs down, in order to meet the demands of competition. For workers, the result was devastating. As fashion merchandising grew, the domination of jobbers over subcontractors was firmly implanted in the garment industry; patterns of low pay and fragmentation of the work force became the norm.

Amid this structure, the American garment trades grew dramatically. Between 1880 and 1889 alone, the value of the product increased from thirty-two to sixty-eight million dollars; capital investment grew from eight million to over twenty-one million dollars. The number of manufacturers increased from 562 to 1,224, and the number of workers employed in the trades increased from 25,192 to 39,149. Of these latter, 23,030 lived and worked in New York City.[98]

> Immigrants unused to industrial conditions would work fragmentarily in their homes. They bought sewing machines and supplied the foot power to run them. Contractors organized immigrant labor, maintaining their isolation, extracting labor from them in their tenement homes.[99]

Securing a dominant position within the garment industries, jobbers took on the role of fashion enterprisers. By 1920 women's fashion comprised 76 percent of the product of the industry, and was produced according to established seasonal patterns. Two times each year, jobbers would map out merchandising plans for the coming season. Designs were developed according to an emerging "market for styles"; fashions were derived from a variety of places: copying, "self-design," and purchase of pre-cut patterns. After buying cloth from mills, the jobber would then farm out its manufacture. "The method is that of consignment. The jobber sells his materials on consignment to the sub-manufacturer and buys back the finished goods.''[100] Within this apparatus, labor exploitation was virtually ensured. Louis Levine, in his classic study of the International Ladies' Garment Workers' Union, explained the characteristic burden carried by laborers in the trade.

> It is to the advantage of the jobber to increase the number of sub-manufacturers in order to pit one against another. But the sub-manufacturer cannot carry on production without transmitting the pressure of the jobber. Having "figured" the cost of a garment of a certain style, the sub-manufacturer is anxious to produce the garment at that cost. If he finds that the standards and wage rates fixed by the union will not permit this, he tries in every way open to him to evade union restrictions. If he cannot succeed in that and maintain a fair shop, he removes to a less desirable district and decreases the size of his shop.[101]

This general situation, described by Levine in the early 1920s, has continued, attested to by the subsequent migration of garment production to the non-union South, and then to Hong Kong, South Korea, and elsewhere.

This was the structure of an industry that through its mass selling, its appropriation of imagery, and its national advertising was promoting dreams and propounding misery as well. As hand-crafted clothing was displaced by a garment industry, the home made a transition from self-production to contracted labor. Shops grew up in tenement buildings. Inside them, investigators such as Jacob Riis found "men and women bending over their machines or ironing clothes at the window, half naked." Riding the Second Avenue elevated train through the "sweaters' district" of New York City, one was flanked by a perpetual row of tenement sweatshops. "The road is like a big gangway through an endless workroom where vast multitudes are forever laboring. Morning, noon, or night, it makes no difference; the scene is always the same."[102] In the mid-1880s, as sweatshop labor multiplied in New York and Chicago, sixty- to eighty-four-hour work weeks were common, and even after this, many workers took "material home and worked until two and three o'clock in the morning."[103] Wages were meager and days were consumed in dark and filthy quarters.

During the 1890s, tenement sweatshops came under attack by reformers and by legislation. The general tenor of legislation was to develop a clearer separation between work districts and residential areas. In the aftermath, after 1900, production began to migrate to a "more distinctly manufacturing district." Foot power was replaced, to some extent, by steam and electricity. New machinery "such as the braiding machine, the cording machine, the seaming and binding machine" came into shops, as did more advanced tools for cutting and pressing. With these developments, eastern European Jews were joined by Italian immigrants as laborers in the industry. Despite all this, Levine concludes, "the general condition of the trade and of the vast majority of workers showed little improvement."[104]

Between the 1880s and 1920, a large proportion of the people working in garment production were women. The necessity of industrial labor among vast numbers of immigrant women cut deep into traditional patterns of home production, and on the most basic level forced women not only into the production of industrial goods, but into their consumption as well. Mass-produced clothes were a necessity, increasingly, among women whose lives were circumscribed by long hours of wage labor or piecework. Against the backdrop of a middle-class morality that inscribed women with delicacy and home service, the industrial city drew women of poor, immigrant families into the complex tendrils of the marketplace. Women found themselves in circumstances that, more and more, defined them as consumers, a basic category of industrial life.

The backrooms of "fashion" were scenes of extreme exploitation and monotony. While the garment industry drew women into the social world, it was a socialization that was marked by the repetitions and futility of the shop. At the very moment that the garment industry was giving shape to an important archetype of industrial oppression, so too was it creating social and psychological conditions that inspired widespread demands for social change. This happened in other early-twentieth-century industries as well, and by 1909 the United States was gripped by widespread labor agitation. Caught in a wave of anticapitalist feeling, much of this agitation looked beyond immediate economic issues, and evoked visions of a better world, often reflecting tenets of anarchism, socialism, syndicalism: economic equality and industrial democracy.

Within the garment industry, in response to its daily humiliations, labor activity was conspicuous and often militant. As early as 1885, the Knights of Labor made inroads into the garment trades of New York and Chicago. In August of that year, "the entire cloak trade of New York was thrown into a 'general strike' which lasted two weeks." Strikes followed in Chicago, also under the banner of the Knights of Labor.[105] Pushing for unionization in 1902–3, the youthful ILGWU encouraged and orchestrated boycotts of goods not bearing the union label.[106]

Deeply influenced by radical ideas, and receptive to the socialist and anarchist perspectives voiced by many immigrant intellectuals, the militancy and vision of garment workers grew midst an interchange and climate of "worker education."[107] From 1905 until 1909, when many shops were closed down by their owners, the Industrial Workers of the World gained a presence in some shops, "advocating 'the abolition of capitalism,' by means of 'class struggle.' "[108]

A massive strike of shirtwaist makers in New York in 1909 and 1910 lasted nearly three months. It involved twenty to thirty thousand women, most of them young women of sixteen to twenty-five.[109] In 1910, sixty thousand cloakmakers walked off the job over wages and conditions. In that same year, in Chicago, forty thousand tailors struck Hart, Schaffner and Marx in Chicago.[110]

Industrial conditions were wretched and inflammatory in the garment industry and elsewhere. The demand for industrial democracy, for greater social equality, was in the minds and on the lips of countless working people. A wave of industrial warfare shook the nation.

Yet in this climate, labor struggle was not the only avenue of change that was presenting itself. Ironically, the very garment industry that existed as a site of misery and exploitation was also generating a provocative array of goods that sounded their own trumpets for social equality and industrial democracy. Sidestepping the fundamental issues of social power and the distribution of wealth, fashion posed a spectacle of change. Despite the limits of the spectacle, its lure was powerful, even among those whose labor produced it. If garment production provided an arena of social discontent, there were other elements of urban, industrial life that encouraged an immigrant, laboring population to embrace the promise of mass fashion. While sweatshop labor dampened the hopes of many who had sought a land of freedom, there were other, provocative elements of urban America that encouraged one to "dress for success." Forsaken in the promised land, working people saw mass-produced fashion as one key to the mastery of a new world. The terms of that world can be reduced to a single word: *appearance*.

Beyond coping with the specific terms of their employment, migrants to industrial cities found themselves embedded in the unfamiliar terms of a swelling urban culture. If mobility had brought immigrants into the city, it was also a powerful component within the urban chore-ography. People, en masse, were constantly on the move; the city was a rush of mobile people, mobile wealth, mobile ideals. Likewise, if customary existence was one in which the people you confronted on a day-to-day basis were familiar to you, the metropolis was a society of strangers; unknown faces were commonplace. The concentration of people in streets, in manufacturing districts, in dance halls and other urban entertainments, confronted people with an unremitting parade of stran-gers. These were, and still are, the terms of mass life. Within it, one was continually forced to make silent, often unconscious decisions, based on outward appear-ances. There was no time, no possibility, to get to "know everyone." Judging and presenting appearances became stocks in trade.

Within such a context, appearances entered the rhythm of existence at almost every turn. They were essential to a sense of security as one turned a corner. They became a vehicle of employment. In a strange environment, they separated the "greenhorns" from those who knew their way around. As personal life be-came increasingly mobile and private, one donned ap-pearances as a prelude to public expeditions.

The increased accessibility of fashion fit the terms of urban life like a glove. In a theater of perpetual quick judgment, one was encouraged to assemble an effective response to the judgments of others. The city, a flourish-ing seat of commercial activity, set the terms for the commercialization of the self. In her 1929 study of the psychology of dress, Elizabeth Hurlock put it this way:

> No one likes to be considered mediocre, or to be so like every one else that he is passed over unnoticed.

> From the cradle to the grave, no one is totally free
> from regard for the opinion of others. . . . One of the
> chief values of clothing is that it enables people to
> advertise themselves in a way that will win the atten-
> tion and admiration of others. Many who lack any
> ability and could not hope to rise above the "average"
> on their merits alone, find a satisfactory outlet for this
> desire for recognition through the medium of dress.[111]

Clothes filled a vacuum, provided an effective medium of
exchange, in a milieu where the density of population,
the jaggedness of time made careful scrutiny less and less
possible.

The atmosphere of the city, itself, reinforced this. It
was a jungle of display, an unrelenting spectacle, a circus
of facade. Signs and lights shouted for attention. Window
displays cried "Look and see!" It wasn't just a "habi-
tat," it was, by its form, a self-promoter. With electricity, the promotion grew and became magical in its capti-
vation. It was forbidden fruit . . . asking to be eaten. To
be a part of this amphitheater, one imbibed its principle
of display. Under its lights, within its motion, fashionable clothing became an imperative medium of engagement.

The urban stage not only offered a continual spectacle, it also generated continual opportunities for people
to see themselves as part of the cityscape. As the metropolis took on its modern dimensions, it became a
collection of glass and mirrored surfaces, unavoidable
occasions for seeing oneself as a sight. Anne Hollander,
looking at the relationship between clothing and images,
has said that the mirror "is the personal link between the
human subject and its representation." In front of it, or
as we catch a glimpse of ourselves as we pass by a shop
window, we engage in "the imaginative act of making art
out of facts: the aim is to mold the reflection into an
acceptable picture, instantaneously and repeatedly, with

no other means than the eyes themselves. . . . Behind the reflecting surface is something waiting to be born.''[112] If the ''facts'' of life for many among the urban population were constituted by endless toil and the anonymity of the streets, fashion provided a symbolic medium of escape. It offered a way of molding reflections, of making art out of facts, of transcending the forces of circumstance by embracing the tools of display. In a world of strangers, such devices entered the realm of common sense.

8 / Avenues of Display

THE CITY provided a fertile soil within which mass fashion took root. As a mobile and personalized form of display, fashion was particularly suited to a society characterized, more and more, by mobile individuals. It played a major part in the ensemble of outer features that has come to be known as "personality."

The emergence of mass fashion, however, was not an idiosyncratic development. As it shared complementary capacities with chromolithography; as it reflected and transmitted the priorities of urban existence, it was an integral component within a symphony of social developments. It was an important feature of an industrial, consumer culture that was taking hold across the American landscape. It contributed to tangible social change. It also reflected the change. Yet its propagation was dependent upon a broad range of other institutions, which were part and parcel of a consumerist mode of life. As the imagery of fashionability moved through cities, then on into small-town and rural America, it did so upon pathways cut by other, new vehicles of display.

Within the city, an essential publicizer of fashion was the department store. Itself a child of industrial merchandising, its presence gave testimony to the journey from itinerant peddler to palaces of consumption that had taken place in the area of retailing across the nineteenth century. In the mid-nineteenth century, department stores had begun to appear, simultaneously, in Paris, London, and New York, led by Frenchman Aristide Boucicaut, who established the reknowned Bon Marché in Paris in 1852.[113]

The American department store was the offspring of numerous patriarchs: A. T. Stewart, Lord and Taylor, Rowland H. Macy, B. Altman, and Bloomingdale in New York; John Wanamaker in Philadelphia; Marshall Field in Chicago; William Filene, first in Lynn and then in Boston, Massachusetts.[114] For the most part, department stores were founded by immigrants from Britain; Jewish émigrés from Germany and then Eastern Europe; and by "descendants of Quaker families settled in New England in the seventeenth century."[115]

From their beginnings, these establishments were purveyors of clothing. Some dated back to the era of "slops." The chain of Browning, King & Company got its start supplying clothes to forty-niners in California.[116] Relatively soon, however, these stores became purveyors of more fashionable goods. Selling clothes in a range of prices to a corresponding range of customers, department stores provided a dazzling atmosphere for their wares.

If ready-made clothing became increasingly ornamental over the latter part of the nineteenth century, the principle of department store design was similarly elegant. The engagement was reciprocal, reinforcing each other. Ready-made clothing put the imitative symbolism of wealth in reach of more and more people, to be worn as an emblem of achievement. Similarly, the department store created an architectural environment that was palatial, a mimicry of space and style that was, by custom, a prerogative of opulence. New York's first department store, pre-dating the age of mass fashion, was A. T. Stewart's "Marble Dry-Goods Palace" at Broadway and Chambers Streets. Fifteen years later, Stewart's erected a new store, utilizing a cast-iron building facade, a cheaper, lighter mode of display, which was painted to approximate the weight and substance of stone. A democracy of surfaces was being erected through architectural innovation.[117]

Internally, these "palaces of consumption" were true to the principles of appearance and display. In 1853, Lord and Taylor built a store at Grand and Chrystie Streets, which defied the crowded terms of urban space. Built before the introduction of electric lighting, the illumination of such a structure was always a problem. Gaslights, though bright, were extremely dangerous, particularly in an establishment where crowds would risk the sudden apocalypse of fire and explosion. The Lord and Taylor store introduced a pattern that was replicated elsewhere. "The new store incorporated a large central rotunda with glass dome which allowed daylight and air to penetrate into the building."[118] The resulting structure provided a dramatic diversion from the crowdedness of urban life that was generally experienced by its clientele. The rotunda design created a spectacle of air, space, and light that provided a symbolic retreat from the terms of an increasingly congested city life. Such innovations of structure and display provided a seductive and promising context for the retailing of industrial wares. Within such an arena, the din of the sweatshop, the filth of the factory, the monotony of work were masked. The buying environment complemented the claims and conceits of the goods themselves, often defying experience.

These temples of Mammon were particularly effective places for the display of industrial "plenty." They reiterated its optimism and, at least symbolically, avoided its costs. As ready-made garments became conspicuous vehicles of style, they found a suitable home within the big stores. Making their first appearances in the latter decades of the nineteenth century, by 1915 ready-to-wear departments were entrenched as features within the stores. The distribution of these goods was further aided by the founding of the United Parcel Service in 1907, a basic metropolitan delivery service.[119]

While department stores took hold in cities in the 1880s, most Americans still lived in the country. In 1880 the United States was still mainly rural; agriculture was still the predominant area of employment and production. Yet these farm areas and people were inoculated by the spectacle of industrial goods as well. A dynamic medium of urban images and goods was the mail-order catalog. Beginning in 1869 with E. C. Allen's "People's Literary Companion," a catalog displaying a diversity of items, the mail-order approach to merchandising was perfected by Aaron Montgomery Ward, who became the official supplier to the Grange, an organization of farmers. Rural social networks were becoming an infrastructure for the establishment of industrial merchandising networks. Ward's success was followed by that of Sears, Roebuck & Company whose catalog was dubbed, simultaneously, "The Farmer's Friend" and "America's Dream Book." The pages of Sears' catalog were glutted with pictures and print. For an audience used to open spaces, these pages offered a crowded representation of city life; Chicago was the home-base of Sears, Roebuck. Yet if the experienced crowdedness of the city was often marked by deprivation, the pages of the catalog were cornucopian.

Richard Sears and Julius Rosenwald combined an understanding of rural, pre-consumerist social values with an expertise in mass retailing. The catalog posed an inviting advertisement for this combination; sympathetic to the hesitancy of farm folk to deal in distant markets, ostentatious in its proselytizing for consumer goods. With Rosenwald as the curator of Sears' fashion display and manager of its immense corporate structure, clothing stood prominently within the catalog. If in turn-of-the-century catalogs timepieces were featured first within its pages, by the 1920s fashion goods for women held that honored spot. Read and re-read throughout the American countryside, Sears, Roebuck catalogs carried the imagistic message of the garment center into the outer reaches of the society.[120] It offered the wherewithal and the definition of modernity: *ready-made*.

Mail-order catalogs were just one of the ways by which ready-to-wear was spread through printed literature and images. The growing institution of mass-circulation newspapers also carried the tidings of fashion. From the late nineteenth century onward, advertising for ready-made clothing became a part of the printed vernacular of the city. Advertising methods adhered to the principle of display. Beyond being an originator in department stores themselves, Rowland Macy was also innovative in the area of journalistic advertising. His store utilized an advertising mode that broke many of the conventions of printing, and grabbed the attention of its viewers. Departing from "the usual straight lines of letterpress," Macy instead opted "for an arrangement of words into patterns and the use of repetition of short, incisive phrases—all to catch the reader's eye."[121] Such verbal techniques were enhanced, increasingly, by pictorial displays. In addition to showing readers what a garment looked like, pictures afforded the occasion to place the garments within a setting, offering occasions and atmospheres that linked the product with privilege and leisure, whether available to the consumer or not. Beyond newspapers, such mass magazines as Edward Bok's *Ladies' Home Journal* promoted the ideals of fashion, and gave fashion advice to a growing audience of readers. Slick pages enhanced the glamor of pictorial display.

Techniques developed by chromolithographers figured heavily in the graphic broadcasting of fashion. As chromos could approximate the rich density of oil paints, so too could they enhance the look and textures of cloth. A cultural system of cross-referencing was established in the array of artistically rendered reproductions; on paper, in cloth. One of the most interesting uses of chromolithography in relation to fashion was in the printing and selling of paper dolls, which expanded around the turn of the century.

Fashion miniatures had a long history. Early in the nineteenth century, and before, American women of wealth purchased "fashion babies" from Europe. These were dolls, produced on the Continent, wearing fashions as models for imitation by dressmakers. They were accouterments to the spread of fashion among the rich. Later on, these costly models were replaced by "pantines," paste-board dolls that served a similar purpose: providing models for imitation by seamstresses.[122] These items were part of a tradition that equated fashion with class privilege.

By 1900, with the spread of fashionable ready-to-wear, "fashion babies" experienced a similar democratization. While early examples had been exclusive models and dressmakers' aids, chromolithographed paper cutout dolls were children's toys. Cheaply produced yet elaborately colored, paper cutouts spread the imagery of fashion to little girls of different backgrounds and circumstances. The generational implications are suggestive. Even if older generation rural or immigrant parents adhered to austere traditions in dress, paper dolls introduced fashion to their little girls at an early age, setting the desires of impressionable youth against the resistant conventions of age.

For people living in certain American cities, a wave of large public expositions provided another spectacular arena of display. These elaborate fairs, offering a utopian panorama of industrial and artistic achievement, were themselves facades of "monumental grandeur." Their architectural motifs were testimony to the principle of superficial display. One of the grandest was the Columbian Exposition, held in Chicago in 1893. At an estimated cost of forty-six million dollars, Chicago businessmen attempted to construct an environment that mirrored the distinction of European neoclassical design. Mimicking the perpetuity of Renaissance ideals, a mule-team of architects put up a city that was primarily surface, true to the priorities of the age. Historian John F. Kasson has described the telling combination of classical ideals and temporary construction:

> The Columbian Exposition offered architects, artists, and patrons an opportunity to construct an ideal that would purify the gross materialism of American culture, order its chaotic energies, and uplift its taste and character. Out of their united efforts, they aimed to create a monumental White City, an image of Venice purified and reborn. As an ideal, the White City would be a Dream City, rising in less than two and a half years out of the Chicago mire to flourish for a few seasons, and then in 1896 to be dismantled.

The exposition, like the fashions it propagandized, reflected a characteristic discovery of consumer capitalism: turning sow's ears into silk purses. "On closer inspection," Kasson points out, "the gleaming white marble of the Exposition buildings turned out to be staff, a compound of plaster and fibrous binding, clothing wood and steel" as an armature.[123] The vistas of privilege were produced, for a sightseeing public, and then disposed of. This disposable environment, beyond its adherence to the principles of appearance and display, was also a testimony to the logic of consumption, so essential to the industrial system that spawned it. In the world of ever-changing fashion, in particular, the consumerist ethic—continually using things up—was an intrinsic component.

Within the halls of expositions, fashion was an important exhibit. At the Centennial Exhibition in Philadelphia (1876), the propagation of style was part of the show. Particularly for visitors from the West, what they saw was filled with new and unfamiliar goods: "finer things in fabrics, apparel, furniture, home furnishings and other lines of goods used in the arts of living, goods that had formed but a small part of their thought up to that time."[124] Likewise, the Columbian Exposition promoted new trends in fashion among a large mob of visitors.

In their form and in their content, expositions interacted with the products of the garment industry and reinforced their aura. Display, as a notable element of urban existence, was magnified and utopianized in the shadowless dazzle of the White Cities.

By 1920, the most powerful agencies of mass impression, the movies, were playing their part in the rise of fashion. Shown in movie palaces, which—like department stores and expositions—were grand monuments to elaborate facades, films riveted the imagination. In their study of Middletown, Helen and Robert Lynd noted that, by the mid-twenties, among high-school-age youths, the "sharp figures on the silver screen are always authoritatively present with their gay and confident designs for living."[125] Anne Hollander elaborates:

> Movies taught everyone how ways of walking and dancing, of using the hands and moving the head and shoulders, could be incorporated into the conscious ways of wearing clothes.

Hollander continues, implying that film, in its magnification of motion, contributed to the diminution of cloth in women's fashion following the First World War:

> After about 1920 the fact that women's clothes showed such a reduction in overall volume was undoubtedly partly due to the visual need for the completely clothed body to be satisfactorily seen *in motion*.
>
> The still body that is nevertheless perceived as ideally in motion seems to present a blurred image—a perpetual suggestion of all the other possible moments at

which it might be seen. It seems to have a dynamic, expanding outline.[126]

As a basic source of Americanization, film provided a visual manual to urban and rural people. It magnified ideals of consumption, of motion, of beauty, and of dress. Writing in 1929, fashion analyst Elizabeth Hurlock commented on the impact of film over the preceding decade:

> In recent years the popularity of the cinema and its far-reaching effects have made screen stars more powerful in the determination of presentday fashions than the actors and actresses of the legitimate state. The nation-wide publicity which is given to them, has made them the popular heroes and heroines of the day. What they do, say, think, eat, or wear serves as a model for their devoted followers.[127]

If screen stars were thin and mobile, so too would be their imitators. The 1920s became an era of dieting and thin, skimpy styles. If the screen images were luminescent white and black, fashions, likewise, moved toward black and white; "color drained out of elegance, and was replaced by the whole black and white spectrum" during the twenties.[128] The silver screen brought fashion imagery to everyone, and set it before them in terms larger than life. A pattern of interaction between screen stars and popular desires was taking hold. In baroque palaces, sculpted of plaster and horse-hair, in a flood of publicity and fan magazines, people confronted stars as models for sexual fantasy, excitement in life, consumption. Fashion stood at the surface of this confrontation.

By the 1920s, there was a massive interaction of fashion display. Countless new institutions carried the message and repeated each other's chants. Yet the rise of mass fashion was not the result of a series of discrete avenues of display. It came amidst a broad and general development that encompassed the flowering of mass production and mass consumption. Within this general development, mass fashion went beyond the reproduction of styles, adapted from the modes of nineteenth-century wealth. A reciprocity, an interaction began to develop, between fashion and the industrial structure that was propagating it on a mass scale. If mass production affected the construction of clothing, it also left its imprint on design. Approaching the 1920s, fashionable clothing was already marked by the new, mobile terms of a mass, industrial society.

9 / New Patterns

FROM THE TIME of the Civil War, the connective tissue between fashion and industrialism spread the look of finery beyond its formerly insular sanctums. As mass production appropriated the imagery of fashion, the imagery of fashion, itself, was irrevocably affected by that intercourse. By 1863, mechanical reproduction had made its mark even on the handcraft traditions of home-produced clothing and dressmaking. Where beforehand each garment was patterned and cut individually, now printed paper patterns were commercially available. Developed by a New England tailor named Butterick, the principles of standardization had insinuated themselves into the home. Such patterns were also employed in factories, establishing a link between public and private spheres of production.[129] As in so many other areas of life, the conceptualization of a product was gravitating from the imagination of the producer to the designs of commerce.

By the early decades of the twentieth century, the proliferation of ready-to-wear clothing began to coincide with dramatic changes in the silhouette of fashion itself. Patterns of sumptuosity and conspicuous consumption of cloth were costly both in terms of the amount of cloth and the labor they required. Textile yardage decreased, as simpler, less fulsome styles began to appear. In a world of mass fashion, questions of cost increasingly invaded the realm of design. In 1913 an average women's outfit required 19¼ yards of fabric in its production. By

1928, with more and more women donning fashionable products from the garment center, the average outfit consumed only 7 yards of cloth.[130]

While the diminishing amount of cloth may be partly explained as attempts to minimize productive costs, other aspects of industrial society also left their imprint on style. As fashion became a staple among women who entered into the outer world of work, designs that were predicated on docility and enforced leisure became patently restrictive. Among rich women, sport and city life denoted a need for more mobile styles. Among poor women it was wage labor. If the first generations of ready-to-wear had provided working-class women the opportunity to emulate the fashions of the rich, by the 1920s fashion had begun to emulate the logic of industrialism. The fashion ideal for women increasingly became that of "the young, agile, long-limbed girl, whose naturally shaped body is well suited to the working requirements and mobility of the modern world. Her well-proportioned figure is easily clothed by a standardized manufactured garment."[131] Among fashion designers, it was the "King of Fashion," Paul Poiret, whose Parisian workshop legitimized and advocated simple and comfortable dress. Avoiding any link between fashion and social utility, however, Poiret asserted that he was merely expressing an "Oriental influence."[132]

Despite such disclaimers, the connection between simple dress and the terms of twentieth-century life is clear. The increasing worldliness and mobility of women, and their engagement in wage labor, were accommodated and symbolized by a style of dress that foreswore the sedentary ideals of Victorianism. Style reflected a kinetic potential: lean, taut, with emphasis on the legs. Reverberating against the staunch sexual dualism of the nineteenth century, the entry of woman into the world of work, or the world of public life in general, was seen as her masculinization. Fashion reflected this metamorphosis of gender, dramatically. Where nineteenth-century corsetry had molded women to emphasize their reproductive functions, styles moving toward the 1920s were productive in orientation. The idiom of action and of masculinity began to transform the ideals of young womanhood. Industrial ideals of youth and physical endurance infected the terms of beauty. If film and entertainment were vehicles of fashion ideals in the public consciousness, they were also ideals of mobile industrialism and efficiency. In a memoir on fashion, Cecil Beaton waxes eloquent on the beauty of Irene Castle, a star of the years around 1915. As a feminine ideal, dancer Castle is a repudiation of the delicate uselessness of Victorianism:

> Irene Castle's appearance was unlike anyone else's, yet overnight people accepted it and emulated her wherever possible. The primary effect that she created was one of an exquisite grace combined with an extraordinarily boyish youthfulness. There was something terrifically healthy and clean about her. In her whiplike and taut bearing she hinted at the wonderful play of muscles beneath the surface, as a fine-bred horse betrays its beauty by a ripple. There was something bladelike and steely about her muscles and her limbs. She used her hands with such a bold grace that one had the notion that she gesticulated rather than gestured. . . . She walked with very long strides, with no daintiness, swinging along with wonderful, live, big gestures. She invented a whole balance of movement, with the pelvis thrust forward and the body leaning backwards. . . . It was as if a gyroscope were inside her, always stabilizing the body's framework no-matter on which tangent it moved off.[133]

Beaton's imagery is that of the mobile, engaged woman of the industrial age. The cushioned, parlor-bound woman of the past was now described in metallic and mechanical terms. Still an object of masculine passion, that passion was now evoked by the power of

motion and of strength. Unencumbered by trails of ring-
lets from her head, she now was capped by a short,
boyish haircut, known by those who copied the style as
the "Castle bob." In the turbulent motion of mass industrialism, fashionable women were increasingly attuned to
its demands. Lean and sinewy, the flapper style of the
1920s provided a unified principle of work and leisure.
Whether dancing or wage-earning, the flapper was a
model of endurance.

While hardly scanty, men's clothing after the turn of
the century also reflected the primacy of endurance. If
the cloak of morality, denoting entrepreneurial austerity,
had informed the construction of men's suits throughout
much of the nineteenth century, the masculine ideal un-
derwent certain changes in the years after 1900 as well.
Describing the shift, Paul Nystrom spoke of how "the
styles of clothing for men seemed to aim at emphasizing
size and physical strength. Men in the clothing of the
period from 1900–1905 looked like giant athletes."[134] If
women's clothing intimated strength and motion, the
steel-worker physique inculcated in the imagery of men's
fashion also had a symbolic intimacy with the priorities
and proximity of labor. The magnetism of fashion, born
in the consumption patterns of a leisure class, had now
evolved to reflect the life patterns of its latest practi-
tioners: working-class women and men.

Insofar as fashion took on the imprint of industrial
modernity, it reflected a variety of influences. Work and
mobility were major factors in the delineation of new
styles, but there are also myriad, elusive aspects to the
wiles of fashion. Some questions are suggested but unan-
swerable. The entry of vertical lines and geometric patterns evokes the translation of the body into the architectural forms of the urban edifice. The thin and taut ideal,
while linked to mobility and action, may also engage the
anxieties and anomies of modern existence. It is hard to
be conclusive, but important to speculate on such paral-

lels of meaning. The conspicuous consumption of cloth, now joined by the conspicuous consumption of human energy as a fashion ideal, however, was clearly an outcome of industrial modernity. As Henry Adams once observed, the virgin is replaced by the dynamo as a sensuous ideal.

Not all interactions between fashion and industrialism were symbolic in their origin. During the First World War, for example, concrete social and material priorities had a direct impact on style. The war that drew legions of men onto the fields of battle also drew unprecedented numbers of women into factory work. Within such a development, the move toward more mobile fashions was expanded as a necessity among women. In addition, as war production demanded the channeling of essential materials toward military ends, the War Industries Board established a series of regulations regarding clothing:

> Shoes for both men and women were made with shorter tops, the limit allowed being eight inches, and no leather linings. Coats for men were shortened and the cuffs removed from their trousers as a means of conserving woolen material. The steel, formerly used for women's corsets, was needed for wire cables to hoist guns and munitions over the peaks in the Alps, and the result was that corset manufacturers were summoned to Washington where they were told that a decrease of one-fourth in the amount of wire used for stays must be made at once.

The war created social and material demands that gave further impetus to trends begun beforehand, dramatizing the symbiosis between fashion and material life.

In the early decades of this century, as social life and structures of survival took on a new shape, patterns of sartorial meaning were altered. While earlier mass fashion had mimicked the displays of elites, now the idiom of display took on the trappings of common life. Industrial labor and production made inroads into the visual language of fashion. An emulation of the proletarian lot now joined the emulation of elites within the patterns and energies of style. The democratization of access to fashion had now injected fashion with a more democratic ethos, setting the stage for a time when the once-scorned clothing of miners would carry the labels of couturiers.

10 / The Sirens of Style

"WHY DID I choose to come to America?" begins the father, a Roumanian immigrant, in Mike Gold's classic *Jews Without Money*. "I will tell you why," he continues, "it was because of envy. . . ." The envy was a product of tales told in his native village, but it also had roots in pictures he had seen in the window of a shop that sold Singer sewing machines. Here, in the pictures, were representations of a world that transformed the inequities of experience. Presumably, this world was made possible by sewing machines.

> One picture had in it the tallest building I had ever seen. It was called a skyscraper. At the bottom of it walked the proud Americans. The men wore derby hats and had fine mustaches and gold watch chains. The women wore silks and satins, and had proud faces like queens. Not a single poor man or woman was there; every one was rich.

For Mike Gold's father, clothing was decisive in a vision of opportunity that stood, far away, in America. Clothing told him that in this distant land, "the poorest ragpicker lived better than a Roumanian millionaire."

"In America," he believed, "people did little work, but had fun all day." The democracy of the image presented an inviting promise, and he embarked upon his pilgrimage, his mind reeling with the expectation that now, he too might "wear a derby hat."[135]

While Mike Gold's tale is ultimately one of painful disenchantment, the availability of fashion mesmerized immigrants upon their arrival in America. Its apparent power seemed to overturn the conventions of ages. It offered the possibility to assume the bearing and carriage of people who, in the old country, had had an exclusive claim on sartorial grace. Mass fashion afforded immigrants the possibility to "be somebody" in a new world, rejecting the indignities of the past, and accommodating themselves to the world of display in which they sought their future.

For Italian immigrants in New York, donning ready-to-wear broke ancient taboos. As peasants from the southern tier, they had learned that certain lines should not be crossed: "No woman of the poorer classes," for example, "dared put on a hat. She would have been the laughing stock of her community if she did. To don a hat was the privilege of the signora [woman of the landowning gentry], or the whores."[136] In America, a war broke out over such customs. While older women held to the conventions of the past, wearing scarves over their heads and shawls over their shoulders, young Italian women eagerly ate of the formerly forbidden fruit. These were the accouterments of the New World. Not only were they the means of survival for those who made them; they were a symbolic ascendency to the level of the signora; or, perhaps, to the freedom from family constraints represented, once more, by the finery of "shameful love." If work was long and tedious and housing decrepit, clothing afforded the illusion of stepping out of one's circumstances. Those who held to the lure of the past looked askance at those who adopted the idiom of fashionable democracy. Among one Sicilian community on New York's Lower East Side, women who learned the vernacular of ready-made were chided:

> In the old country she used to carry baskets of tomatoes on her head and now she carries a hat on it . . .

> look at the daughter of so and so. In Cinisi [a village
> in Sicily] she worked in the field and the sun burnt her
> black. Here she dares to carry a parasol.[137]

For an older generation schooled in the indignities of
sumptuary law, fashion was proscribed from desire. For
their children, it represented a transcendent escape. It
was one of the few areas in which the promises of industrial plenty could, at least superficially, be met.

The promise of industrial democracy had early been
expressed in terms of clothing. Clothing had long been a
device in the elevation of classes. For the bourgeoisie,
fashion had been an important emblem of their arrival;
for laboring people the expectation was similar. As New
England farm girls made their first forays into the cotton
mills of Lowell, Massachusetts, they were seduced by a
"hoisting of false colors." Labor recruiters, scouting
rural Vermont and New Hampshire, promised girls that
they would tend their machinery dressed in silks, and
would work at a leisurely enough rate so as to "spend
half their time reading."[138] Some girls did in fact return to
family farms, arrayed with "new silk dresses"—an effective advertisement to those girls who would come
next to work in the factories.

By the turn of the century, with the deluge of ready-
to-wear, the lure held out many decades before to the
Lowell mill girls was a visible claim made across the
broad tawdry horizon of a developing consumer culture.

For people "caught between a longing for love and
the struggle for the legal tender,"[139] cheap, evocative
ready-made clothing fed the hungry fires of social wish
and personal desire. It made the often tough journey into
the modern industrial world seem all the more promising.
For hard-working, ill-housed immigrants, despised by
the middle-class "natives," clothing offered one of the
few avenues by which people could assume a sense of
belonging. In a world of strangers, the ability to construct appearances, a disguise, was one of the most es-

sential lessons. It could be observed as one moved from tenement district to tenement district; from wretched ghetto to screaming tenderloin. The abundance of cheap ready-to-wear was one of the first acquisitions of the urban poor, often procured before some things more necessary, but less visible.

In the 1890s, the area of New York City between 27th and 40th Streets at Seventh Avenue was known as "African Broadway," the quarter in which a large number of the city's black residents lived. Most were recently arrived from the South, what W. E. B. Du Bois called "country bred." These were the children of slaves, refugees from a land in which plantation aristocrats dressed in the style of conspicuous elegance, while blacks—like all poor rural folk—wore overalls and other "slops." Yet there, on African Broadway, the availability of mass fashion was widely evident:

> Always and invariably on "dress parade" is the new quarter (reported by the *New York Tribune*, October of 1895). . . . The younger women, arrayed in gowns that are wonderfully good imitations of the fashions, though heaven knows how they can afford them, walk in pairs and trios up and down Seventh Avenue. . . . The people . . . are poor, with only a dollar or two standing between them and starvation most of the time. . . . (Nonetheless, one sees a) daily promenade of gayly dressed girls and *sprig* [sic] young colored men. Yellow is the prime tint of the young colored girls' clothes. The favorite dress of the young men "in style" is a glossy silk hat, patent leathers, a black suit with a sack coat of remarkable shortness, and a figured waistcoat. Paste diamonds are *de rigueur*.[140]

In a world of degraded housing, racism, and general economic deprivation, clothing afforded these recent migrants from the South one of the few avenues by which a selfhood could be publicly expressed, one consistent with principles of appearance and display.

The power of the lure of finery is heard in the lament of Mamie Craven, a laundress quoted in Ruth True's study of New York's poor West Side in 1914: "Oh . . . you don't know *how* I want a chinchilla coat." This from a young woman not content to see her earnings eaten up by rent, food, fuel.[141]

The immigrants' desire for fine clothing was the object of ridicule and moralizing by the middle class. Unable to appreciate the meaning of clothes to those who were denied nearly all else, they would refer to these fashionable poor, walking up the avenue, as a "Monkey's Parade." What they condemned were the "shop apprentices, the young work girls, the boy clerks, and so forth, stirred by mysterious intimations, spending their first-earned money upon collars and ties, chiffon hats, smart lace collars, walking-sticks, sunshades . . . "[142]

Bertha June Richardson, in her 1913 study of "the woman who spends," explained the impulse toward finery among immigrant girls in city settlement houses. Speaking to a middle-class audience, concerned with "uplifting" these "misbegottens," she says:

> Did you ever go down to one of our city settlements full of the desire to help and lift up the poor shop girl? . . . There must be some mistake, you thought. These could not be poor girls, earning five or six dollars a week. They looked better dressed than you did! Plumes on their hats, a rustle of silk petticoats, everything about them in the latest style. You went home thoughtful about those girls who wasted their hard-earned money on cheap imitation, who dressed beyond their station, and you failed to see what enjoyment they got out of it. In time you learned that it was only an attempt "to bridge the difference" between themselves and those with larger opportunities by imitating all they could see.[143]

Thorstein Veblen once argued that emulation was the fuel that energized fashion. For an urban poor, raised in the traditions of sumptuary law and dazzled by the expanding array of mass-produced imagery, the tools of emulation were now increasingly available. Middle-class women who worked in the social-work movement of the early twentieth century were often perplexed at the vigor with which poor immigrant girls picked up these tools. Social workers often came from affluent backgrounds; their lives did not so require the erection of appearances. Like Jane Addams, such a person "may afford to be very simple, or even shabby as to her clothes, if she likes." As many of these women were carrying on their own battles against the constraints of Victorianism, a simple approach to dress was not uncommon among them. But Addams understood the imperative of dress among working girls:

> But the working girl, whose family lives in a tenement, or moves from one small apartment to another, who has little social standing and has to make her own place, knows full well how much habit and style of dress has to do with her position. Her income goes into her clothing, out of all proportion to the amount which she spends upon other things. But, if social advancement is her aim, it is the most sensible thing she can do. She is judged largely by her clothes. Her house furnishing, with its pitiful little decorations, her scanty supply of books, are never seen by the people whose social opinions she most values. Her clothes are her background, and from them she is largely judged.[144]

The same impulse was noted by Stuart Chase later on, in 1929:

> Not long ago I walked along New York's East Side where the more poorly paid workers live. The buildings were old, slatternly, ugly and depressing beyond description. Yet out of a ramshackle doorway would come a child in a brand-new overcoat; a girl in silk

stockings and furs. The contrast struck one between the eyes. It serves to typify the whole uneven, lateral development of American living standards.[145]

Emerging was a basic pattern of American consumer culture. Produced in a variety of price lines but imitating the look of affluence, mass fashion provided a means by which poor people could develop an appearance of upward mobility, construct a presentable, public self by which that mobility might in fact be actualized. The remarkable success of the fashion industry was built on such aspirations, which by the late 1920s enveloped the lives of almost everyone. Writing in 1929, Elizabeth Hurlock proclaimed:

> Never in history has fashion held such power as it does today. Never have fashions been so varied and so fleeting. Never has fashion's sway been so universal that to be out of fashion might literally be interpreted to be "out of the world."[146]

Hurlock's last phrase reveals the tyranny of fashion. If clothing presented people with the possibility of concealing their origins and if fashion was a tool of outer display for more and more people, it was also true that the new world *demanded* the "Americanization" of the self. Fashion and presentability were, increasingly, categories imposed upon modern industrial citizens. To turn away from the pull of fashion was to remain alien and different; to stand "outside the gates." To embrace fashion was to move ahead with society. Leonard Covello, an immigrant from Italy, described his sartorial Americanization with an ironic sense of contradiction:

> My long European trousers had been replaced by the short knickers of the time, and I wore black ribbed stockings and new, American shoes. To all outward appearances I was an American, except that I did not speak a word of English.[147]

Bertha June Richardson argued that the tyranny of fashion, among middle- as well as working-class people, undercut the principles of *nature,* substituting individual consumption for the common good. To Richardson, the elaborate structure of fashion set people against one another in a ritual of "purposeless imitation." The ritual wove itself through the classes of society, elevating personal gain above social needs:

> The shops imitate each other and dictate to the woman just the line of imitation she shall follow, without a thought for her needs. The Fourth Avenue shop says to the Fourth Avenue buyer: "Behold my clever imitation. For less than you could pay in a Fifth Avenue shop, I can give you a perfect imitation. You would not be behind the styles, I know. I can make you look like the real peacock, so buy here." The Third Avenue shop . . . say(s) the same to its customers. The First Avenue shop has a still cheaper imitation, and in Hester Street, on the pushcarts, ghosts of the real are "Going, going, going" for thirty-nine cents.

In Richardson's estimation, this journey of the imitation downward merely turned people's minds to the worship of worthless things, while essential needs were overlooked. Invoking *nature* against the dominion of style, Richardson cautioned that "*She* will teach you to struggle for and to imitate those things which make for life, the highest life, the best life, *not for yourself alone,* but for all to whom you are bound by the common ties of life"[148] (emphasis added). For all its utilitarian moralism and stuffy contempt, Richardson's was a potent insight. If fashion was a powerful device, requisite to modern life, it was also an element in the social process by which common bonds of community and commitment were subverted by the individualism of a consumer society. Mass fashion was providing more and more people with the idiom of sartorial expression, but it was a vernacular punctuated by the lingo of social competition.

Other critics of mass fashion spoke from the platform of the old elite monopoly. Cecil Beaton argued that images that were once unique and mysterious were now being "reduced to journalistic commonplaces." Fashion imagery greeted everyone at breakfast, in the morning paper. To Beaton, the traditional magic of fashion had been based on its rarity, its spontaneity. "Without mystery," he bemoaned, "magic disappears. . . . If distance lends enchantment, then there is little distance in our contemporary world." Celebrities, carrying fashion into the public domain of popular consciousness, had, for Beaton, robbed fashion of its imagination.[149]

In line with this, Karlyne Anspach reported that as late as 1967, elite New York department store Bergdorf Goodman expected its employees to avoid looking overly stylish. Committed to upholding an air of mystery, magic, and originality for their clientele, Bergdorf's instructed its employees: "We don't want our sales people mistaken for customers."[150] The availability of mass fashion made it all the more important for purveyors of elite fashion to hold on to the apparent province of uniqueness.

Another source of concern over the homogenization of style was the elite fashion designers themselves, who saw ready-to-wear as the Waterloo of the imagination. Paris designer Paul Poiret felt that the trend to mass fashion was ultimately a fetish for labels:

> Another thing which the American traders appeared to me to practise was to pack mediocre merchandise under a distinguished label. In that country they will have labels, and as they have no understanding of the value of objects, they go by labels only. To sell common merchandise under the name of Poiret seems to them a happy and fortunate notion.[151]

The current mode of "designer jeans" is the ultimate expression of the fetishization Poiret decried. To him,

American garment manufacturers were servile copyists; "their absolute lack of imagination prevents them from conceiving the unforeseen and the hypothetical."[152] His heir in the leadership of Paris fashion, Christian Dior, put it somewhat more delicately during the 1950s:

> [Americans'] clothes, hair, nails and shoes are all impeccable. This is true of all classes of society from the millionaire down to the elevator operator . . . but I must at the same time admit that in the end there was something uniform about it.[153]

Though these criticisms sprang from the self-interest of elites, they contained more than a grain of truth. If fashion gave more and more people access to a language of individual expression, its mass production tended toward the opposite: mass expression. Rooted in the production of industrial and military uniform, the ready-made fashion industry also created a mode of uniformity, though touched by the elegance of style.

Defenders of mass fashion, during the decisive period of the 1920s, described it as a force of great political and social magnitude. Paul Nystrom, an architect of modern fashion merchandising, waxed eloquent on the imprint of fashion on the popular sensibility.

> Once the pursuit of the wealthy and aristocratic few, [it] is now followed by the masses. . . . Fashion is one of the greatest forces in present-day life. It determines both the character and the direction of consumption. Fashion makes men shave every day, grow moustaches, cut their hair in certain ways, wear certain colors in hats, clothing and shoes, certain shapes in collars, four-in-hand neck-ties, trousers creased, and low shoes all the year round. For women it changes the tint of the face powder, the odor of the perfume, the wave of the hair, the position of the waist line, the length of the skirt, the color of the clothes, and the height of the heels. . . . Fashion causes all of these changes and, at the same time, makes people like it.[154]

To Elizabeth Hurlock, fashion liberated people from the burdens of the past:

> It has prompted nations to advance at a pace never apparent in those bound by rigid custom. It stimulates industry and inventiveness. It tends to break down the barriers between classes, lessens the feeling of national differences, and decreases the tendency toward national superiority, which is apt to develop when nations are differently clothed.[155]

For Hurlock, the homogenizing influence would be a predicator of international understanding; common goals and aspirations, common bonds of commodities would allow people to transcend ethnic identities and social economic differences. Fashion, it was argued, offered the promise of equality. It created a common aesthetic symbolism, which if, at first, provided an idiom of class identity, would increasingly provide an idiom of national and then international identity, transcending class.

Clearly, fashion did not deliver the same goods to everyone. Depending on who one was and where one shopped, fashions came in a variety of prices and qualities. The ready-made fashions that greeted immigrants to America, early in the century, were usually of "the cheapest and poorest quality. . . . The clothes wore badly and had frequently to be replaced."[156] But in a society presumed to embody a variety of experiences and possibilities, the institution of mass fashion helped to construct what Anspach had termed "a common subjective life."[157]

Despite fashion's promise of equality, the structure of the industry itself pointed up the inherent contradictions of the promise. Ready-to-wear fashions appeared in a variety of forms and prices reflecting concrete, economic inequities of society. Yet the common element, established within the variety, was its most visible element: its surface, its style.

The proliferation of these symbolic surfaces, in a variety of prices and qualities, was structured—formally and informally—within the developing garment industry. Counterfeiting and "style piracy" are as old as mass fashion. They are an "underworld" without which mass fashion would not have come about. In the twenties Paul Nystrom exclaimed, "The copyist is everywhere," conceding that it was unavoidable. "Almost every one deplores design copying in principle, but, lacking any legal check, copying continues openly and brazenly as a dominant fact in our economic life."[158] For designers of originals, it was very difficult to protect against the piracy of styles. One of the few mechanisms of protection was the elevation of the label, the registered trademark, to an element of style itself. This tendency is widespread today, where many fashions are conspicuously marked by labels. Even here, piracy is possible, although legally more risky. When one steps into a pair of fifty-dollar Calvin Klein jeans, there is always the possibility that they are counterfeits.

Beyond style copying, the proliferation and gradation of varieties of fashion have heavily depended upon the development of synthetic fabrics. Beginning with rayon, the ability to capture the look of luxurious fabrics and to reproduce it on a mass scale with the use of chemicals has been a key to the egalitarianism of the image.

If piracy and copying were the early means to the spread of mass fashion, by the late 1940s the high-fashion houses themselves were joining in the proliferation of fashion. In 1947 Christian Dior entered into a partnership with Marcel Boussac, a French manufacturer of cotton textiles, to produce a line of mass-produced clothing, offering various levels of quality. Thus, they countered style-piracy by creating an institutional amalgam of original design and mass production:

> Dior and Boussac did not stop at top fashion; they founded a whole industry around it. . . . The main

> business of Christian Dior commences with the selling
> of models at the fashion shows twice a year. Some-
> times a model is sold one hundred times. . . . A buyer
> from overseas can do one of three things: he can buy a
> paper pattern of the model, but he may not label it
> Christian Dior; or he can buy a canvas copy and
> change it to suit his purposes naming it "Original-
> Christian-Dior-Copy"; or he can buy the original
> model in material which is the most expensive and is
> permitted to label it "Christian Dior." The more the
> buyer buys, the greater the discount he receives from
> Dior. Crowds of busily sewing midinettes are responsi-
> ble for the quick finishing of garments so that the buyer
> can soon travel home with his new models safely in his
> suitcase. Exact drawings and reproductions of the new
> fashions are first allowed to appear a month after the
> fashion shows.[159]

The structure revolutionized haute couture and established pathways by which the imprimatur of designers
could, in a variety of forms, reach a range of markets.
For American, French, and Italian designers today, the
pattern set by Dior is the basis of their success. The
pattern has been refined and has evolved, but the principle continues. Today's designers give their franchise,
their label, to manufacturers of garments whose factories
may be in Southeast Asia, and whose customers feel
blessed to have acquired something above the common
cut. If the bourgeois tradition in clothing began at a time
when the wearing of finery, after the French Revolution,
was a risky business, today's fashion industry owes its
existence to the fact that the wearing of finery became a
right of citizenship.

From the period of 1917 to the present, a stock criticism of "Communist" countries has been the absence of
finery: "drab," "dull," "unimaginative!" While socialist movements proclaimed struggle against social and
economic inequity in the name of the people, capitalist
enterprises were developing their own, curiously appeal-

ing respite from inequity by denying its existence and backing this up with a democracy of images and universal fashion. The success of this phenomenon is irrefutable; the allure of fashion crosses the boundaries of social system and political ideology.

Youth, more than any other segment of the society, was caught by the windy voice of fashion. It was a language young people listened to, which cajoled them at every turn, and one they learned to speak for themselves. By 1922, as shown in a survey taken among readers of the movie fan magazine *Photoplay,* teenage girls were assuming an increasingly decisive and autonomous role in the selection of clothing. Patterns of family budgeting were now subjected to the preferences and demands of adolescents. Of the girls surveyed by *Photoplay,* about half of them shopped for clothing alone, "without any guidance or aid from their parents." Personal tastes and the desire to attract the interests of young men were seen as the main considerations in the purchase of clothes. New principles of appearance and display had implanted themselves in family life. This trend marked a stark contrast to patterns that had predominated only a short time before; practices by which "women of mature years and experience"—mothers— had done most family shopping for clothing. Such a transformation not only altered family patterns of consumption; it was of enormous marketing significance to the clothing industry itself. By 1922, nearly all categories of garments found their primary markets among people under thirty years of age:

> 55 percent of the buyers of "dress goods" were
>   under thirty;
> 53 percent of the buyers of ready-to-wear were
>   under thirty;
> 61 percent of the buyers of underwear . . .
> 65 percent of the buyers of hosiery[160]

Clothing manufacturers responded to and reinforced these trends, aiming merchandise primarily "to capture the interest of the younger generation." To those in the business of marketing mass fashion, daughters were far more receptive to the rhythms of the market than their mothers, whose impulses were more likely budgetary. Youth, embroiled in the "free market" courting practices of modernity, was perceived as a market whose "most absorbing problem is that of personal adornment." Merchants and manufacturers of the twenties fostered youthful, fashionable ideals, geared toward people for whom the "practical has little appeal." "Youth," it was perceived, "lives in today and allows tomorrow to take care of itself."[161]

Such a definition of "youth" cast the young as ideal consumers, unconcerned with questions of profligacy or waste; committed to an understanding of needs that placed them within the confines of a continually changing marketplace. As the older generation was often attuned to a different logic, issues of clothing and consumption occasioned considerable family conflict, then as now. Whereas in *customary* society elders taught the young, the consumer society reversed this physics, encouraging elders to look to youth for guidance. The marketplace reinforced this, needless to say, through advertising and goods, so that by the 1920s Elizabeth Hurlock noted that it was not uncommon for the young woman of between eighteen and thirty to influence the selections made by her mother.

Among immigrants, where parents held fast to tradition, this trend placed children in the role of Americanizers, instructing their parents in the ways and means of modern life. Anthony Mangano, in his autobiography, *Sons of Italy,* tells of the time when his sister finally convinced his mother to abandon the dress practices of her past: "What a triumph it was when she succeeded in persuading her to wear a hat instead of a scarf over her head, and to put away her old shawl and wear an American coat.''[162]

The finger-knowledge of the future was the province of youth, and only by following the dictates of the young could parents hope to be anything but mired in the past. In the wisdom of the garment industry, ''youth was extremely suggestive and easily led.''[163] What better group to serve as fashion leaders for the rest of society? The implicit logic, which extended beyond clothing to almost all areas of life, was that the ''first duty of the citizen is to be a good consumer.'' This was the modern patriotic wisdom of David Cohn, a former Sears executive, and a chronicler of ''morals and manners'' in the consumer age. It was a patriotic wisdom that assumed the triumph of youth over age, of the *new* over the *durable*.

Even during the Depression years, ''commercial pressure for 'correct' clothing impaled the imaginations of the young.'' As the Lynds looked at ''Middletown'' again during the 1930s, they discovered that while fewer people could afford to buy new clothes, the high school was still a scene of driven fashion consciousness, of unrelenting ''social pace.''[164]

Seen in retrospect, the interaction between fashion and youth has been a double-edged sword. Learning the idiom of fashion may make one more susceptible to imagistic propaganda of the fashion industry, but one may also employ the vernacular of dress in one's own terms. This is a sidelight of fashion consciousness. If youth was wishfully described as suggestible, it was also true that youth employed, and has continued to employ clothing as a form of rebellion. The fervor that accompanied the uses of fashion as a wedge against the ancient customs of family life has likewise been unleashed against the dictates of contemporary life.

In instructing manufacturers and designers on the intricacies of merchandising, Paul Nystrom was keenly aware of young people's capacity to *set* styles:

> The conflict of youth with convention grows out of the difficulty of learning the rules of society as set down by custom. . . . In the field of dress, as well as popular thinking and government, changes and new styles are generally sponsored by youth, and even in dress these new styles are often offered with all the ardor of revolution. The new fashion is promoted by appeals to freedom.[165]

The tendency of youth in revolt to appropriate the social language of dress has been an important feature of the last hundred years. It played a role in the dismantling of traditional social bonds, but also within social movements, both cultural and political. It is a part of the modern political sensibility, a visible statement of resistance.

The visibility of the statement, however, contributes to its ambiguity. While it serves the energies of resistance, it also can feed the smolderings of consent: as a reproducible surface, it can, itself, be merchandised; its meaning, changed. As this happens, freedom becomes something to be bought, alone. Collective origins of the image are hidden. While much of today's fashions still emulate upper-class styles, the emulation of the rebellious, self-motivated uses of the fashion vernacular is also widespread. As clothing is employed, spontaneously, to burst through the confines of convention, it can also be magnified by the channels of mass production, by the modern instruments of communication. It then becomes part of a new consensus. A voice of outrage and self-determination becomes a whimper of docile uniformity. When this process takes place, and objections are raised, the industry shrugs its shoulders and says: "The people set the styles." Most often, when this happens, the price goes up: the final insult.

11 / The Commerce of Choice

THE MAJOR accomplishment of the mass-fashion industry was its ability to plumb the wells of popular desire. Against a backdrop of historic denial, its dazzling array of wares offered the symbolism of a world turned upside down. As it became increasingly available, it was embraced with energetic fervor.

Fashion, once the prerogative of those who enjoyed leisure and economic privilege, became the insignia of freedom, available to all. Yet fashion was really an odd admixture. As it intertwined with the instruments of mass production and consumption, its "freedom" was underlined by uniformity. The success of the industry was in its capacity to produce and distribute standardized goods, laced with the lingo of individual choice and self-expression.

The contradictions that lay within the institution of mass fashion did not escape the critical eye of Paul Poiret, a designer of the old, elite school of couturiers. Poiret believed fashion design to be an art, its aura dependent upon originality and spontaneity. Mass production, he contended, robbed it of its meaning. As Walter Benjamin noted in his essay "The Work of Art in the Age of Mechanical Reproduction," when a piece of art is reproduced its commercial potential may be enhanced, but it loses some of its aura. As originals are mass-produced, Benjamin argued, the elite lose their hold on a traditional province of imagistic power.

Visiting the United States in the early years of the century, Poiret was disturbed by the translation of fashion into items of mass consumption. While respectful of America's ability to produce goods *en masse,* he saw the society as lacking in "artistic spirit." The women of America, embroiled as they were in the lure of mass fashion, seemed to lack "personality."

To Poiret, these failings were unavoidable. Massive in size and population—unlike the "little land of France"—the United States was not amenable to the "licence or libertarian customs" that were necessary to artistic creativity. America was best at displays of energy and endurance—"sport and business"—but lacking in "poets, musicians, or painters."

Looking over American society and its institution of mass fashion, Poiret concluded that there was a suppression of "feelings," a tendency toward "control."

> Its population must be canalized into rigidly straight channels, like the roads there, and protected from all risk of meeting with accident. . . . Let them not say that they expect in the future a generation of aesthetes and lovers of art.[166]

While the development of mass fashion was predicated on the coexistence of spontaneity and uniformity, this combination escaped Poiret's sensibility. Poiret's experiences, as he traveled across the country, a celebrity of fashion, only reinforced his cynicism.

Visiting a school in Chickasha, Oklahoma, Poiret was enlisted to address a group of three thousand girls on matters of color coordination. When he found that the girls had difficulty understanding his advice, he was forced to perform personal consultations for half of the audience.

> The girls' Directress gave permission to the pupils of the senior class to parade past me in order to learn from my own mouth which was the color that each

ought to adopt. Thus, I saw file by in front of me 1,500 virgins, into whose eyes I stared to discover the color of their irises, and I had to say immediately, like a seer, the tone that suited them. I said: "Blue, green, garnet," and the young ladies withdrew content.[167]

The tale evokes the unity of the assembly line and the promise of individual choice implicit in the ideology of mass fashion. From the vantage point of the girls, they were receiving the tools of individuality; for Poiret they were a parade of barely indistinguishable numbers, demanding discipline and regulation.

By the 1920s, the merchandising of individuated styles had gone beyond Poiret's parade of virgins. Fashion was increasingly promulgated by more sophisticated marketing and merchandising techniques. Insofar as "the people" had a voice in the delineation of fashion, that voice was increasingly monitored and studied to promote more effective retailing. The reconciliation of individuality and standardization demanded an elaborate and imaginative structure. Concerns like those raised by Poiret had little place within it.

As clothing was an important arena of popular expression—often a self-defined voice—the fashion industry depended on access to that expression. Access often began with the development of fashion research departments within clothing concerns. These departments, utilizing the methods of style-consulting committees, boards, or juries, kept watch on new designs before they went into production.[168] "Trends of taste" were examined, and employed more and more in the design of goods.

Fashion, perhaps more than any other area of consumption, was a piece of the marketplace that displayed an interaction between spontaneous choice and mass-produced goods. The process by which social desire was translated into commodified forms was more present within the realm of fashion—on the surface of things—than anywhere else in the unfolding consumer society. This is why the term "manipulation" is inadequate to describe fashion merchandising, although the corporate profit motive certainly plays its part in the drama. The capitalist process of producing fashion on a mass scale, rather, was a fusion of expressed, popular desire and the powerful ability to replicate that materialization in a mass-produced, mass-marketed form.

Beyond monitoring popular innovations in style, the analysis of consumer patterns took on the shape of modern consumer survey research. Past sales records were screened; sales tests and direct inquiries were pursued in the form of personal calls and field studies. There was a general development of modern retailing techniques: stock controls; inventories; customer and sales counts; unsuccessful sales studies; store-by-store customer-control studies—all were ways of attempting to measure changing tastes.[169]

While these methods may be seen as ways of trying to "paralyze the critical powers of an individual with the result that he or she follows the lead, whatever that lead may be," fashion merchandisers attempted to surround the actual sales process with an aura of individuality.[170] "One of the most important points in selling fashion goods is the necessity of individualizing every sale and of avoiding any attempt to handle either merchandise or customers in a mass way," warned Paul Nystrom.[171] Many retailers—particularly chain and department stores—ignored Nystrom's dictum; but more recently his approach has been adopted enthusiastically. Even in large department stores, serving vast herds of customers, the trend has been toward a "boutique" style of merchandising, creating the aura of a small shop within an arena of mass selling. If clothing is a symbolic route to individual freedom, all connections to the mass are best denied.

Concerned with developing responsive markets, fashion merchandisers of the twenties began to develop a more refined consumer typology. If the first clothing typology was rooted in sizing, the new typology plumbed the diversity of psyches. Attitudes and approaches to life were sorted out into a manageable bunch of personality types; each was then correlated to a fashion type.

Bullock's Department Store in Los Angeles "devised a list of personality types which [was] . . . fairly representative of the work done in this line."[172] The store developed six categories of customers, and divided women's fashion sales among them. The six were

1. Romantic—slender, youthful;
2. Statuesque—tall, remote, blonde;
3. Artistic—enigmatic, suggestive of the "foreign";
4. Picturesque—soft outline;
5. Modern;
6. Conventional—older, stouter, economical.

While definitions of types varied, all were geared toward the routinization of sales, unifying the vagaries of desire with the conformity of the marketplace. A new way of understanding oneself, in relation to society, was emerging. Linked to matters of personal decoration, it broke from a past in which *who you were* in society was a matter of social and economic class. The new structure was more superficially defined, and one's classification was, ostensibly, a matter of choice. Some might choose "Romantic," others "Artistic." Social identity, according to the schema, was there on the racks, to be bought.

Consumer types were often correlated to an appeal to intrinsic human motives and instincts, much as the advertising industry of the twenties was attempting to sell a broad variety of goods by appeal to instinct, impulse, and fundamental hungers.[173] As they developed, these "hungers" were linked to a historical tradition. Fashion, as in the bourgeois tradition of the nineteenth century, was primarily defined in terms of women. Types, styles, and colors proliferated in women's clothes, while men's clothing continued to be relatively sedate, a "cloak of morality." Along with mass fashion, women were sold a moral code of family life. Even if poor women were forced by circumstance to work outside the home, the fashion ideal was one of docility and uselessness. Women, as they bought a wardrobe and were coached to follow the lead of ever-changing fashion, became family symbols of success. Like the wives of nineteenth-century bourgeois before them, they carried the wealth, or more precisely in their case the *look* of wealth, of the family. Clothing was an objective representation, for each woman, of her husband's ability to provide for her. Mass fashion made such a display all the more possible, if, at the same time, all the less meaningful.

To Paul Nystrom, fashion represented a ray of light, a seasonal panorama of promise and change, in what was otherwise an often dismal present. Separated from customary bonds, the hunger for meaning weighed heavily over the lives of modern Americans. They were, he felt, subjects of an existential philosophy of "futility"; the burdensome reverie of mass, industrial existence. It was this condition, he argued, that made fashion-merchandising techniques so successful. The engineered individuality and aesthetics of mass fashion were, if thoughtfully merchandised, a vitalizing tonic to the "fatigue and boredom" that plagued the mass of people, caught as they were, questioning "the purpose of life itself."[174]

While Poiret had decried American mass fashion as a failure of imagination, the garment industry erected a market based on the stifled imaginations of its clientele. Within such a context, mass fashion developed as a primary channel of expression and desire. Methods of selling and of gauging the market, though predicated on productive uniformity, were geared to responding to the cries of individual and social need. As Nystrom said, evaluating the appeal of fashion:

> It is not easy to jump out of oneself, but in the effort to make such changes as are possible, it is easy enough, particularly for people who have the means, to change one's dress, and the mental effects of change of clothing are quite remarkable. . . . The desire for new sensations and the spirit of adventure . . . are powerful forces.[175]

Where it might be argued that the desire for change would be more meaningfully pursued in the realms of concerted social action, fashion offered a continually changing outlet that located personal fulfillment, a sense of self, alongside the canals of social conformity.

12 / *History and Clothes Consciousness*

WITHIN the fashion codes of nineteenth-century bourgeois life, it was a woman's role to display the economic and social success of her husband's virtue and enterprise. Though relegated to the status of a passive emblem, she was also a clarion of the moral order, proclaiming its legitimacy and its historic mission.

In the twentieth century, amid a growing challenge from socialism, the florescence of a fashionably dressed working class has served a similar function. Where working people had once looked as poor as they were, now they were able to take on the appearance of abundance. Not only did the evolution of ready-to-wear fashions appeal to the ancient desires of people schooled by scarcity; it also became one of the most splendid and cited examples of capitalist society's claim to deliver the goods, to respond to human needs. Even in the midst of dire poverty, the iconography of fashion is ubiquitous and casts its spell. Clothing has become—for more and more people—an arena of social dialogue in which desires are expressed, and symbolically met. Within the expansive parameters of fashion, questions of *class; sexuality* and *gender;* and conflicting vectors of *resistance* and *conformity* have played themselves out visibly and dramatically. In a consumer society, the language and meaning of objects are fused with those of the marketplace.

The unlikely interaction between the images of freedom and spontaneity and the uniformity of mass production and merchandising stands at the heart of this development and is the dynamic of mass fashion. But beyond this, the interaction raises fundamental questions about the industrial culture in which we live, its achievements and its contradictions. The tensions between spontaneity and uniformity speak to the issue of what it means to be a person, living in the shadows of commercial enterprise, striving for the democratic objective of self-determination for all. Adjacent to the world of fashion lies a turbulent society in conflict. Fashion bears the imprint of its dissonance and outrage, but it also temporizes.

Over the last three decades, discord and social clash have been evident upon the landscape of fashion, as they have in American culture as a whole. The 1950s, in the United States, was a period lit by the radioactive afterglow of war. If the fact of the atomic bomb made for a new sense of horror in the general consciousness, it was also—with its unfathomable expression of energy and waste—a decisive metaphor for a mature consumer culture. Insofar as *consumerism* represented the principles of conspicuous waste and the domination over nature, the atom was a potent symbol for the new way of life that was unfolding. Under the immeasurable weight of *impending doom,* a consolidation of commercial power and the growth of consumer industries gave shape to a way of life.

Fueled by the postwar economic boom, an "American way of life," permeated by the democracy of images, took hold for unprecedented numbers of people. Material circumstances changed; the architecture of daily life assumed new forms; new and uniform symbols moved beyond marks of prosperity, to being marks of *loyalty*.

Many of these new circumstances and symbols centered on the rise of suburbia. Swiftly populated by a migration of millions, the suburbs were seen as a refuge of family life away from the exigencies of urban existence. These new developments placed people, particularly women and children, away from the centers of production and commerce. The initial attraction of suburban living was that it responded to the deeply felt needs of the population—desires for autonomy and space. Against the noise, dirt, and multitude of the industrial cityscape, the suburbs claimed to elevate "family life" as a safe and private reserve, immunized from the corruption of the metropolis. Once the ideal of wealthy Victorians, "family service" was canonized as the universal feminine ideal, responsive to trends in the labor force, which were pushing women out of jobs they had assumed during the war years. Suburban plots offered a miniaturized, mass-marketed mimicry of the estates of a landed gentry. Suburban homes were standardized parodies of independence, of leisure, and, most important of all, of the property that made the first two possible. The American ideal, in the era of postwar growth, was that of the *landed consumer*. "Castles" were offered in a variety of models, each tied to a romantic, pre-industrial motif: *ranch, colonial,* and so forth.

Yet the independence and escape offered by suburban ideology never took one very far from the scrutiny of one's neighbors. The vertical configuration of the city was made horizontal, but the seclusion of the land was illusory. Consistent with the world of appearance and display, images were deceptive. Predicated on the notion of individualism, yet erected as a parade of repetition, the search for a community of individuals was overwhelmed by the imperative of display once again. "Keeping up with the Joneses" became a cliché of suburban living. Entrenched in a commitment to prosperous leisure, suburban families became a spawning ground for fierce, social competition. "Presentability" imposed its tyranny on manicured lawns, and, more and more, on manicured people. Presentation of self was an essential activity, displayed through the "picture windows" of new "developments."

Within this new theater of appearance and display, and in the lives of its inhabitants, clothing played an important part. Americans were expected to dress a certain way, and the avalanche of commercial imagery that accompanied the postwar boom—magazines; film; advertisements; and the new "Information Bomb," television—supplied constant reminders. Doris Day, *Father Knows Best*, Betty Furness, *Ronald Reagan for General Electric*—these were the voices and imagistic role models of suburbanization.

As the appearances of land and housing were supposed to be romantic replicas of the estates and ranches of a nineteenth-century landed class, clothing followed suit. The world of home and the world of work were dramatically cleaved from each other. This was echoed in the sartorial separation of women and men. Women's clothing ideals in the fifties, as materialized by the garment industry, struck close to the spirit, if not the specific prescriptions of Victorian womanhood. Leisure, delicacy, and, at times, the preponderance of cloth were marks of suburban womanhood. For "knocking around," Bermuda shorts, sports shirts, and the like provided the beginnings of a massive leisure-wear industry. Dressing up, women drew from Victorian prescriptions more specifically. Skirts flowed over stiff underlayers of crinoline; pastel colors provided a symbolic immunity from the proximity of grime and work, as it did from the exotic hues of *shameful* sensuality. Even at wifely "chores"—it was rarely referred to as "work"—women turned to the ambiguous symbolism of the "frilly apron." Sweaters, push-up bras, and girdles conspired together, focusing their effects on the reproductive components of a woman's body, not unlike the declaration made by nineteenth-century corsetry. For leisure, women wore "sneakers," like the kids. Otherwise, high-heeled shoes—to the extreme—added to the hobbled presentation of American womanhood. Amid an ideology of unsullied chastity, women were reduced to a primarily sexual identity, or to the identity of a child. Makeup, deodorants, and other visual and olfactory barriers were set up to protect womanhood from personhood. Identity was, by prescription, no more than the assembling of a "self."

Insofar as a woman held to the prescribed ideal, she became an advertisement for her own inadequacies in the world of paid work, concurrently advertising her husband's adequacy as a provider. True to the sexual ethics of Victorianism, she was delicate, childlike, unsuited for worldly engagement, the bearer of her man's (and her nation's) economic success. At the same time she was a patriotic symbol; fashion and modern appliances shared the spotlight with automobiles in the theater of national destiny.

In the emanations of the mass culture, the suburban wife was also characterized as the bearer of the guilt of sin. While the culture encouraged her to buy and assemble a fashionable veneer, her commitments to the marketplace were simultaneously ridiculed as wasteful and frivolous. Situation comedies of the time were populated by a parade of women whose primary identity was that of "mad shopper." Hobbled, decorated, infantalized, isolated, and scorned, she was ensnared in a trap not unlike that against which Jane Addams and other expatriates from Victorianism had rebelled. Within the "snare of preparation" of suburban womanhood, women were at best the receptacles of male adoration; at worst, the targets of male frustration.

The masculine ideal was also true to nineteenth-century bourgeois patterns of attitude and dress. Wearing a cloak of morality, the man went off to work in the enervating whirl of the city, giving of himself to sustain the suburban dream. The austerity of the business suit—gray flannel, pin-striped, and so on—expressed a uniform commitment to hard work, dedication to family and society, and explicitly denied spontaneity. For men, war and prosperity were intertwined by recent memory, and their sense of "duty" and economic pursuit coalesced into a style. To defend the rights of the folks "at home against the Communist threat," men were expected to submit to the terms of uniformity right down to the crewcut that was fashionable in the period. Unswerving loyalty to nation, to home, to place of work, and to the principles of consumerism was the sartorial message. So unimaginative, unemotional, indistinguishable, so bland was this masculine ideal that by the late fifties, the men's clothing industry embarked on a special campaign to sell more goods, to expand masculine interest in fashion. As the masculine ideal had been permeated by an ethic of denial, marketing strategy attempted to reach men through women: "Mothers, wives, girl friends, and secretaries," reasoned Pierre Martineau, "can do a tremendous job of exerting pressure on a man to make him dress right." The men's apparel businesses, unhappy with the economic implications of the suburban ethic, sought to mold men into a "seasonal, volatile, style-conscious class."[176]

Children in the 1950s were expected to emulate their parents, and did. The successful and popular suburban girl was a "clotheshorse"; each day at school would show her envious classmates that her closets were bulging with an endless supply of color-coordinated outfits and accessories. Boys had somewhat more latitude, since rough-and-tumble was a rite of passage on the route to the austere responsibilities of manhood. Colors were muted; cut was simple, double-reinforced at the knees; sensible—"clean-cut." If the display of cloth and decoration was requisite among girls, it was not the case for boys. An eighth-grader in 1957 made the mistake of going to school one day in a pair of red pants, bought for him by a mother unschooled in sartorial logic. As he entered his first-period math class, his pants caused an immediate commotion among classmates. His teacher was so outraged by the transgression, and so committed to the role of disciplinarian, that the boy had five points immediately subtracted from his average. At midday the boy was sent home for causing a disruption. Needless to add, he never wore his red pants again. Schools underwrote the dictates of propriety by enforcing unwritten dress codes, maintaining the standards of fashionable decorum, of social order.

On the surfaces of suburban life and in its panoply of imagery, the imprimatur of purchasable "leisure" was in force everywhere. Here was a world far from the corruptions of the city and the scarcities of a rural past. True to the patterns of Victorianism, home was a retreat from "the real world." Mass fashion adapted to this suburban motif, under the rubric of "leisure wear." All could now aspire to the symbolic language of affluence, and the postwar consumer industries were standardizing a symbolically charged mode of life that fulfilled aspirations on the monthly installment plan. "Landed" consumers had little of the social wealth or power of those whom they emulated, but they could wear the emblems of wealth and power. These emblems formed the panoply of a new, suburban conformity, beacons that illuminated an unfolding definition of American prosperity. Suburbs were an abundant theater of commodities and display.

Fortune magazine, in a marketing profile of the suburbs in 1953, noted that residents were "sharply sensitive to group opinion"; had a "large and growing 'discretionary' income" with which to buy a wide variety of consumer goods; and were psychologically "preoccupied with spending problems . . . particularly with expenditures on items that are not necessities."[177] Increasingly, argued *Fortune,* suburbs would be "the clue to the future" as far as marketing went. Here was the "average American group," which national merchandisers should target for their goods. In clothing, in automobiles, in appliances and home furnishings, suburbia provided an ideological template for the shaping of a uniform, national market. The "mythical individual" at whom businesses were encouraged to aim their products was the *suburbanite*. In a period of rapid economic growth and the intense political suspicion of McCarthyism, suburbia provided a tyranically strident and uniform measure of who *belonged* and who didn't.

Yet, ironically, as the suburban lifestyle was promoted over and over, its limits became increasingly manifest. Here was the language of "individualism," carved out of slavish conformity. "Happiness" was ghettoized in the shopping centers of regimented acquisition. In many ways, the leisure-time motif of the suburbs amounted to a philosophical statement of the contradictions of twentieth-century American development.

The suburbs were a watershed in the unfolding of Americanization and consumption. They were the "intrinsic outcome" of a society of "mobile individuals," living in an environment where production and consumption were—to all appearances—unconnected, shorn of their past, existing only for the present. Suburbia canonized an industrial system in which goods were invested with potent symbolic meaning by the marketers and promoters, a symbolism that totally obscured their source of origin. The suburban lifestyle was one in which consumption was a patriotic duty, encouraged with no hint of the social or environmental costs involved. Separated from the world of work, suburbs were islands whose inhabitants were virtually blind to the reality of the surrounding seas. Suburbia existed for itself. The rest of the world had no other function than to feed its appetite for goods.

It was this lack of vision, this insularity, that ignited a massive disaffection from the conformity of suburban

existence. While the suburbs offered a consumable apparition of leisure, they did not easily allow for an understanding of that which lay beyond its codes. Both urban
and rural existence, in spite of their shortcomings, had
made a broad world available. Their inhabitants understood much about what was inscrutable in the suburbs.
Rural Americans, and migrants from rural pasts elsewhere, had understood the ecological laws of survival.
Living off the land, depending directly upon it for their
continuity, they shared a respect for the earth, for the
nature, which bound them to the millennia of human
experience.

The cities provided a reference from this sensibility
and functioned to enlarge a world-view in other ways.
Cities did not hide the world, but gave it new dimensions,
in the flow of migrations, in a mosaic of cultures,
languages and skin tones that reverberated in the streets.
Sexual possibilities were expanded by the very proximity
of bodies. Different worlds were always in contact and
collision, as work and life commingled, inexorably intertwined. Both the country and the city, in their own ways,
brought people in touch with the world, its breadth of
cultures, its primordial drives, its terms of survival.

The suburbs were divorced from the understandings
of either. The great claim of suburban living was escape—from work, cultural multiplicity, passion—and it
set itself against the notion of land as a resource necessary to survival. In the suburbs, land itself had entered
the realm of total display. Suburbia perpetrated a vision
of the world according to the narrow categories of consumerism; it was an arena of appearance, of spending, of
retreat.

As the pre-eminent cultural ideal of the fifties, suburbia came increasingly under attack from those beyond its
margins of concern. Its conformism ate away at many
who lived, desperately and discreetly, within. The lack

of vision; the mindless spending for its own sake; the merchandised conformism began to alienate suburban youth by the end of the fifties.

Insofar as suburbia was elevated—commercially, culturally, politically—as the embodiment of "typical" America, its limits came to be seen as America's limits, and people began crying out against America. Voices banished, suppressed, or ignored in the pacific motifs of the leisure-time dream were being heard articulating an increasingly provocative critique and alternatives. The land of consumer plenty was being characterized, more and more, as one of spiritual impoverishment, sexlessness, of "one-dimensionality." Image was attacked by rhythm. Hidden cultures emerged. Music, poetry, political chants heralded the coming of resistance.

"America," wailed poet Allen Ginsberg, in a poem dated January 17, 1956, "I've given you all and now I'm nothing." To Ginsberg, and other voices of artistic opposition, America was the thief of passion and compassion; the robber of personhood, of freedom.

> *I can't stand my own mind.*
> *America when will we end the human war?*
> *Go fuck yourself with your atom bomb.*
> *I don't feel good don't bother me. . . .*
>
> *America when will you be angelic?*
> *When will you take off your clothes? . . .*
>
> *America why are your libraries full of tears?*
> *America when will you send your eggs to India?*
> *I'm sick of your insane demands.*
> *When can I go into the supermarket and buy*
> *   what I need with my good looks? . . .*
>
> *Your machinery is too much for me.*[178]

As clothing had been central to the elaboration of a suburban uniformity, it was also central to its undoing. As "Beat" poet and playwright Michael McClure explained his art, it was a vital resistance, against the backdrop of a forbidden climate of conformism.

> It was like being on an elevator containing a lot of people with crew cuts and pin-striped suits. As I looked around them, I realized that I couldn't get off the elevator unless I discovered some alchemical or superhuman way of doing it. The way to escape was to create poems that were living creatures. My hope was that my poems might become alive, become living organisms through the energy that I threw into them. I wanted poems to grow their own eyes, ears, noses, legs, and teeth.

> My poetry was not the expression of the ideas that I'd been taught by the culture, but the expression of the fleshy facts of myself that I'd discovered in spite of the culture. And I think that's what all of us were doing— we were in the act of discovering ourselves, not what we had been instructed to discover by the culture.[179]

Mass life and suburban existence were seen as strait-jackets; sartorial codes especially put the mind in uniform. Adjacent to the Beat revolt and to its powerful musical counterpart—rock 'n roll—a new style of dress was adopted. Spontaneous choices asserted themselves against the uniformity of national symbols. Pastel sports shirts were answered by denim pants and black turtlenecks, as suburbia was answered by the underworlds of work and bohemianism. Antifashion became a conspicuous weapon of outrage.

Others raised a jagged edge against the smooth informality of suburbanism. The struggle of blacks to overturn the burdens of racism and oppression was heard as a dissonant rumble against the contented quietude of suburbia. As this rumble mounted to a roar, the culture of black America shook the underpinnings of the *mainstream*. First the flashy finery of the "tenderloin," worn by such entertainers as Little Richard, then Afros, dashikis—symbols of the roots of Afro-Americans—expanded the sartorial revolt. Through music, politics, through the geyser of the *countercultural* refusal, passions suppressed or obfuscated by the consumerist conformity of the fifties erupted into the field of vision. By the mid-sixties, the world at large was battling the suburban sensibility. Peasants of Asia and Latin America, Africans, shaking the chains of colonialism, dissonant and disaffected young Americans and Europeans were collaborators in a rhythmic panorama of revolt against the values enshrined in the suburbs of the United States.

The clothes that played such an important role in this revolt were assembled from the assorted cultural battlefields upon which the process of Americanization had been fought. Self-consciously nonconformist, uniforms of work and alienation, of distant cultures and angry underworlds came together as a symbolic rejection of the bland consumerism of "typical" Americanism. Blue jeans, peasant blouses and frocks, army surplus collaborated to repudiate the standardized "democracy" of images in a return of repressed realities, worn as conspicuously as possible. These were drawn from the countless worlds scorned by the enforced compact of leisure and abundance. Labor, war, and the neglected cultures and subcultures of America (Native-American, hipster, ethnic, nudist, juvenile delinquent) inspired a revolt of sartorial sensibility. In a society predicated on the marketing of images, images became a weapon of resistance.

In the 1960s, young people appropriated outrageous admixtures of clothing as a popular form of expression. The most potent, the most sensual, the most theatrical idioms of design erupted in spontaneity and diversity along with the worlds from which they came. Almost overnight, the consumer industries of mass fashion were out of step, "out of fashion." Where fashion industries did make waves, it was on the crest of the wave of social movement. The miniskirt was an outrageous expression of rejection, aimed at the prim niceties of suburbia and fueled by an impassioned popular mood. Yet it too was part of a fashion cycle that aimed at achieving a regularity, a conformity in the market. The counterculture made such regularity elusive and unmanageable. Diana Vreeland, editor of *Vogue* magazine since 1962, described the breakdown of the fashion mainstream during the sixties:

> A youthquake was starting. High society had disintegrated incredibly . . . suddenly it seemed everyone had gravitated to his own private world and the center was lost. Meanwhile, the young did things their way without regard to the old world. And anyone who wasn't with them made no difference at all.[180]

The fashion industry, successful for decades in dictating the sartorial definitions of democracy on a seasonable basis, was now chasing the public from behind. Fashion, or antifashion, was riding the crest of popular initiative. Images and meanings were actively constructed; clothing was increasingly an exercise in imagination, in unpredictability. A proliferation of new and powerful surfaces represented a shift of creative initiative, from the design rooms of industry to the emancipated intuition of people in search of autonomy and personhood.

Yet if it appeared for a time that mass fashion had been overturned by this outpouring of popular expression, the sixties was *rather* a period in which the machinery of mass fashion was forced to confront its limits, to adjust itself.

The culture of the fifties was built on the ability to fabricate images and meanings and to distribute them *en masse*. A uniform and mass-produced culture was inoculated by the imagery of casual leisure, sold as a national product. Yet the superficiality of suburban identity made it eminently vulnerable. Piercing through the veneers of suburban life, many people confronted the general discontent, the cultural price paid by people in an industrial, consumer culture: standardization, monotony, the eradication of social bonds and understandings, a "philosophy of futility."

If the power of surface imagery sustained the development of the suburban landscape, it also contributed to its undoing. The ability to assume surfaces of meaning provided radical youth in the sixties with an essential tool of revolt. The revolt established alternative imagery, alternative information, alternative meaning as the conspicuous agents of political and cultural display.

Clothing was a prime vehicle of repudiation. If the mainstream imagery propagated a sharp demarcation of gender and the insularity of a nuclear family, alternative imagery challenged notions of gender and raised the question of communalism to the fore. If the dominant culture clothed gray industrialism in the Dacron pastels of suburbia, the counterculture examined the principle of play in the cotton garments of work. If the fifties was a time when to be "un-American" was to be immediately suspect, the sixties assumed the vestments of unassimilated ethnicity, particularly of the Third World. If the fifties had promoted the nobility of the cowboy and his expansionist violence, the clothing of the sixties spoke up for the Indian with beads and headbands. The staunch sexual divisions of suburban life were answered by motifs that made gender increasingly ambiguous. The olive-drab of war was turned against itself, becoming a uniform of pacifism. The capacity to give images and meanings to objects, so exploited by the vernacular of the consumer society, was turned against itself with a vengeance. Clothing of revolt became all the more possible among people schooled by a world in which meanings and images were infinitely manipulable. The consumer society, with its heavy implantation of imagery, had supplied its opposition with the visual terminology of revolt.

The phenomenon of mass fashion had begun nearly one hundred years before, at a time when capitalism was under widespread attack as a social system. For laboring people, squalor and exploitation had marked the emergence of the industrial system. "Wage slavery" and vast chasms of possibility shaped their experiences. Slowly the modern ready-to-wear garment industry emerged, sharing a potent image-making capacity with other emerging industries of mass impression. A democracy of images, compelling and promising, began to define the landscape of a new industrial, consumer culture.

Rising from a world in which formal and informal sumptuary laws had predominated, mass fashion appropriated the symbolic codes of status and made them available on a mass scale. For people nurtured by denial and living in a world increasingly defined by the principles of appearance and display, mass fashion served as a powerful lens of expectation. The democracy of images came together, promising to fill the thirsty wells of hope, of long-standing desires.

By the 1950s the tradition of mass fashion was deeply entrenched. The ability to standardize the imagos of leisure and status had been refined, reaching a point where these had become the clichés of a mass-produced existence. The lure of mass fashion, heralded in the twenties as the apotheosis of an industrial capitalist democracy, was now under assault as a desert of perpetual sameness.

The 1960s, in a cultural insurgence, redefined the terms of opposition, of challenge to industrial life. Where mass fashion had once appealed to the hungers of new, industrial citizens, now it evoked a sense of cultural famine. The sartorial radicalism of the sixties posed an articulate statement of alienation from the confines of suburbanism, establishing new sartorial idioms. These reflected, far more than the uniform fabrications of the fifties, the wishes and desires, the concerns and aspirations, of Americans coming of age during the post–

World War II era. Donning blue jeans offered an egalitarian repulsion against the symbolic luxuries of imitation. Putting on a dashiki was a turning away from the western European aesthetic, which had motivated fashion and dominated the marketplace. Peasant blouses celebrated the simplicity of rural life above the artifices of modernity. Responding to Ginsberg's wail, when America took off its clothes, it repudiated the conventional promises of mass fashion. Sartorial revolt provided a brilliant imagistic rendering of social demands and popular expressions.

Within this context, fashion merchandising evolved a response, attempting to appropriate and reproduce its visual language of resistance. As mass fashion in the nineteenth century had engaged the hopes of an industrial population, the marketers of the 1970s engaged, more and more, the critique of industrial uniformity. A mass fashion has emerged, over the past ten years, which draws its style and structure from the questions of the sixties. Images of refusal, autonomy, and cultural diversity, permeated by patterns of sexual liberation and working-class culture, are the warp and woof of recent fashion marketing. The language of diversity and revolt, born in an outrage against a merchandised reality, has entered the parlance of merchandising. The genius of a consumer society, to translate popular aspirations into the terms of the marketplace, has asserted itself once again.

The sartorial revolt of the 1960s was not merely a presentation of different clothing styles. It was also a voice of people whose lives could not be lived within the constrictions of the fifties' cultural conservatism. The radicalism was, to a large extent, a statement by people of who they were, who they had become, how the terms of American society had made the dictates of suburbanism impossible for them. In assuming a new way of dressing, people were saying much about who they were.

Though the voices are quiet today, the visual and conspicuous statement of sixties radicalism provided a wide range of industries with a powerful lesson in marketing, in diversification. If within the clothing styles of the sixties lay new and critical understandings of family life, sexual life, notions about work and consumption, and questions of cultural identity, the fashion industry from the early seventies onward has produced goods that are, largely, a response to this challenge. The sartorial mode of resistance produced the pattern by which the clothes of the present are cut and sold. T-shirts; jeans; pants-suits for women; peasant, gypsy, western and outlaw styles; the embroideries of non-western ideals, the influence of homosexual culture within the styles worn in the culture at large; all of these trends have been drawn from the critical repository of the sixties.

A look across the pages of fashion magazines reinforces the pattern. Today there is no fashion; there are only *fashions*. The diversity of revolt has been translated into a diversity of markets. The entire historical and cultural panorama of clothing is available. Blue jeans are high fashion; emblems of egalitarianism become weapons of social competition and sexual struggle. Discos enforce sumptuary laws, requiring clientele to be dressed in the now elevated finery of "designer jeans"; laws of exclusivity persist, turned on their heads. Original meanings are lost or rearranged, as designer Calvin Klein proclaims: "Jeans are sexual. Why do you think people buy jeans?" Alongside designer jeans, the delicate armors of Victorian womanhood can be purchased. With women increasingly entering the work force, mannish clothing becomes the garb of employability, shorn of its earlier, rebellious meaning. Even the styles of the "Ivy League" fifties have made a comeback in the pseudo-tongue-in-cheek form of the "Preppie look."

Elsewhere are the notorious garments of "shameful love." Sold boldly from shop windows, such items are also available at suburban buying parties, not unlike those formerly reserved for such domesticated items as Tupperware. Against the sharp challenge of cultural and political diversity posed in the 1960s, recent developments in fashion have seen an unfolding of market diversity. The images come from everywhere. The history of fashion, in all its contradiction, has imprinted itself, in symphony, upon the surfaces of the marketplace. Its multiplicity of display dazzles—a break from the convention of standardized ideals—while the objective terms of daily life become increasingly dull, decreasingly promising.

Today's fashions are completely impregnated by the claim that they too make war against uniformity; they enhance one's ability to "do one's own thing." Matched ensembles, once a garment-industry staple, have given way increasingly to interchangeable components. In fashion pages, women are encouraged to blaze a "personal path through the plethora of current fashion" in assembling the styles that fit their lives.[181]

Looking back to a time when fashion codes were inviolable, Enid Nemy writes that the old rules no longer stick. "The old signals aren't working, and there aren't any new decipherable ones. . . . Women now are wearing what they like, not what they're told to like."[182] In a flourish of libertarian lingo, fashion writers inform readers that "all of the old rules for what to wear, when to wear it and where, have been tossed out."[183] Such statements come in magazines, flanked by ads that likewise promise freedom, independence, uniqueness, status.

No rules, only choices is the current claim; selling goods is still the game. The parameters of freedom are circumscribed, once again, by a renovated strategy of the market. Learning a lesson from the outbreak of sartorial autonomy that characterized the fashion vernacular in the sixties, today's fashions offer the weapons of resistance and compliance in one, ready to wear. Image and information, recast and readapted to the machinery of fashion marketing, to the politics of culture, assert a revolt against conformity once again. A multiplicity of imagery abounds; meaning is lost. The sartorial tools of social revolt provide the fashions and surfaces of a society gripped by quietude. Next to them, on the shelves, lie the sartorial tools of constriction, the cloaks of morality. It is all there. Everyone can be anyone.

In fashion, as in much of the imagery of a mass culture, we confront the echoes of our own desires. The history of mass fashion is one of a powerful conjuration, implanting the idiom of people's longings upon the outer textures of corporate enterprise; beneath the surface lies a continuity of frustration, a squelching of initiative. A perpetual vernacular of critical, popular expression—torn from the confines of the marketplace—is the only alternative to the echo of mass fashion, to the claims made by a democracy of images.

Part Five

Mass Culture and the Moral Economy of War

1 / Through a Glass Darkly

IN 1835 there occurred a fateful event in the history of modern consciousness. In late August of that year, the *New York Sun*, one of the first mass, commercial newspapers, published a series of articles on astronomer Sir John Herschel's telescopic surveillances of the moon from his observatory at the Cape of Good Hope, Southern Africa.

The first in the series described the telescope in some technological detail. The machine was a hybrid of science and magic: Its lens was "24 feet in diameter, and weighed nearly 15,000 pounds after it was polished; its estimated magnifying power was 42,000 times." Herschel, the *Sun* reported, believed that his instrument would make him a seer amid the unfolding of technical discovery. It would allow him "to study even the entomology of the moon, in case she contained insects upon her surface."[1]

The installments that followed were a temptation in the religion we call "progress." Readers were provided with a description of the lunar surface and of the shady vegetation that flourished there. Then, in a wooded valley, the scientist "beheld continuous herds of brown quadrupeds, having all the external characteristics of the bison."[2]

The articles were the work of Richard Adams Locke, a relation of John Locke, and star reporter for the *Sun*. Needless to say, the articles were a hoax. The alleged source for the articles, the Edinburgh *Journal of Science,* was—at the time—defunct. Herschel, himself, continued his work at the Cape of Good Hope, totally ignorant of the stories' appearance. He was a victim of a new development in communication: the mass-circulation, commercial press. It would be decades before he could have been promptly informed by another: submarine telegraph lines. As he sat there at the tip of Africa, the stories about him took on the character of *fact* in New York City. Despite the fictional roots of the articles, the most important thing about them was their *facticity.* People believed them. The burgeoning network of printed newspapers spread the word further. Whatever doubts there were were expressed cautiously. Academics sought out the printed accounts, in the spirit of inquiry. A media audience took shape.

By the time the silken, copper-colored humanoids appeared, the whole world was watching. Unlike the busy, urban, industrializing people who were reading about them, these moon creatures glided on diaphanous membranes linking hand and foot; they were "winged creatures" who, far from being "engaged in any work of industry or art . . . spent their happy hours in collecting various fruits in the woods, in eating, flying, bathing, and loitering about upon the summits of precipices."[3] At the far end of mechanical science—it might have been argued—lay paradise. People toiled under the *truth* of it.

What was so believable about this world that stood beyond the edges of common sense? Clearly this is a question of historic significance. It speaks to the structures of perception and understanding that germinated in the industrial epoch. The mass media placed their version of sense and order upon existence. The ability to forge *reality* was an early capacity of print, a capacity constantly enlarged by subsequent devices for storing and disseminating information. As the *word*, as the *image* is reproduced, again and again, it becomes *fact*, known simultaneously by strangers. It is the lifeblood of a mobile world-system employing standardized meanings and requiring standardized understandings. *Fact!* is seen, over and over again, repeated by itself, repeated by others. When it is stored, it becomes a history. Against the random and irretrievable quality of daily life lies the tangible evidence of the printed word, of the graven image, of the fact. Its presence is awesome, and the tale of Richard Adams Locke's "moon hoax" reveals this power as a discovery.

The mass media are basic to the modern secular system of belief. Although the printed Bible stood at the center of the Protestant revolt, its claims were primordial. The printed, widely circulated daily newspaper, on the other hand, was also a child of modernity. Its spectacle was the forerunner of all the media spectacles to come. Its audience was one increasingly tossed in a mobile and expanding world; experience provided only a hazy tunnel of perception. Literacy was ennobled as the tool of liberty, while the newspaper began depicting the world in broadside. Thomas Paine or Frederick Douglass could reveal the emancipatory promise of literacy; but the "moon hoax" revealed its awful power, even in a time when today's commercial networks of images, messages, and audiences were only first taking hold.

The publishers of these papers, scions of early industrial capitalism, were aware of their mighty force. James Gordon Bennett, publisher of the *New York Herald*, waxed eloquent about the historic potential of the daily "penny press." In the light of the "moon hoax" and its impact, Bennett's puffery takes on a menacing wisdom.

> What is to prevent a daily newspaper from being made the greatest organ of social life? Books have had their day—the theatres have had their day—the temple of religion has had its day. A newspaper can be made to take the lead of all these in the great movements of human thought and human civilization. A newspaper

> can send more souls to Heaven, and save more from
> Hell, than all the churches and chapels in New York—
> beside making money at the same time.[4]

Benjamin Day of the *Sun* expressed similar goals for
the penny press. Mobilizing and standardizing opinion
stood at the height of his journalistic aspirations. Speaking in terms of New York's "laboring classes and the
mechanics," Day claimed that "already we can perceive
a change in the mass of the people. They think, talk, and
act in concert."[5]

If Herschel's miraculous instrument couldn't find insects on the surface of the moon, the nascent mass media
could and did. With the moon hoax we see the inner life
of "objectivity"; the ability of a universal marketplace,
and its structures of communication, to construct webs
of meaning, a panorama of perception. The ubiquity of
the image became the groundwork for a new and compelling *truth*.[6]

To this day we still experience the reverberations of
this "moon hoax" syndrome. It has become normal.
Consumable facts, words, and images are generalized
and infinite. Media images permeate the fabric of perception; they are among the weighty facts of our lives. With
the addition of each new realm of mediation—photography, radio, computers, and the entry of new elements
into the vernacular of understanding—there is a major
eruption of the syndrome. One hundred three years after
the moon hoax had consecrated the believability of the
commercial press, Orson Welles and the Mercury Theater of the Air did the same for radio, with their news-
broadcast rendition of H. G. Wells' *War of the Worlds*.
Within eighteen years of radio's inception as a commercial institution of mass listenership, it had penetrated the
human sensibility. This time, the general anxiety of the
modern world-rhythm was tapped by a Martian landing
in New Jersey, believed to be true by many.[7]

So in tune are people to the ability of media to verify the fantastic, to assemble truth out of motive or fantasy, that the 1969 landing of men on the moon was viewed by many as a trick, performed in a television studio: skepticism underwritten by self-conscious gullibility.

In written histories of the media, the above survive as anecdotes with a comical edge. Yet they are significant. Within an industrial regime, they serve to map out the modern terms of knowledge and information. Imagination becomes domesticated as the raw material of the "fact." The terrors and hopes of the imagination are channeled by the positivity of the fungible fact; structured by its reproducible certainty.

2 / *Channels of Fear*

A COVER STORY in the April 1980 issue of *Esquire* announced a shift in the American sensibility. Coming out of the Vietnam war and a decade or more of social activism, the magazine noted America had lapsed into an era of poignant self-examination. "We paid attention to us," said the *Esquire* article. "Us. U.S. was us, and U.S. acknowledged it—'You, you're the one.' " The scope of this sensibility was broad. Social, political, economic, spiritual, and personal lives were permeated by an ethic of ME-ism.

As *Esquire* saw it, geopolitical events brought an end to all that. While moralistic condemnations of the "culture of narcissism" served to intensify the personal guilt associated with structured individualism and self-centeredness, *now*, at last, we had been *"Saved!"*

> *Saved!* by the man in the turban and *Saved!* by 80,000 Soviet troops but mostly *Saved!* by . . . [the] discovery of the new ethic and language about to color our view of the nation. No longer did we hear about a government "as good and honest, decent, truthful, and competent and compassionate and as filled with love as are the American people." . . . Suddenly we heard about strength and power and superpower and cold war. . . . And not only was it cold, it was mean. Cold war meant toughness. It meant suspicion. It meant aggressiveness and competitiveness and firmness. It meant team play. . . . It meant business. It

> meant Hard Line. In short, enlisted men and women of
> the Western world, it meant—means—exactly the op-
> posite of what you've been used to for the last few
> years.[8]

Insofar as "narcissism" had become a central theme
in the media broadsides and pop culture of the seventies,
Esquire's estimation of the situation was correct. Spectacles of national sensibility, as well as tirades of moral
outrage against them, seem to rise and fall like so many
other campaigns emanating from national advertisers
and image-makers. In the annals of the spectacle, each
moment has its brand name, its trademark. Those who
worried over the preponderant idiom of *self* that characterized the latter part of the seventies were able to take
heart, for it appeared that the good old world of authority
and discipline might return.

Yet while the mass culture may tend to generate a
nomenclature for every present, as it eradicates the past,
the social phenomenon called "narcissism" is of special
concern—neither as the bevy of activities, commodities,
and slogans that celebrate "MY needs," nor as a criticism of others, but rather as a structuring of needs and
desires through self-involved (mobile-individualistic)
terms of gratification. Narcissism has been symptomatic
of a general trend in the emergence of *mass culture* itself
since the seventeenth century. More specifically, the rise
of a world-market system; the development of the Protestant ideal of salvation and individual mobility; the development of industrial cities, factories, bureaucracies;
the *enlightened* abandonment of community structure
and ritual; and the universal penetration of a wage system of survival—all have generalized the *self* as the
highest form of existence. In personal and productive
life, as Warren Susman has argued, "the rituals of the
external church grew feebler, while the needs of the
inner self grew stronger."[9] Bearing one's own cross may

be the signal of rugged individualism, but it is also neu-rotic. In Freud's view, the elimination of totemic struc-tures did not do away with their function; it only person-alized that function and loaded it upon our tattered and isolated souls.[10]

The historic fragmentation of social life is a basic component of our understanding of the character of a *mass culture*. The displacement of collective modes of living, work, ritual, and sensibility makes room for the elaboration of a media panorama, consumed and under-stood by people individually. Ultimately, within a rising, universal marketplace, *consumerism* is the basic social relationship replacing customary bonds. It is sanctified by the Puritan admonition that salvation is a matter of *you*, and *you alone* . . . before God. It is secularized as the social form of a mass culture, of modernization. The universe of the commodity looms large with pain and promise over *the consumer*. Much of what we experi-ence reinforces this, particularly within the framework of urban, industrial life. The *self* becomes the haunted re-pository of sensitivity, vulnerability, and emotion, of need and desire. The *commodity* increasingly invades the realm of satisfaction. The utopian struggle is caught between the two.

The very term "mass culture" underwrites this per-spective. Mass culture is founded in the mass production of *the word*, and its dissemination as a commodity. As the self stands alone, the word of God, or the printed word, or media in general, or the facts, confront one with a universal image. Mass culture is for those who have become masses. The viability of a capitalist mass culture is predicated on the assumption that all others—other than ourselves—are strangers. Often, experience gives meaning to this perception. As Raymond Williams has put it:

> The masses are always others, whom we don't know, and can't know. Yet now, in our kind of society, we

see these others regularly, in their myriad variations; stand, physically beside them. They are here, and we are here with them. And that we are with them is of course the whole point. To other people, we also are masses. Masses are other people. . . . In an urban industrial society there are many opportunities for such ways of seeing.[11]

There is another side to the problem of "narcissism," or to the ways in which social life has been fragmented and plundered. Precisely as capitalism's rise has meant the decline of many of the customary bonds of mutual dependency, it has erected and elevated new systems of unification and dependence: systems of communication and transport; agencies of mass production and mass impression. The "moon hoax" reveals their sensual potency at an early age. These systems are highly unified and collectivized in their own terms. Advertising, for example, has been called upon to organize masses of strangers into reliable, national markets of consumers. As former head of the National Endowment for the Humanities Ronald Berman has approvingly observed, "Advertising is engineered social order."[12] The goal of the advertising industry is to link the isolated experience of the spectator with the collectivized impulses and priorities of the corporation. The contingencies of the *self* will be thwarted by the unity of the commodity and the facts of the marketplace. In the commodity lies a newly realized self, the promise of community. It is the most widely disseminated interpretation of *what could be*, and it, too, is a hoax.

Insofar as media imagery constitutes a system of unification, it has been employed to organize populations for patriotism, for self-denial, and for war. The general structure of a mass culture makes such mobilization increasingly possible. Recent times have witnessed such a development: a convergence of ominous imagery of different, vastly different sorts, which we will simply call "the coming war." This is not a prophecy, but a metaphor for the broad panorama of mass culture that has recently emerged in the United States. It is important because it is what people see; it links people to an understanding, or a misunderstanding, of the world.

Whether or not there will be an actual war is a matter to be settled by our coming history. But either way, "the coming war" has emerged as a basic thread in much of what we consume in the way of image and information. In *its* broadside, *Esquire* has announced this as a shift in sensibility, a new spirit of *team play* replacing concerns for *self*. But surely, without prejudice toward *Esquire*, one has not replaced the other. Within a mass culture, they perpetually coexist. On the one hand, the current war hysteria may be understood as the rise of a national jingoism; a collectivized—albeit dangerous—sensibility. On the other, we are informed that a more aggressive U.S. presence around the world may be the only defense for our "standard of living." That is to say, for the "narcissistic," consumerist, and estranged style of life promulgated within the tableau of American consumer society.

3 / *Individualism as Conformity*

AS capitalism has evolved a consumption-oriented mass culture, social, economic, and political power have become increasingly coordinated and consolidated. To a large extent, the rise of modern management, communications, production, and distribution has been dependent on the appropriation and mobilization of technical and organizational capacities by a ruling, monopoly-capitalist class, administered by an emergent sector of professional/managerial intelligentsia.[13] This increased coordination at the top levels of society has entailed increasing fractionalization throughout the remaining, popular majority. In this systemic, organizational inequity, the appeal of advertising, for example, must be understood in a cultural context in which the social status, employment, and even survival of people are separated from customary networks of skill and association. In a world of strangers, survival is to a large extent a matter of appearance and surface impressions. Already by 1899, Thorstein Veblen noted that the constant mobility of an industrial population places people in a context where they are judged, more and more, by their ability to "display goods."[14] The atomized self becomes the vehicle for general conformity.

Yet the examples of this organizational inequity are not limited to the arenas of the consumer marketplace. The unity of the atomized self and general standards of conformity, which may at one moment fuel our critique of consumer narcissism, may in the next find its complement in the political mobilization of a population toward war. Here, too, we observe the aesthetic resources of capitalist society converging to address a culturally scattered population. Their reunification will be seen in the cemeteries and veterans' hospitals.

In the 1930s, evaluating the rise of German fascism, Walter Benjamin argued that "war and war only" could engender mass action on such a broad scale, while at the same time "respecting the traditional property system," and the popular disunity it engenders. In Benjamin's estimation, war was the apotheosis of mass culture, the ultimate expression of a politics rendered aesthetic. If *economic* consumerism tends to organize disconnected individuals into coherent and predictable markets, it is *political* consumerism that defines the current state of western democracy seeking to create a vast patriotic unity—a unity without solidarity. To Benjamin, the mass culture of war was one that could generate mass mobilization while at the same time posing no evident threat to the property system.[15]

The current situation in the United States provides ample support for Benjamin's argument. At a time of general dislocation, when social fragmentation is rampant and aggravated, the re-emergence of a military nationalism is threatening to become the basis for a new-found unity. The panorama served up by the mass media is increasingly and variously oriented toward the possibility of war—particularly fateful as U.S. capitalism experiences a general crisis in its ability to deliver on the post–World War II promises of suburban abundance. Where Jane Russell was once the image-embodiment of the Marshall Plan—her bountiful breasts exported as a filmic promise of American nurturance on screens around the world—today's media images present a leaner and more tortured ideal.

The powerful role played by the mass media in modern life is both a function and a reflection of a society in which customary culture has been dismembered. Despite widespread but fragmented opposition, the various media provide people with a blistered way of understanding, of seeing the world they inhabit. Given a renewed war euphoria, it is important for us to look at that window, to see the ways it has contributed to this development, the ways it frames what is then called "reality." Through the media, we see the most available and imposing panorama of the social world.

4 / *Windows on the World*

TABLOID JOURNALISM in New York City presents an urban population with a mediated vision of their own environment and experience. Using the police blotter as the source of information, these papers magnify the horrors of city life; they trivialize acts of compassion under the rubric *good samaritanism*. Collective escape from the terms of the commodity-society is represented characteristically by stories about Jonestown and the People's Temple; alternative culture is eternally equated with barbarism. Daily life at its most atomized level—where others are not merely strangers, but predatory strangers—becomes the mediation of *experience* via the press. A half-hour with the *New York Post* each evening, and one feels lucky to have arrived home alive that day.

Overall, the media present us with a vision of chaos and disorganization. The disjointed format of "objective" news reporting—whether in the *National Enquirer* or the *New York Times*—adds to the chaos, and poses it as truth. Comprehensibility, connections between seemingly disparate items, is—for the most part—taboo. Some of what we see is distant, other is close to home; yet what unifies everything is its disunity. The vision is that of a world gone mad, a vision not unconnected to the choreography of our daily lives. The chaos of the media world is one that speaks to the chaos of existence, and meets our glance in a world where alternative networks of analysis are few and far between. The world-view of chaos—as projected by the media array—is intrinsically *narcissistic*, not in the sense that it talks about the self, but in that it re-enacts the shattered experience of the self on the level of a spectacle, a spectacle to be consumed. Mass life provides fertile soil for the consumption of the media panorama. In the media, "free-floating anxiety"—the psychopathology of everyday life—is made visible, is objectified before our eyes. Disconnected thoughts are organized into stories, each of which floats on pages enacting a general climate of danger, fear, and desire. Inner life is paraded before us, validated by a format that calls itself "objective."

In our eyes, in our ears, in our minds, the disparate images of a mass culture rendezvous to create a coherent vision of incoherence. Both our experience and the general media panorama underwrite the need for some kind of unity, some kind of bond, some kind of solution; an action or re-integration that will settle the chaos. Yet insofar as the mass culture posits and reflects a narcissistic disunity, it also generates its prescribed terms of order. In multiplying the evidence of fragmentation, it also, now, begins to articulate the terms of assimilation into order. The terms are war, or—more precisely—authoritarianism: the *moral economy of war*.

Glaring from the headlines, from the advertising pages, from the business section, from "sports," the terms of unification are established. Some of this may come to us in the form of centralized directives—administration policies broadcast as moralistic admonitions:

CARTER . . . SEES NEED FOR PAIN AND DISCIPLINE,

reads the front-page headline of the *New York Times*, March 15, 1980. Budget cuts in the public sector; increased military expenditure; Carter, Reagan, or Central Casting's candidate for president, John Anderson . . .

all these become the social infrastructure for unity, for moral fiber, for a population making a collective pilgrimage toward austerity. Unity will be built on the shoulders of personal guilt. To believe the editorial rhetoric, we are paying the wages of sin for the self-indulgent seventies, the activist sixties, and the fabulous fifties.

The front page of the *New York Post*, January 18, 1980, declares:

WHITE HOUSE TALKS OF NUCLEAR WAR.

Apocalypse is the news of the day. On page three, where the story begins, we learn that "no White House official has discussed such a possibility on the record," and that even in private, discussions have focused for the most part on conventional military response. Given the structure of the message, we are relieved. There will be merely WAR, not NUCLEAR WAR! Opening with the proposition of total annihilation, we are continually comforted by the restraint of those in power. In life there is chaos; in authority, and on the editorial pages, there is order. This has been a convention of commercial journalism since the mid-nineteenth century. A relation of power is reaffirmed in the structuring of information: coordination of those in power, fragmentation for the rest of us.

The moral economy of war is also general and indirect: an ether through which the senses are informed. Much of what we see tends to generate a social and political climate *associated* with war crises, and with the mobilization of unity. Popular literature undergoes metamorphosis. The *Wall Street Journal* (March 9, 1979) informs us that "Joseph Heller gave war a bad name in his best-selling novel [*Catch 22*]. So did James Jones with *The Thin Red Line* and, more recently C. D. B. Bryan with *Friendly Fire*. They made it all sound so grim and antiheroic." The *Journal* indicates that recent trends in mass-market paperback publishing are reevaluating this negativism. "Now the war-book market is rediscovering glory and idealism." Bantam Books is leading the way, we are informed, toward a more pro-war position. Military literature, as published by Bantam, is moving toward a more "positive" definition of war. World War II will provide the proper context for this rediscovery. Quoting the general editor of the Bantam war-book series, the article informs us that "Men were admirable [in World War II]. They weren't just sitting around blowing smoke and listening to rock bands all day. They were admirable men." Among the alternative role models being offered are Nazi war heroes. Says another editor of the series, "There's something to be said for valor and for war, no matter whose side you're on."

Elsewhere, the advertising column of the *New York Times* (December 4, 1979) reports on a speech delivered by Lawrence Fouraker, dean of the Harvard Business School. Speaking to the Association of National Advertisers, Fouraker suggested that those who sit on the boards of major "news gathering organizations—both print and broadcast—should supervise the editorial as well as the business side" of the operation. Corporate direction of news and information finds its roots in war (i.e., George Creel's notorious Committee on Public Information, established during the First World War), and is projected as a legitimate curtailment within the context of war. The further consolidation of the agencies of mass impression can be seen in the lately announced merger of J. Walter Thompson, the world's largest advertising agency, with Hill and Knowlton, the world's largest public relations firm, into what newspapers have described as a "monster image machine," a "giant image-making conglomerate handling many of the country's most powerful corporations." Against the chaos of the media panorama, the merger promises a move toward the greater unity of images.

The racial component of war mobilization has been

introduced with the news that one or more Nobel prize winners—America's wise men—have donated their wizened sperm for the purposes of fathering a master race. In war, historically, issues of racial purity and racial mission provide a particularly pernicious basis for unity. The marriage between wars of conquest and wars of racism is too long to chronicle here, even within the limited horizon of American history.

The terms of unification are broadcast in a wide range of policies. Of particular interest are those policies aimed at dealing with hunger. For years, the corporate-liberal ideology hung on the notion of "the pursuit of happiness." It was fundamental to the rhetoric of the American dream, and continued—in distorted fashion—into the rhetoric of the 1970s. Where food shipments were once the generally proposed response to famine, today's picture increasingly suggests the feasibility of an alternative solution: genocide. *Triage* is presented as "responsible" social policy. The term has military roots in the First World War—the wounded were divided into three groups, with the most seriously wounded left to die. Today the terminology has gained currency within the civilian context, applied as a solution for East Bengal, for the South Bronx. The logic of war, with its conspicuous consumption of human life, becomes a source for the conceptualization of peace.

The above examples, culled from the media, offer direct and indirect ways in which policies of corporate and state authority are played out as visions of unification and order against the general mural of chaos. The media also have mechanisms for organizing our personal lives—though they may be isolated and insular—into the semblance of unity. If social dislocation is the way modern life is experienced—narcissistically—there are times that the media hold before us a vision, an image of ourselves, collectively, in union. Against the isolation of experience, there is something rather compelling about these spectacles of coherence, if not of camaraderie. These spectacles come in a variety of forms, but the general tendency is to create an "objective" environment of opinion, to pose a window on "reality," which sets the terms of some kind of fictional public discourse.

While in our day-to-day lives, in our thoughts, in private discussions among friends, there is little sense that we are engaged in a general, democratic process, this is reified for us within the public displays of the mass culture. One day, Carter announces the reinstitution of the draft registration. The next day the media, using a "man in the street" motif, tell us that America's youth support this move. Scattered interviews with "representatives" of "America's youth" express a willingness, a fervor regarding the question of the draft. Who are we within this imaginary context? If we agree, the media has represented and unified our voice. If we disagree, we feel isolated, under siege.

The most prevalent form of this kind of "vulgar populism" can be found in the proliferation of polling, the most characteristic mode for American democracy. We are confronted with numbers, with percentages. They are us; we are them. The subjectivity of critical judgment reverberates against a wall of "evidence." Here, sociology is revealed—in the most general sense—as the underpinning of ideology: Positivism and quantification erect an edifice of incontestability. An example is drawn from a nationwide ABC News–Harris survey of early February 1980. As reported in the papers (*New York Post*, February 27, 1980), we see ourselves, unified, integrated within a tangible body of public opinion:

AMERICA WOULD GO TO WAR
TO HALT REDS ABROAD

In one of the most dramatic public opinion reversals ever, most Americans now say they'd back the use of U.S. troops to defend nations facing a Soviet invasion. Solid majorities in a new poll would support armed intervention to protect Western Europe, the Persian Gulf, Pakistan and Iran. . . .

In the mid-1970s, the vast majority of Americans were unwilling to support the use of troops almost anywhere in the world.

That sentiment remained in vogue until Moslem militants in Teheran took Americans hostage last November.

Now, the poll of 1198 likely voters, conducted early this month, found these views:

• If the Red Army moved into Western Europe, 67 percent say the use of U.S. troops would be justified; 23 percent say it would not. . . .

• By 75–18 percent, a wide majority backs the new Carter doctrine to use troops to defend the Persian Gulf oil routes.

• A 53–35 percent majority favors armed intervention to help defend Pakistan in the event of a Soviet attack.

• Remarkably, in view of the continuing hostage crisis, a 53–37 percent majority would back sending troops to Iran to fight Russians.

Within the framework of the poll, the source and framing of questions comes from policymakers, those in power. They establish the terms of what might happen. Yet the sociological component of the story is the most essential. In this and in other polls we see ourselves, brought together into groups of people, groups that don't exist. The individualized structure of experience is mirrored within a palpable collectivity that claims to reflect the voice of the people, yet generally reflects the interests and agendas of corporate and governmental policy. As Ann Landers gives us samples of how we feel individually, the polls tell us how we feel collectively. The abstraction of numbers, by which we see ourselves, reproduces our own abstraction from the contexts of community, and from active, political collectivity. We must turn to the polls, because they provide a symbolic escape from the provinciality of experience, as they provincialize our experience. In the polls, we become a part of the spectacle, of the primary, allowable unity, the universal idiom of a mass culture. Yet as we do this—as we are spectators to our own opinions—we are rarely cognizant of the ways in which sociology is one of the most potent legitimizations of ideology, codifying militarism as the ostensible will of the people.

If polls provide a cold and "objective," numerical escape from the qualities of private experience, the media also use the idiom of personal life as a way of symbolically humanizing what are cold and objectivist decisions coming from the highest levels of collectivized power. An example is a *New York Times* article (December 2, 1979) that cited "administration officials, members of Congress, specialists on foreign policy and others, liberals as well as conservatives," projecting their perspective as an estimation of what is euphemistically called "public opinion."

Yet where "public opinion" is sometimes presented in sociological terms, in this example it is couched completely in the idiom of the individual psyche. The article, in which policymakers offer their estimation of the broad "attitudinal" implications of the "Hostage Crisis" in Iran, uses the lingo of narcissism continually, yet establishes it in a context of solid conformism. Iran, the article contends, represents a "political and psychological watershed far more important than the immediate concern over the American hostages in Teheran. [Policymakers] view the situation as a pivotal event marking the close of the post-Vietnam era." The article continues:

> "In terms of domestic politics, this has put an end to the Vietnam syndrome," said a senior official who has served several Administrations.
>
> George W. Ball, a former Under-Secretary of State who is still called to counsel policymakers, captured the sense of many here when he said that the nation

was overcoming "its sense of guilt, its complexes" over the Vietnam war. Another policymaker said that "we are moving away from our post-Vietnam reticence."

Still others speak of "a turning point in our attitude toward ourselves, and there is a feeling that we have a right to protect legitimate American interests anywhere in the world."

Such journalism represents a containment policy directed against any systematic discussion of what are called "legitimate American interests." It employs a terminology completely wed to the narcissistic social structure. Vietnam becomes an attitude. A nationwide resistance movement is disassembled by the language of the individual. The antiwar movement is the symptom of a neurotic, national individual. A war fervor is enunciated in terms of self-realization and therapeutic breakthrough. When a world-political view is essential to our understanding, the language of personality is adhered to, and the memory of a social movement evaporates gradually in its wake. As the above samples show, the language of narcissism and collectivity interact in the depiction and accentuation of a war hysteria, and of the American political framework in general.

The structural confusions of the mass culture also permeate the imagery of the civilian consumer economy, where personal choice and conformity have long operated in unison, and advertising utilizes the realm of war to inform its mode of perception. Take the example of the recent vodka war. The issue: Russian vodka. While the buying of Russian vodka has rarely been a political choice, current circumstances encourage such a link. The battle is the battle of the two communisms: Russian and Chinese. Here, within the ads, political alliances become the basis for individual consumer choice. "Is Tsingtao winning the cold war?" asks the ad, as a picture shows two bottles of vodka—one Tsingtao (Chinese) and the other Stolichnaya (Russian)—being poured into separate glasses of ice.

Here the logic of the personal realm is completely invaded by that of power politics. After all, Stolichnaya was not drunk for political reasons, but because of its touted quality. China has no long tradition of vodka production, so one might just as well buy vodka produced in Newark as in China. But the general climate of the media panorama encourages such displacements, such comparisons. To buy Russian vodka is to support the invasion of Afghanistan. To buy Chinese vodka is to support Chinese-American friendship. Personal taste and political directives become interchangeable.

The greatest impact seems to have been upon domestically produced vodkas, which have long projected an image of authenticity through the use of Russian names and advertising motifs. Now these image policies smack of disloyalty, causing havoc among U.S. vodka producers. The business section of the *New York Times* (March 13, 1980) reported that "vodka marketers are making great efforts to show they are unaffiliated with the folks who sent troops into Afghanistan." Gordon's vodka launched a campaign, advertising itself as "the smoothest vodka on our native tongue," while Smirnoff, after years of capitalizing on its Russian name, proclaimed the ultimate fidelity to an aggressive American jingoism in a full-page ad that in boldface announced:

> **SMIRNOFF VODKA SALUTES**
> **THE UNITED STATES HOCKEY TEAM.**
> (*New York Times*, February 25, 1980)

While personal independence has long been the theme of peacetime American advertising, the current trend is characteristic of wartime advertising, notably the First and Second World Wars, as the patriotic imperative reorganizes the world of commodities and consumers.

The forms of this development are varied, and while some are overtly political in tone, there are a wide range of images that serve—subliminally—to organize the moral economy of war. The area of women's fashion is particularly telling as fashion and fashion imagery have throughout history been connected to issues of social struggle and/or social conformity. From the sixties onward—continuing a clothing "reform" dating back to the mid-nineteenth century—the trend in women's clothing has been toward a freer garb, less constricting, less dramatic in its enunciation of gender. Yet now, fashion increasingly reappropriates traditional styles, styles from the past. One variation of this development is in fact called the "Retro" look, an abbreviation of "retrogressive." One ad invites women to "Retrogress with *Givency!*" The look is an approximation of the wartime forties styles; severe and highly defined in terms of gender. Elsewhere we see the reappearance of the Gibson Girl of the early 1900s. While at that time the Gibson look was a step forward from the hobbling and corsetry of an earlier era, in the current context it is no less than a return to the time when men were men, and women were women. Tight at the waist, broad at the breast and hips, the Gibson style accentuates the reproductive functions of women at a time when many women have been struggling to transcend the limits of such a primary self-definition. This return to "femininity" is part of a broad cultural counterassault against issues raised on behalf of women's rights; it is also an essential component of the war mentality, since women, in their customary domain—hearth and home—historically have provided men with a pretext to fight. The reconstitution of a home-bound woman within the symbolic realm of fashion places the logic of the battle more securely within the hearts and minds of men. The collapse of the idea of a sexually integrated draft in the winter and spring of 1980 may have had as much to do with assembling the ideological conditions of war as it does with the refusal of many women to see the "plum" of a male/female draft as a meaningful gain in sexual equality. In any event, the rejection of the idea of drafting women was a step toward reinstituting the draft for men.

An ad for the Gibson look reasserts the romantic vulnerability of womanhood:

> The Gibson girl. She's romantic. Spirited. Witty. An inspiration for today. All this, for her. From you. . . . Ribbon her waist . . . Her tender nights. . . . Give coquettish innocence. . . . Give her a white gardenia. . . . High drama, our boa to wreathe her. . . .

The ad, which appeared in December 1979, was aimed at men, suggesting Christmas gifts for women. The gifts were to mold a mood, a relationship; the idiom of male protection and female vulnerability permeated the message, as it asserted the sexual climate/cliché of war.

5 / Billboards of the Future

THE ARRAY of media images is so broad, so diverse, so universal, that any discussion of them must end abruptly. They go on as a landscape. As a landscape, the media panorama—to a large extent—provides us with a credible "reality." It is far-reaching and disparate, but it is also—particularly in moments when social and political alternatives are reduced to dogmatism and despair—able to provide people with the semblance of a unified world-view. The media panorama is a mass-consumed charade of a totality. Its only meaning is in our ability to make sense of it in our own terms. If the mode of a mass culture is to appropriate the popular imagination into a facticity of words and images, it is our task to confront this facticity with a critical and transcendent imagination.

Since the rise of print, the idea of democracy has been closely associated with the availability of the word, that all might have access. Democratic struggles have long been associated with the idea of an informed citizenship, capable of critically interpreting the world. This idea has stood as a bedrock against tyrannies. Within the media panorama we see the truncation of this principle. Images and words proliferate; all people have access, yet increasingly, the interpretations are ready-made, alternatives already expelled—a kind of democratic despotism. The media panorama is an issue of political moment. In it we see phantoms of ourselves, living out a political life, a material life, and a dream life within the terms of the social marketplace. Like the proverbial children, we are seen but not heard.

Too often, critics of capitalism turn away from the analysis of ideological power. It is as if the analysis would assert some kind of determinacy, foreclosing the possibility of resistance. Each time the question of hegemony is raised, a story of resistance is told, as if the very raising of the question of ideology threatens the populist fantasy of an autonomous and perpetually heroic "common folk" (read—sometimes—"working class").

To demand that reality be only perceived in the frame of successful struggle, resistance, and popular heroism is a dangerous and deceptive game to play. It may stand in the way of political thought and action. The social and historical dynamics of contemporary capitalism should not be obscured in favor of a "working class" that is at the same time downtrodden and autonomous; plundered yet ideologically self-determined. This is the stuff of Hollywood.

The role of media and mass culture both *in* war and *as* war—their ability to mobilize popular sentiment—has a hazardous and instructive history. Its successes have been founded in the ability to define the realm of popular literacy, the terms of that literacy.

Beyond continual political analysis, it is necessary to challenge that dominion. The challenge must take place within the realm of popular literacy and vision. Only if the mass culture is understood in terms of a battle to redefine the boundaries of social space can political struggles begin to break through the chaos. If war, or the moral economy of war, takes place on the level of the cultural panorama, it is on that level that resistance must take place.

A lesson to be learned from the underground press of the sixties is that of its cultural vision. Recognizing and battling the petrification of dominant cultural imagery, the underground press—within its limits—dramatically reclaimed a place within the realm of popular literacy and vision. The word jumped out of its columns, became visual; the image became conceptual. For a moment, the media panorama was invaded, and its most dazzling lights came from among the forces of opposition. Imagination was pitted against the *facts* of life, inverting the familiar logic of cultural domination.

Such an alternative form and vision are crucial today; there is need to reclaim a place within the vernacular arena of literacy, which now lies under military siege. The images that bombard and oppose us must be reorganized. We must figure out how to present these images imaginatively, so as to give a critical order to the chaos. Literacy, in general, must be extended in the area of critical cultural analysis and understanding. The spectacle must be acted upon, collectively.

Likewise, we must seek to be visionary, utopian. If our critique of the commodity culture points to better alternatives, let us explore—in our own billboards of the future—what they might be. At a time when people are individually aware of the hazards of the consumer culture, the absence of coherent alternatives is tragic. Socialist reveries must be liberated from the confines of esoteric debate. As William Appleman Williams said recently, we must begin to imagine what a "world without empire" might be like. The absence of such dreams is conspicuous within the accessible panorama of today's culture. We read our words over, and we feel the weight of this absence.

NOTES

PROLOGUE

1. This newspaper article was brought to our attention by journalist Les Payne, speaking at the American Writers Congress, New York City, October 10, 1981.

ONE: The Bribe of Frankenstein

1. Mary Wollstonecraft Shelley, *Frankenstein, or The Modern Prometheus* (1831 ed.). New York, 1961, p. 41.
2. *Ibid.*, pp. 142–43.
3. See Langdon Winner, *Autonomous Technology: Technics-out-of-Control as a Theme in Political Thought,* Cambridge, 1977, for a review of literature on technology superseding human power.
4. Carlo Cipolla, *Clocks and Culture, 1300–1700.* New York, 1967, p. 34.
5. Raymond Williams, *Keywords: A Vocabulary of Culture and Society.* New York, 1976, p. 167.
6. John F. Kasson, *Civilizing the Machine: Technology and Republican Values in America, 1776–1900.* New York, 1976, pp. 161–65.
7. Elizabeth Eisenstein, "Some Conjectures About the Impact of Printing on Western Society and Thought: A Preliminary Report." *Journal of Modern History,* x1, pp. 1–56, 1968. Further study along these lines has led to the recent appearance of a major, two-volume study by the same author; see Elizabeth Eisenstein, *The Printing Press as an Agent of Change: Communications and Cultural Transformation in Early-Modern Europe,* Cambridge, England, 1979. See also Lucien Febvre, *The Coming of the Book,* London, 1977; Frederick Hamilton, *A Brief History of Printing in England,* Chicago, 1918; Agnes Allen, *The Story of the Book,* New York, 1967; Marshall McLuhan, *The Gutenberg Galaxy,* New York, 1962; S. H. Steinberg, *Five Hundred Years of Printing,* Harmondsworth, Middlesex, England, 1955. For

some provocative thoughts on printing, set within the framework of a more general, contemporary essay, see George Gerbner, "Television: The New State Religion?" *Etc.*, June 1977, pp. 145–50.

8. See Dan Schiller, *Objectivity and the News: The Public and the Rise of Commercial Journalism*, Philadelphia, 1981, for a valuable contribution shedding light on nineteenth-century American developments.

9. Herbert I. Schiller, *Mass Communications and American Empire*. New York, 1969. Also by Schiller, *The Mind Managers*, Boston, 1973; and *Communication and Cultural Domination*, White Plains, New York, 1976. Schiller's work, widely read internationally, provides the best rundown on the U.S. information structure currently available.

10. See Immanuel Wallerstein, *The Modern World System* (I), New York, 1975.

11. Frederick Douglass, *My Bondage and My Freedom*. New York, 1969, pp. 145–46.

12. See Christopher Hill, *The World Turned Upside Down*, New York, 1972, pp. 106–7.

13. Thomas Paine, *Common Sense*. Harmondsworth, Middlesex, England, 1976, p. 100.

14. Erik Barnouw, *A Tower in Babel: A History of Broadcasting in the United States*. New York, 1966.

15. Karl Marx, *Capital* (I). New York, 1906, pp. 805, 834.

16. *Survey* Magazine, May 3, 1913.

17. Founding *Manifesto* of the I.W.W., January 1905. In Joyce Kornbluh (ed.), *Rebel Voices: An IWW Anthology*. Ann Arbor, Michigan, 1964, p. 7.

18. D. Schiller, *op. cit.*

19. It is worthy of mention that from its inception in the 1840s, *Scientific American* had been one of the most prominent voices of free enterprise. Rarely, throughout the nineteenth century, had it veered from its enthusiastic commitment to the mechanical world-view. Amid the rise of factory capitalism, its lack of social concern was conspicuous. See James Shenton (ed.) *Free Enterprise Forever! Scientific American in the 19th Century*, New York, 1977.

20. Albert A. Hopkins (ed.), *The Book of Progress* (I). New York, 1915.

21. See Stuart Ewen, *Captains of Consciousness: Advertising and the Social Roots of the Consumer Culture*, New York, 1976, pp. 77–80.

22. Erik Barnouw, *The Magician and the Cinema*. New York, 1981.

23. Hopkins, *op. cit.*
24. If *Scientific American* envisioned the transcendent capacity of cinema images as consistent with maintaining industrial discipline, it should be mentioned that others did not. For some, in those early years of the movies, the ability of screen imagery to battle the constraints of daily ritual pointed toward its potential as a revolutionary tool. For Dziga Vertov, the revolutionary Soviet film director whose brother performed his labors in Hollywood, the movie camera provided a device by which the chains of oppression could be broken; dominant modes of perception, transcended. Here, in an essay of 1923 (taken from John Berger, *Ways of Seeing,* London, 1972, p. 17), Vertov assumes the voice of the camera:

> I am an eye. A mechanical eye. I, the machine, show you a world the way only I can see it. I free myself for today and forever from human immobility. I'm in constant movement. I approach and pull away from objects. I creep under them. I move alongside a running horse's mouth. I fall and rise with the falling and rising bodies. This is I, the machine, maneuvering in the chaotic movements, recording one movement after another in the most complex combinations. . . . Freed from the boundaries of time and space, I co-ordinate any and all points of the universe, wherever I want them to be. *My way leads towards the creation of a fresh perception of the world.* Thus I explain a new way the world unknown to you.

There is a discomforting similarity between Vertov's description of the camera as a machine in the service of social revolt, and *The Book of Progress'* interpretation of the camera as a mechanism of illusion and control. For one, the ability to rearrange reality suggests that same ability to its audience. For the other, the ability to rearrange reality placates and structures its audience. While there is a wide range of powerful and compelling cinema, providing new and expansive ways of seeing, Vertov's revolutionary hopes are, as of yet, largely unmet.

TWO: Consumption as a Way of Life

1. Interview with Anna Kuthan done by Karen Kearns, on file with the Oral History Project, CUNY, New York City.
2. Elizabeth Gurley Flynn, *The Rebel Girl.* New York, 1955, p. 134. See also Grazia Dore, "Some Social and Historical Aspects of Italian Emigration to America," originally in *Journal of Social History* (Winter, 1968); as reprinted in Francesco Cordasco and

Eugene Bucchioni, *The Italians: Social Backgrounds of an American Group,* Clifton, New Jersey, 1974, p. 20.

3. Herbert Gutman, *Work, Culture and Society in Industrializing America.* New York, 1977, pp. 174–75.

4. For the site of the New York Stock Exchange see Matthew Josephson, *The Robber Barons,* New York, 1956, p. 16. For the role of slavery in the development of capitalism, see Eric Williams, *Capitalism and Slavery,* New York, 1966, and Immanuel Wallerstein, *The Modern World System,* New York, 1975.

Slavery as a capitalist labor system is a theme developed by George Rawick in *From Sundown to Sunup,* Westport, 1972. This is one of the few books on the subject of slavery to address this issue frontally. Also, William Eric Perkins, in discussion, helped to shed light on this subject. Regarding the question of the capitalist roots of American agriculture, William Appleman Williams has most clearly preceived and addressed the connection. His *Roots of the Modern American Empire: A Study of the Growth and Shaping of Social Consciousness in a Marketplace Society* is an important contribution. Lawrence Goodwyn's *Democratic Promise: The Populist Movement in America,* New York, 1976, also provides important insights into the rise of American capitalist agriculture and the radical response.

See also Sigfried Giedion, *Mechanization Takes Command,* Part IV, New York, 1948, for an analysis of the importance and almost vanguard role of the American mechanization of agriculture. For contrast, see William I. Thomas and Florian Znaieki, *The Polish Peasant in Europe and America,* Vol. 1, Boston, 1919, or Leonard Covello, *The Social Background of the Italo-American Child,* New Jersey, 1972.

5. The obvious significant exceptions to this general pattern were Eastern European Jews whose migration to the United States was permanent.

6. See John Berger and Jean Mohr, *A Seventh Man: Migrant Workers in Europe,* New York, 1975, for a vivid portrayal of current conditions among Europe's migratory workers.

7. Mike Gold, *Jews Without Money.* New York, 1930, p. 151. See also Antonio Mangano, *Sons of Italy,* New York, 1917, p. 23; Antonio Stella, "Tuberculosis and the Italians in the United States," *Charities and the Commons,* vol. 12 (1904), pp. 486–89; and Isaac Hourwich, *Immigration and Labor,* New York, 1912, p. 272, for discussions of the social contradictions of being simultaneously engaged in the old and the new worlds.

8. Raymond Williams, *Keywords: A Vocabulary of Culture and Society.* New York, 1976, pp. 68–70.

9. Raymond Williams, "Problems of Materialism." *New Left Review*, Number 109, May–June 1978, p. 8.
10. Edgar D. Furniss, *Labor Problems*. Boston, 1925, p. 176.
11. Simon Lubin and Christina Krysto, "Cracks in the Melting Pot." *Survey*, vol. 43, 1920, p. 258.
12. Robert E. Park, "The City: Suggestions for the Investigation of Human Behavior in the Urban Environment." In Robert Park, Ernest Burgess, and Roderick McKenzie, *The City*, Chicago, 1925, pp. 16–17.
13. *New York Times*, November 10, 1979.
14. *New York Times*, January 22, 1980.
15. Edward Devine, *Charities and the Commons*. Vol. 17, 1907, p. 502.
16. See J. R. Dolan, *The Yankee Peddlers of Early America*, New York, 1964, for a discussion on the many-faceted activities of peddlers.
17. See Robert Hendrickson, *The Grand Emporiums*, New York, 1979, Chapter 1. For a firsthand account of the general store, see P. T. Barnum, *Barnum's Own Story*, New York, 1961, pp. 12–27.
18. Dolan, *op. cit.*, pp. 254–55.
19. *Ibid.*, pp. 245–47.
20. Barnum, *op. cit.*, p. 26; Hendrickson, *op. cit.*, pp. 206–7.
21. Hendrickson, *op. cit.*, p. 223. For a history of Montgomery Ward, see Hendrickson, pp. 205–233.
22. Gordon L. Weil, *Sears Roebuck, U.S.A.* New York, 1977, pp. 5, 25–27. This book offers an informative account of the Sears, Roebuck Company. See also Norman Cohn, *The Good Old Days*, New York, 1940, and Hendrickson, *op. cit.*, pp. 236–53.
23. Weil, *op. cit.*, pp. 62–64; Hendrickson, *op. cit.*, pp. 212–17.
24. For a description of Wanamaker's, see Hendrickson, *op cit.*, pp. 75–81. See also the excellent article by Susan Porter Benson detailing the development of American department stores, "Palaces of Consumption and Machine for Selling: The American Department Store, 1880–1940," *Radical History Review*, Fall 1979, pp. 199–221. For Macy's ad as well as another description, see Sheila Rothman, *Woman's Proper Place*, New York, 1978, pp. 18–22.
25. Simon Patten, *The Consumption of Wealth*. New York, 1892, p. 51.
26. *Ibid.*, p. 34.
27. *Ibid.*, p. 51.
28. J. Strummer, M. Jones, "Lost in the Supermarket." Recorded by The Clash, *London Calling*, New York, CBS Epic Records, 1979.
29. Quoted in *The New Yorker*, May 18, 1981, p. 35.

THREE: City Lights

1. Some of the material used in this essay comes from Elizabeth Ewen, "Immigrant Women in the Land of Dollars, 1890–1930" (Ph.D. dissertation, State University of New York at Stony Brook, 1979). The references are primarily to the experiences of Italian and Jewish women migrating to New York City during this period. In order to highlight the mother-daughter relationship, the role of fathers in family life has been deemphasized. For an exploration of this theme, see Alice Kessler-Harris's introduction to Anzia Yezierska's *Breadgivers* (New York: Doubleday & Co., 1925; reprint ed., New York: George Braziller, 1975), as well as the novel itself. The source material documenting the lives of immigrant women comes mainly from three sources: contemporary novels and autobiography, social work material, and oral history. Extensive use was made of the archives of the *Oral History Project: 1890–1930,* City University of New York, New York City, directed by Herbert Gutman and Virginia Yans-McLaughlin from 1974 to 1976. For secondary materials, see Virginia Yans-McLaughlin, *Family and Community: Italian Immigrants in Buffalo, 1890–1930* (Ithaca, New York, 1977); Charlotte Baum, Paula Hyman, and Sonya Michel, *The Jewish Woman in America* (New York, 1976); and Judith Smith, "Our Own Kind: Family and Community Networks in Providence," *Radical History Review* 17 (April 1977): 99–120.

2. Viola Paradise, "The Jewish Girl in Chicago." *Survey* 30 (1913), 700–703; see especially p. 701.

3. Malcolm Wiley and Stuart Rice, "The Agencies of Communication." In *Recent Social Trends in the United States: Report of the President's Research Committee on Social Trends,* New York, 1933, p. 209.

4. For Italian women, see Phyllis Williams, *South Italian Folkways in Europe and America,* New Haven, Connecticut, 1938, pp. 19–24; Leonard Covello, *The Social Background of the Italo-American School Child,* Totowa, New Jersey, 1967, pp. 210–20; Yans-McLaughlin, *op. cit.,* pp. 25–35. For Jewish women, see Baum *et al., op. cit.,* pp. 66–74; Mark Zborowski and Elizabeth Herzog, *Life Is with People,* New York, 1952; reprint ed., New York, 1972, pp. 131–35.

5. Louise More, *Wage Earners' Budgets: A Study of Standards and Cost of Living.* New York, 1907; reprint ed., New York, 1971, p. 28.

6. Mary Simkhovitch, *The City Workers' World.* New York, 1917, pp. 79–80.

7. Robert Chapin, *The Standard of Living Among Workingman's*

Families in New York City. New York, 1909; reprint ed., New York, 1971, pp. 249–50.

8. Elizabeth Gurley Flynn, *Rebel Girl.* New York, 1973, p. 133.
9. Elsie Clew Parsons, "The Division of Labor in the Tenements." *Charities and the Commons* 15 (1905): 443.
10. Since men were more irregular in turning over their wages in full, the mother-daughter bond was vital to the economic viability of family life (see E. Ewen, *op. cit.,* pp. 123–31; and Louise Odencrantz, *Italian Women in Industry,* New York, 1919, pp. 175–77). For cultural conflicts see E. Ewen, pp. 276–323; Marie Concistre, "A Study of a Decade in the Life and Education of the Adult Immigrant Community in East Harlem," Ph.D. dissertation, New York University, 1943, reprinted in part in Francesco Cordasco and Eugene Bucchioni, *The Italians,* Fairfield, New Jersey, 1974; Belle Israels, "The Way of the Girl," *Survey* 22 (1909): 494–97; Baum *et al., op. cit.,* pp. 115–17.
11. Lewis Palmer, "The World in Motion," *Survey* 22 (1909): 357.
12. Lewis Jacobs, *The Rise of American Film,* New York, 1939; reprint ed., New York, 1969, p. 12.
13. Antonio Mangano, *Sons of Italy.* New York, 1917, pp. 6–7.
14. Cited in Russell Nye, *The Unembarrassed Muse.* New York, 1970, p. 365.
15. Palmer, *op. cit.,* p. 355.
16. Cited in Irving Howe, *World of Our Fathers,* New York, 1976, p. 213; see also Odencrantz, *op. cit.,* p. 235; and P. Williams, *op. cit.,* pp. 117–18.
17. Jacobs, *op. cit.,* p. 17; see also Sklar, *op. cit.,* pp. 18–30.
18. Jacobs, *op. cit.,* pp. 69–71. Robert Bremer, *From the Depths: The Discovery of Poverty in the United States* (New York, 1956), argues that the early movies made a real contribution to the social understanding of poverty as environmental (see pp. 110–12).
19. For another account, see Jacobs, *op. cit.,* pp. 47–48.
20. *Ibid.,* pp. 70–71.
21. John Spargo, "Common Sense of the Milk Question." *Charities and the Commons* 20 (1908): 544–96; see esp. p. 595. For another account of this powerful movie, see Lindsay, *op. cit.,* pp. 70–71.
22. See Jacobs, *op. cit.,* pp. 71–72.
23. Maria Ganz with Nat Ferber, *Rebels: Into Anarchy and Out Again.* New York, 1919, pp. 77–78.
24. Mike Gold, *Jews Without Money.* New York, 1930, p. 94.
25. Cited in Edward Wagenknecht, *The Movies in the Age of Innocence,* Norman, Oklahoma, 1962, p. 41. See also Sklar's discussion of the relationship between comedy and audience, *op. cit.,* pp. 104–21. For a feminist counterpoint, see Molly Haskell,

From Reverence to Rape, Middlesex, England, 1973, pp. 61–74.

26. See Alice Kessler-Harris, "Organizing the Unorganizable: Three Jewish Women and Their Union," *Labor History* 17 (Winter 1976): 5–23.

27. Ruth S. True, "The Neglected Girl." In *West Side Studies,* ed. Pauline Goldmark, New York, 1914, p. 116.

28. Jerry Mangione, *Mount Allegro.* Boston, 1943, p. 228.

29. Sophonisba Breckinridge, *New Homes for Old.* New York, 1921, p. 175.

30. True, *op. cit.,* p. 112. See also Breckinridge, *op. cit.,* p. 170; and P. Williams, *op. cit.,* p. 36.

31. Oral interview with Agnes Mazza, CUNY Oral History Project, May 1975. See Yezierska, *op. cit.,* pp. 35–36, for a fictional rendition of this theme.

32. See Robert Park and Herbert Miller, *Old World Traits Transplanted,* New York, 1921; reprint ed., New York, 1971, pp. 79–80; Baum *et al., op. cit.,* pp. 116–17.

33. Sklar, *op. cit.,* pp. 88–91.

34. True, *op. cit.,* pp. 58–59.

35. *Ibid.,* p. 67.

36. Interview with Filomena Ognibene, March 1975.

37. Interview with Grace Gello, April 1975.

38. For a particularly useful analysis, see Sumiko Higashi, *Virgins, Vamps and Flappers,* Montreal, 1978. See also Haskell, *op. cit.,* pp. 42–89.

39. Wagenknecht, *op. cit.,* p. 181.

40. Cited in Higashi, *op. cit.,* p. 61.

41. For accounts of Theda Bara, see Wagenknecht, *op. cit.,* pp. 179–81; Higashi, *op. cit.,* pp. 55–62; and Jacobs, *op. cit.,* pp. 266–67.

42. Mary Pickford, *Sunshine and Shadow.* New York, 1955, p. 31.

43. Higashi, *op. cit.,* p. 43.

44. James Card, "The Films of Mary Pickford." In *"Image" on the Art and Evolution of the Film,* Marshall Deutelbaum (ed.), New York, 1979. For accounts of Mary Pickford that stress this theme, see also Higashi, *op. cit.,* pp. 41–52; Haskell, *op. cit.,* pp. 58–61; Wagenknecht, *op. cit.,* pp. 159–63; and Jacobs, *op. cit.,* pp. 264–66. Card, Higashi, and Jacobs all stress Pickford's popularity with working-class audiences.

45. Pickford, *op. cit.,* pp. 350–51.

46. Higashi, *op. cit.,* pp. 1–15; Haskell, *op. cit.,* pp. 49–57. For a discussion of the ambiguities of the virgin theme, see Russell Merritt, "Mr. Griffith, *The Painted Lady* and the Distractive Frame," in Deutelbaum, *op. cit.,* pp. 147–51. In *The Painted*

Lady, Blanche Sweet, as the good girl, is driven mad by sexual contradictions, caught as she is between a repressive father, an unscrupulous lover, and the new sexual world represented by makeup and clothing. For analysis of the good-bad girl, see Martha Wolfenstein and Nathan Leitesm, *Movies,* New York, 1950, pp. 25–46.

47. See Stuart Ewen, *Captains of Consciousness,* New York, 1976; and Helen Lynd and Robert Lynd, *Middletown,* New York, 1929.

48. Benjamin Hampton, *History of the American Film Industry.* Covici, New York, 1931; reprint ed., New York, 1970, p. 221. For an analysis of this change, see Hampton, *op. cit.,* pp. 197–215; Sklar, *op. cit.,* pp. 88–92, 122–34; Jacobs, *op. cit.,* pp. 287–301; and David Robinson, *Hollywood in the Twenties,* New York, 1968, pp. 26–41.

49. Hampton, *op. cit.,* p. 222.

50. Higashi, *op. cit.,* pp. 136–42; Hampton, *op. cit.,* pp. 220–26; Sklar, *op. cit.,* pp. 91–96; Haskell, *op. cit.,* pp. 76–77; Jacobs, *op. cit.,* pp. 335–41, 401–3.

51. Wagenknecht, *op. cit.,* p. 207.

52. Hampton, *op. cit.,* p. 224.

53. Cited in Jacobs, *op. cit.,* p. 401. The sexual relationships depicted in these films bear a striking resemblance to the critique of male-female relationships developed by Charlotte Perkins Gilman in *Woman and Economics,* Boston, 1898. Gilman argues that male capitalist greed and gain in the market and female "sex attraction" in the home constitute the grid of dependency relationships in modern society and create a market for "sensuous decoration and personal ornament" (p. 120). See pp. 110–20.

54. See also Michelle Mattelart, "Notes on 'Modernity': A Way of Reading Women's Magazines," in *Communications and Class Struggle,* Armand Mattelart and Seth Siegelaub (eds.), Paris, 1979, 1:158–70. She argues that "change, in as much as it affects women, becomes synonymous with integration into the 'modern.' And it is the image of the happy woman, the woman dazzled by the desires and possibilities of consumption, and progress . . . which is the best publicity for modernity" (p. 160). See also Higashi, *op. cit.,* p. 142.

55. Hampton, *op. cit.,* p. 225; Higashi, *op. cit.,* pp. 102–4.

56. Interview with Maria Zambiello, January 1976.

57. Interview with Maria Frazaetti, March 1976.

58. Interview with Filomena Ognibene, March 1975.

59. Sklar, *op. cit.,* pp. 44–45. See also Nye, *op. cit.,* pp. 377–79; and Hampton, *op. cit.,* p. 172.

60. Cited in Nye, *op. cit.,* p. 378.
61. Lloyd Lewis, "The Deluxe Picture Palace." *New Republic* (March 1929), pp. 174–76; reprinted in George Mowry, *The Twenties,* New Jersey, 1963, p. 59.
62. *Ibid.,* p. 58.
63. Walter Benjamin, "The Work of Art in the Age of Mechanical Reproduction." *Illuminations,* Hannah Arendt (ed.), New York, 1968, p. 223.

FOUR: Fashion and Democracy

1. A fairly detailed description of the rise of the blue jean may be found in Ed Cray, *LEVI's,* Boston, 1978.
2. Paul H. Nystrom, *Economics of Fashion.* New York, 1928, p. 278.
3. Estelle Ansley Worrell, *American Costume: 1840–1920.* Harrisburg, Pennsylvania, 1979, p. 38.
4. *Ibid.,* pp. 28–29.
5. Horatio Alger, Jr., *Ragged Dick and Mark, The Match Boy.* Reprinted New York, 1962, p. 58.
6. Amy Pagnozzi, "Jeans: No Stone Unturned in Fight to Cover the Rear." *New York Post,* July 15, 1980.
7. William Thomas, "The Jeans of Summer." *Back Stage,* July 18, 1980, p. 1.
8. *Ibid.*
9. Craig Whitney, "Moscow Bracing for Big Influx of Western Influences." *New York Times,* July 3, 1980.
10. Paul H. Nystrom, *Fashion Merchandising.* New York, 1932, p. 31.
11. Ingrid Brenninkmeyer, *The Sociology of Fashion.* Ph.D. dissertation, Fribourg, 1962, p. 115.
12. *Ibid.*
13. Quentin Bell, *On Human Finery.* New York, 1976, p. 141.
14. Thorstein Veblen, *The Theory of the Leisure Class.* New York, 1899.
15. Brenninkmeyer, *op. cit.,* p. 115. Bernard Rudofsky, in *The Unfashionable Human Body* (Garden City, New York, 1974), relates that, according to medieval Christian doctrine, sexual distinctions between Adam and Eve were minimal before the fall from Paradise. Illustrating his contention with a fourteenth-century woodcut, we see Adam and Eve as a "sexless couple," devoid of any clear sexual definition. In another illustration, a thirteenth-century miniature, we see an Adam and Eve both painted with hermaphroditic sexual organs (combination penis and vagina) (pp. 16–17). According to such scriptural in-

terpretations, physiological sexual distinctions were, themselves, largely a result of the fall from grace.

16. Anne Hollander, *Seeing Through Clothes*. New York, 1978, pp. 23, 36.
17. Frances Elizabeth Baldwin, "Sumptuary Legislation and Personal Regulation in England." *Johns Hopkins University Studies in History and Political Science,* Series XLIV, No. 1, Baltimore, 1926, p. 10.
18. Pearl Binder, *Muffs and Morals*. New York/London, 1953, p. 157.
19. Kent Roberts Greenfield, "Sumptuary Law in Nürnberg: A Study in Paternal Government." *Johns Hopkins University Studies in History and Political Science,* Series XXXVI, No. 2, Baltimore, 1918, p. 7.
20. Baldwin, *op. cit.,* p. 23.
21. *Ibid.,* pp. 231–32.
22. *Ibid.,* pp. 228–29.
23. *Ibid.,* p. 228.
24. Brenninkmeyer, *op. cit.,* p. 132.
25. Baldwin, pp. 248–49. Under a law, "1 James I, c25," it is stated that "all acts heretofore made concerning apparel . . . shall . . . henceforth be repealed and void."
26. Bell, *op. cit.,* p. 115.
27. See Werner Sombart, *Luxury and Capitalism*. Ann Arbor, 1967 (1913).
28. Brenninkmeyer, *op. cit.,* pp. 58–59.
29. *Ibid.*
30. Larzer Ziff, *Puritanism in America: New Culture in a New World,* New York, 1973, p. 19.
31. James J. Flink, *America Adopts the Automobile*. Cambridge, Mass., 1970, p. 65.
32. Rudofsky, *op. cit.,* 159–60; Brenninkmeyer, *op. cit.,* 137–38. See also Albert Soboul, *The Parisian Sans-culottes and the French Revolution,* Westport, Connecticut, 1979.
33. See Max Weber, *The Protestant Ethic and the Spirit of Capitalism,* New York, 1958. See also R. H. Tawney, *Religion and the Rise of Capitalism,* New York, 1926.
34. Benjamin Franklin, *Autobiography*. Reprinted New York, 1962, p. 69.
35. Frederick B. Tolles, *Meeting House and Counting House*. New York, 1948, p. 123.
36. Bell, *op. cit.,* pp. 119, 124–25, 148.
37. Hollander, *op. cit.,* p. 75.
38. Brenninkmeyer, *op. cit.,* p. 140.

39. Bell, *op. cit.*, p. 141.

40. Nystrom, *Economics of Fashion*, p. 316.

41. Stuart Chase, *Prosperity: Fact or Myth*. New York, 1929, p. 64. See also Eugene Genovese, *The Political Economy of Slavery*, New York, 1965.

42. Jane Addams, *Twenty Years at Hull House*. New York, 1910, pp. 6–7, 13–14.

43. Allen F. Davis, *American Heroine: The Life and Legend of Jane Addams*. New York, 1973, p. 20.

44. Theodore Zeldin, *France 1848–1945: Ambition and Love*. Oxford, England, 1979.

45. C. P. (Gilman) Stetson, *Women and Economics*. Boston, 1898.

46. See Rudofsky, *op. cit.* See also William A. Rossi, *The Sex Life of the Foot and Shoe*, New York, 1976.

47. Rudofsky, *op. cit.*, pp. 100–111. See also Binder, *op. cit.*, p. 123.

48. Havelock Ellis, *Studies in the Psychology of Sex*, volume II, part I, p. 172. New York, 1942. See also Binder, *op. cit.*, p. 114.

49. Nystrom, *Economics of Fashion*, p. 264.

50. Binder, *op. cit.*, p. 123.

51. *Ibid.*, p. 125.

52. David L. Cohn, *The Good Old Days: A History of American Morals and Manners as Seen Through the Sears, Roebuck Catalogs*. New York, 1940, p. 376.

53. Bell, *op. cit.*, p. 141.

54. Elizabeth B. Hurlock, *The Psychology of Dress: An Analysis of Fashion and Its Motive*. New York, 1929, p. 198.

55. Rudofsky, *op. cit.*, p. 46.

56. Karlyne Anspach, *The Way of Fashion*. Ames, Iowa, 1967, p. 69

57. Burton Y. Pines, "Reagan's Money Machine." *Time*, July 7, 1980. The article reports that while Nancy Reagan enjoys her husband's affluence in five-thousand-dollar dresses, Ronald Reagan "has to be prodded into buying a new suit."

58. "The Very Thing That Makes You Rich," written by S. Bailey, Screen Gems–EMI Music Inc.–BMI. Recorded by Ry Cooder on *Bop Till You Drop*, 1979. Warner Brothers Records, Inc.

59. Cohn, *op. cit.*, p. 309.

60. Hurlock, *op. cit.*, pp. 130*ff*.

61. Hollander, *op. cit.*, pp. 133–34.

62. See Paul Poiret, *King of Fashion: The Autobiography of Paul Poiret*. Philadelphia, 1931.

63. Louis Levine, *The Women's Garment Workers: A History of the International Ladies' Garment Workers' Union*. New York, 1924, pp. 1–2.

64. Egal Feldman, *Fit for Men: A Study of New York's Clothing Trade.* Washington, D.C., 1960, p. 1.
65. Bertha June Richardson, *The Woman Who Spends: A Study of Her Economic Function.* Boston, 1913, pp. 77–78.
66. Robert S. and Helen Merrell Lynd, *Middletown.* New York, 1929, p. 162.
67. Harry A. Cobrin, *The Men's Clothing Industry: From Colonial Through Modern Times.* New York, 1970, p. 19.
68. Pauline Arnold and Percival White, *Clothes and Cloth: America's Apparel Business.* New York, 1961, p. 84. See also Nystrom, *Economics of Fashion,* pp. 411*ff.* There is some dispute as to when slop shops make their first appearance in the United States. While most sources indicate a beginning date of about 1800, one writer places the first slop shop in New Bedford, Massachusetts, in 1822. See Hurlock, *op. cit.,* p. 88.
69. Brenninkmeyer, *op. cit.,* p. 147.
70. Feldman, *op. cit.,* pp. 59–68. See also Brenninkmeyer, *op. cit.,* p. 147.
71. Nystrom, *Economics of Fashion,* p. 408.
72. Feldman, *op. cit.,* p. 49.
73. *Ibid.,* p. 48.
74. *Ibid.*
75. *Ibid.,* pp. 47–48.
76. Nystrom, *Economics of Fashion,* p. 410.
77. *Ibid.,* p. 452.
78. See Christopher Hill, *The World Turned Upside Down,* New York, 1972.
79. See John Berger, *Ways of Seeing,* London, 1972. The entire book makes valuable reading for any student of images; see particularly, pp. 88, 109–10.
80. *Ibid.,* p. 106.
81. Peter C. Marzio, *Chromolithography 1840–1900: The Democratic Art.* Boston, 1979, p. xi.
82. *Ibid.,* p. 5.
83. *Ibid.,* p. 104.
84. Elsa G. Herzfeld, *Family Monographs.* New York, 1905, pp. 14–15.
85. Marzio, *op. cit.,* p. 2.
86. *Ibid.,* pp. 125–26.
87. Brenninkmeyer, *op. cit.,* pp. 145–46.
88. Chase, *op. cit.,* p. 65.
89. Bell, *op. cit.,* p. 31.
90. Nystrom, *Economics of Fashion,* p. 26.
91. Cohn, *op. cit.,* p. 461. See also Gordon Weil, *Sears, Roebuck, U.S.A.* New York, 1977, p. 43.

92. Cohn, *op. cit.*, p. 387.

93. *Ibid.*

94. Allen Devere, "Personal Decoration." *The World Tomorrow.* volume VIII, New York, 1925, p. 77. Cited by Cohn, *op. cit.*, p. 309.

95. Weil, *op. cit.*, p. 42; Cobrin, *op. cit.*, p. 49.

96. Weil, *op. cit.*, p. 43.

97. Cohn, *op. cit.*, pp. 290–91.

98. Levine, *op. cit.*, pp. 12–17.

99. *Ibid.*, pp. 15–16.

100. *Ibid.*, p. 398.

101. *Ibid.*, p. 405.

102. Jacob Riis, *How the Other Half Lives.* New York, 1890, p. 108.

103. New York Bureau of Labor Statistics *Report,* 1885. Cited by Levine, *op. cit.*, pp. 18–23.

104. Levine, *op. cit.*, pp. 171–72.

105. *Ibid.*, p. 37.

106. *Ibid.*, pp. 108–9.

107. *Ibid.*, pp. 30–31.

108. *Ibid.*, pp. 122–23.

109. Arnold and White, *op. cit.*, pp. 104–5.

110. Cobrin, *op. cit.*, p. 105.

111. Hurlock, *op. cit.*, pp. 26–28.

112. Hollander, *op. cit.*, p. 391.

113. John William Ferry, *A History of the Department Store.* New York, 1960, p. vi.

114. See Ferry, *ibid.*, entire; Anspach, *op. cit.*, p. 172.

115. Ferry, p. 23.

116. Nystrom, *Economics of Fashion,* p. 409.

117. Ferry, *op. cit.*, p. 42.

118. *Ibid.*, p. 47.

119. John B. Swinney, *Merchandising of Fashions.* New York, 1942, p. 6. See also Ferry, *op. cit.*, p. 40.

120. Weil, *op. cit.*, Chapter 3.

121. Ferry, *op. cit.*, p. 16.

122. Hurlock, *op. cit.*, pp. 130*ff.*

123. John F. Kasson, *Amusing the Million.* New York, 1978, pp. 17–18.

124. Nystrom, *Economics of Fashion,* pp. 88–92.

125. Robert S. and Helen Merrell Lynd, *Middletown in Transition: A Study in Cultural Conflict.* New York, 1937, p. 175.

126. Hollander, *op. cit.*, p. 154.

127. Hurlock, *op. cit.*, pp. 115–16.

128. Hollander, *op. cit.*, pp. 34–35.

129. Arnold and White, *op. cit.*, p. 91.
130. Nystrom, *Economics of Fashion*, p. 434.
131. Brenninkmeyer, *op. cit.*, p. 163.
132. Nystrom, *Economics of Fashion*, p. 212.
133. Cecil Beaton, *The Glass of Fashion*. Garden City, 1954, p. 116.
134. Nystrom, *Economics of Fashion*, p. 339.
135. Mike Gold, *Jews Without Money*. New York, 1930, pp. 60–61.
136. Richard Gambino, *Blood of My Blood*. New York, 1974, p. 175.
137. Robert Park and W. I. Miller, *Old World Traits Transplanted*. New York, 1919, p. 147.
138. Caroline Ware, *Early New England Cotton Manufacture: A Study in Industrial Beginnings*. New York, 1931; reprinted 1966, p. 215.
139. "The Pretender," by Jackson Browne. Swallow Turn Music/ WB Music. ASCAP.
140. Jervis Anderson, "That Was New York: Harlem," Part I, "The Journey Uptown." *New Yorker*, June 29, 1981, pp. 43–44.
141. Ruth S. True, "The Neglected Girl." *Russell Sage Foundation West Side Studies*, New York, 1914, p. 60.
142. *Ibid.*, pp. 66–67.
143. Richardson, *op. cit.*, pp. 77–78.
144. Jane Addams, *Democracy and Social Ethics*. Cambridge, Mass., 1902; reprinted 1964, pp. 34–35.
145. Chase, *op. cit.*, p. 80.
146. Hurlock, *op. cit.*, p. 3.
147. Leonard Covello, *The Teacher in the Urban Community*. New York, 1958, p. 22.
148. Richardson, *op. cit.*, pp. 75–77.
149. Beaton, *op. cit.*, p. 26.
150. Anspach, *op. cit.*, p. 34.
151. Poiret, *op. cit.*, pp. 265–66.
152. *Ibid.*, p. 275.
153. Christian Dior, *Christian Dior and I*. New York, 1957, pp. 42, 48.
154. Nystrom, *Fashion Merchandising*, p. 31.
155. Hurlock, *op. cit.*, pp. v–vi.
156. Louise Odencranz, *Italian Women in Industry*. New York, 1919, p. 229.
157. Anspach, *op. cit.*, p. 40.
158. Nystrom, *Fashion Merchandising*, pp. 218–19.
159. Brenninkmeyer, pp. 65–67.
160. Hurlock, *op. cit.*, p. 175.
161. *Ibid.*, pp. 176–77.
162. Antonio Mangano, *Sons of Italy*. New York, 1925, p. 21.

163. Hurlock, *op. cit.*, p. 183.
164. R. S. and H. M. Lynd, *Middletown in Transition*, pp. 171, 200.
165. Nystrom, *Economics of Fashion*, p. 73.
166. Poiret, *op. cit.*, p. 271.
167. Cohn, *op. cit.*, p. 285.
168. Nystrom, *Fashion Merchandising*, pp. 43, 47.
169. *Ibid.*, pp. 70–81, 127–53.
170. Hurlock, *op. cit.*, p. 143.
171. Nystrom, *Fashion Merchandising*, p. 189.
172. Nystrom, *Economics of Fashion*, pp. 479–80.
173. Stuart Ewen, *Captains of Consciousness: Advertising and the Social Roots of the Consumer Culture*. New York, 1976. See pp. 31–39, chapter entitled "Mobilizing the Instincts."
174. Nystrom, *Economics of Fashion*, pp. 55*ff*, 67*ff*.
175. *Ibid.*, p. 69.
176. Vance Packard, *The Hidden Persuaders*. New York, 1957, pp. 144–48.
177. "The Lush New Suburban Market." *Fortune*, November 1953, p. 128.
178. Allen Ginsberg, "America." In *Howl and Other Poems*, San Francisco, 1956.
179. Michael McLure, "Nights in North Beach." In Lynda Rosen Obst (ed.), *The Sixties: The Decade Remembered Now, By the People Who Lived it Then*, New York, 1977, p. 28.
180. Diana Vreeland, "Chatting About Style." In Obst, *op. cit.*, p. 146.
181. Carrie Donovan, "The Way to Dress Today." *New York Times Magazine* (Fashion Supplement), August 24, 1980, p. 137.
182. Enid Nemy, "Looking Like Somebody," *ibid.*, pp. 186–87.
183. Donovan, *ibid.*, p. 137.

FIVE: Mass Culture and the Moral Economy of War

1. Frank M. O'Brien, *The Story of the SUN: New York, 1833–1928*. New York, 1928, p. 43.
2. *Ibid.*, pp. 43–44.
3. *Ibid.*, pp. 50–53.
4. Frank Luther Mott, *American Journalism, A History: 1690–1960* (third edition). New York, 1962, pp. 232–33.
5. O'Brien, *op. cit.*, p. 93.
6. An important contribution to our understanding of this question is in Dan Schiller, *Objectivity and the News: The Public and the Rise of Commercial Journalism*, Philadelphia, 1981.

7. The *War of the Worlds* broadcast took place on the eve of Halloween, October 30, 1938. A good general sourcebook on the event is Howard Koch, *The Panic Broadcast,* New York, 1970. Koch was the author of the program's script.

   Another interesting study of this event is Hadley Cantril, *The Invasion From Mars: A Study in the Psychology of Panic,* Princeton, 1940.

8. Peter W. Kaplan, "The End of the Soft Line." *Esquire,* April 1980, pp. 41–47.

9. Warren I. Susman, " 'Personality' and the Making of Twentieth Century Culture." In John Higham and Paul Conkin (eds.), *New Directions in American Intellectual History,* Baltimore, 1979.

10. Sigmund Freud, *Totem and Taboo.* New York, 1950. (1913).

11. Raymond Williams, *Culture and Society.* New York, 1958, pp. 299–300.

12. This sector's development is explored suggestively in Alvin W. Gouldner, *The Future of Intellectuals and the Rise of the New Class,* although the revolutionary potential of this "new class" is too uncritically drawn. See also the work of Barbara and John Ehrenreich on the "Professional-Managerial Class" in *Radical America,* March/April, May/June 1977.

13. Ronald Berman, "Advertising and Social Change in Twentieth-century Advertising and the Economy of Abundance," *Advertising Age* (special issue), April 30, 1980, p. 8.

14. Thorstein Veblen, *The Theory of the Leisure Class.* New York, 1899.

15. Walter Benjamin, "The Work of Art in the Age of Mechanical Reproduction." In *Illuminations,* New York, 1968, pp. 243–44.

INDEX